LIGHT *of* FEARLESS
INDESTRUCTIBLE WISDOM

LIGHT *of* FEARLESS
INDESTRUCTIBLE WISDOM

The Life and Legacy of
His Holiness Dudjom Rinpoche

by

Khenpo Tsewang Dongyal Rinpoche

Samye Translation Group

Prose Translation and Annotation
Khenpo Tsewang Dongyal & Carl Stuendel

Verse and Song Translation
Toy-Fung Tung & Marie-Louise Friquegnon

Snow Lion Publications
Ithaca, New York

Snow Lion Publications
P. O. Box 6483
Ithaca, NY 14851 USA
(607) 273-8519
www.snowlionpub.com

The original Tibetan version of the poetry verses is available for downloading at www.padmasambhava.org.

Printed in USA on acid-free recycled paper.

Paper—ISBN-10: 1-55939-304-1; ISBN-13: 978-1-55939-304-1
Cloth—ISBN-10: 1-55939-324-6; ISBN-13: 978-1-55939-324-9

Library of Congress Cataloging-in-Publication Data

Tsewang Dongyal, Khenpo, 1950-
   [Gter chen Bdud 'joms 'jigs bral ye śes rdo rje gar dbaṅ 'gro 'dul gliṅ pa rtsal gyi rnam thar ye śes rdo rje'i 'od zer. English]
   Light of fearless indestructible wisdom : the life and legacy of His Holiness Dudjom Rinpoche / by Khenpo Tsewang Dongyal ; prose translation and annotation, Khenpo Tsewang Dongyal & Carl Stuendel ; verse and song translation, Toy-Fung Tung & Marie-Louise Friquegnon.
      p. cm.
   Includes bibliographical references and index.
   ISBN-13: 978-1-55939-304-1 (alk. paper) (paper)
   ISBN-10: 1-55939-304-1 (alk. paper) (paper)
   ISBN-13: 978-1-55939-324-9 (alk. paper) (cloth)
   ISBN-10: 1-55939-324-6 (alk. paper) (cloth)
   1. Bdud-'joms 'Jigs-bral-ye-śes-rdo-rje, 1904-1987. 2. Rñiṅ-ma-pa lamas--Biography. I. Title.
   BQ942.D87T76 2008
   294.3'923092--dc22
   [B]
                                           2008020559

CONTENTS

FOREWORD

by

Her Eminence the Dudjom Sangyum Kuzhok Rigdzin Wangmo

*His Holiness Dudjom Rinpoche and Dudjom Sangyum Rigdzin Wangmo
in the 1950s in Kalimpong, West Bengal, India*

YESHE NYING PO, INC.

THE VAJRA NYINGMA SEAT OF HIS HOLINESS DUDJOM RINPOCHE, SUPREME HEAD OF DUDJOM TERSAR

Buddhist Church

His Holiness Shenphen Dawa Rinpoche, Chairman
The Sangyum Rikzin La, Vice-Chairwoman
Ms. Tsering Penzom, Vice-Chairwoman

His Holiness Shenphen Dawa Rinpoche, President
Fay Hibbert, Secretary
Diane Stanley, Treasurer/Assistant Secretary
Andrea Uribe, Assistant Treasurer
Theresa Giorgi, General Manager

Khenpo Tsewang has been a disciple of His Holiness Dudjom Rinpoche for many years. While His Holiness resided in the West, specifically the United States of America, he served as his personal attendant and secretary.

Due to maintaining pure devotion and samayas with this great teacher, His Holiness spontaneously spoke with Khenpo about his life story. Khenpo used that as the foundation for writing a biography of His Holiness which was published in Tibetan in 2004 on the 100th year anniversary of the birth of Dudjom Rinpoche.

Now, Khenpo Tsewang Dongyal has translated this biography into English. I am very happy with his work and hope that this will bring more awareness of the life and achievements of His Holiness Dudjom Rinpoche as one of the greatest Masters and Tertons of the 20th Century.

I am happy to write this acknowledgment because it is the life story of my dear husband.

May this book benefit and bring better understanding of our Buddha Dharma to all.

Dudjom Sangyum Rigdzin Wangmo

September 2006
New York City

19 WEST 16 STREET, NEW YORK, N.Y. 10011 (212) 691-8523 phone/fax, email: ynyingpo@aol.com

His Holiness Dudjom Rinpoche

Author's Introduction

Becoming a Disciple of Dudjom

His Holiness Dudjom Rinpoche has hundreds of thousands of disciples all over the world. I am one of them. I was introduced to this great master in a very ordinary way. I did not have dreams and visions, nor was I informed by another teacher that His Holiness was my destined root guru. Even when I met His Holiness Dudjom Rinpoche for the first time, it did not feel any different from when I met other masters. Meeting His Holiness was like the beginning of a new season, such as the first day of spring, which at the time may not feel particularly momentous. But as the days and weeks proceed, there naturally comes the blooming of spring, then the brilliance of summer. My appreciation of His Holiness's spiritual greatness and extraordinary modesty evolved slowly. His Holiness Dudjom Rinpoche was and is a living buddha, beyond time, but it took time for this disciple to realize it. The story begins long ago, in my home country—Doshul, eastern Tibet—with my simple family in a yak-hair tent.

In 1955 my seminomadic family moved to the upper valley of the very great and sacred Jowo Zegyal Mountain, as we did each summer. The view was spectacular; we were immersed in the beauty of nature. There were glacial and rocky mountains, and valleys filled with colorful wild flowers, thick bushes, fresh-water springs, streams, and rivers. Yaks, sheep, horses, ibex, and many hundreds of mountain goats—protected by a centuries-long ban on hunting—grazed in the meadow and drank from the waters. Occasionally we saw wolves and mountain lions drinking there too. In the sky and trees were ravens, pigeons, magpies, and vultures. All these creatures peacefully coexisted, each pursuing its own style of living.

It was early summer, and the weather was beautiful. My parents and all the other villagers were excited and busy. They seemed to be preparing for something special, and I wondered what it could be. I was five years old and was always interested in having fun. I asked my father, "What's happening? Are we having a big party?" And my father said, "No, not a party. A great lama who lives about a three-day horse ride from here is coming. He has been to our area quite often. He is well loved by everyone, and he is going to bless us."

That day passed and night fell. I went to sleep, close to my father. Often my father chanted prayers all night long. I was certain that all fathers must not sleep, that they must chant through the night just as my father did. On this particular night I woke up repeatedly because I was so excited to see the lama. Rain was falling against our yak-hair tent; it made a beautiful echoing sound that seemed to perfectly harmonize with my father's chanting.

Early the next morning, my mother, Pema Lhadze, was preparing our village nomad breakfast, churning milk to make butter, all the while chanting *calling the lama from afar* according to the great tertön Pema Lingpa. My sisters, Yangzom and Ting Ting Karmo, were sleeping nearby. My father was practicing. I asked him, "When will we see the lama?" He said, "After breakfast." But my father was intensely practicing, and it seemed he would not be done until long after breakfast was finished. My mother said to him, "Gyalchog, won't you go after breakfast? All the villagers are gathering, and the boy is excited." So we ate our meal and off we went.

We walked to where the villagers were gathering and entered the tent in which the lama was staying. As soon as we saw him, we began prostrating. The lama immediately called out, "Gyega, don't do prostrations. Come close to me and sit." ("Gyega" was my father's nickname.) My father and I did a few more prostrations, and then we sat down. I recall the lama being very affectionate to me. He touched my head and rubbed my ears a bit. He even gave me some candy. In our region of Tibet at this time, candy was quite rare, so it was special and dear to children.

This lama was the great siddha and tertön Raya Tulku, the reincarnation of Gechag Tsangyang Gyamtso, a renowned crazy wisdom yogi of the late nineteenth century. Raya Tulku was very famous. He was married and had very long hair, which he wore curled up on his head. His eyes were round, and so was his face; he had dark skin and a fierce appearance. The villagers said he looked like a wrathful deity. But he was actually quite gentle.

A year earlier Raya Tulku had gone on pilgrimage to central Tibet, in particular to visit Lhasa and Samye Monastery. My father knew this; he asked Raya Tulku, "How did it go?" "Wonderful," Raya Tulku replied, and he proceeded to describe some of the places he visited. Then he said, "I had the great opportunity to see Dudjom Tulku." This was the first time my father and I ever heard the name of His Holiness Dudjom Rinpoche. "Who is he?" my father asked. Raya Tulku said, "He is the reincarnation of Dudjom Lingpa, the famous tertön of the nineteenth century." My father wanted to know what Dudjom Tulku looked like. "Very simple and casual," said Raya Tulku. "He is a householder of middle age, and he wears his hair plaited. He is neither tall nor short. He is a great scholar, and very realized." Raya Tulku went on to say, "I asked Dudjom Tulku how long I could expect to live." My father asked, "What did he say?" And Raya Tulku replied, "He said, 'I cannot tell you. You yourself will know.'" Dudjom Tulku must be very special, I thought, to have made such a strong impression upon a master like Raya Tulku.

My father studied and memorized many texts revealed by great tertöns over the centuries that contained prophecies made by Guru Padmasambhava. Guru Padmasambhava forecasted that around this time—the 1950s—the Tibetan people would be overrun by a foreign invader and that they should seek refuge in the south, in Pema Kö. My father knew and repeatedly warned the villagers that the Chinese Communists were coming. "We must leave," my father said. "We must go to Pema Kö." The villagers, some of whom were relatives, laughed and joked about this, saying, "Oh yeah, Gyega? And what other information do you have?" When they saw him they would sing, "Ha Ho, Ha Ho, time to go to Pema Kö." But my father was steadfast; he knew Guru Padmasambhava's prophecies would come true. The villagers tried to prevent our departure. When they realized we were definitely leaving, they told us we had made the wrong decision. Everyone thought my father was unbalanced. We left at the end of 1958. The journey was long and arduous. Then, in early 1960, we entered Pema Kö.

Pema Kö is located in southern Tibet between east India and Burma. There are no modern roads in Pema Kö, or in Tibet as a whole for that matter, but if there were, a two- to three-hour drive to the north would take you to majestic glacial mountains. A similar drive down to the valley would take you to tropical rainforests. There can be enormous climatic variations in Pema Kö, but it is mostly tropical. Rain is plentiful, and bamboo, palm trees, and many types of tropical vegetation grow abundantly.

Pema Kö maintains ancient ways. The people go about barefoot. There are no conveyances—not even horses—so they carry everything on their backs. Farming is the major occupation. The soil is so rich and soft that farmers do not dig—they simply plunge a stick into the ground and drop a seed into the hole. Crops are harvested all year long—in the summer rice, different varieties of corn, and quinoa; in the winter barley, wheat, and lentils. The people speak their own language, which is similar to the language of eastern Bhutan. They do not have their own writing system, so they follow the Tibetan. Tibetan is their second language.

Pema Kö is the hidden land (*sbas yul*) of Guru Padmasambhava. It is, he taught, a refuge for Tibetans during difficult times and a superb place for spiritual practice. He described paths that led from Tibet to Pema Kö. He said that the three staple foods of Tibet, yak meat, tsampa (roasted barley flour), and dairy products, would be found in Pema Kö in the forms of "tree meat, caves of tsampa, and fountains of milk." He also said that because of Pema Kö's mild climate, the people would not have to worry about clothing.

The state of Pema Kö begins where the Tsangpo River, known in India as the Brahmaputra, after flowing eastward from its source near Lhasa in central Tibet, abruptly turns to the south. The river's sudden, dramatic change creates a powerful and mysterious waterfall known as Gyala Shinji Badong, or Throat of Yama, where Guru Padmasambhava and Yeshe

Tsogyal hid many termas, later revealed by Jatsön Nyingpo and other great tertöns. The Tsangpo continues southward through the huge Pema Kö mountains, flowing into Assam, then Bangladesh, until ultimately merging with the Bay of Bengal.

The border and geography of Pema Kö is known as the body print of Vajra Varahi, the secret wisdom consort of Hayagriva. In addition, Pema Kö is considered to be one of the most powerful geomantic energy points on the earth. The native birds often sing the mantras of Guru Padma-sambhava and Avalokiteshvara, as well as other prayers. When people die, rainbows appear around their bodies and in their houses. Rainbows even appear when animals die. At night, the people of Pema Kö see flashing lights and campfires, and hear strange human voices in the hills. In the morning when they investigate, there are no traces of anyone having been there. It is a very mysterious land.

About one and a half months after our arrival in Pema Kö, shortly after the Tibetan New Year, we traveled further south until we reached the mountain atop which His Holiness was born. The mountain was almost vertical, so the ascent was difficult. When we finally reached the summit, we discovered a large, open valley with a beautiful meadow. Here was the village of Terkong Nang, His Holiness's birthplace. There were two monasteries in the village, one for ngagpas and one for ordained monks. Between these two monasteries was a beautiful temple. This temple was where His Holiness resided. During this time I heard many stories about His Holiness. I was told he was traveling—first to Lhasa, then to India.

We stayed in Terkong Nang only about two and a half months. The situation was dire. There wasn't enough food, so although we wanted to stay, it was impossible. After a journey with many hardships we arrived at a Tibetan refugee camp in east Assam in the autumn of 1960. During this time my younger sister, Ting Ting Karmo, died.

In India we met many Tibetan refugees who were devotees of His Holiness, and they talked about him quite often. We learned how widely revered he was and that he was giving many teachings and empowerments of both kama and terma in Kalimpong. My father wanted to take us to

*Kyabjes Chatral, Dudjom, and Dilgo Khyentse Rinpoches
in Darjeeling, India, during the 1960s*

Kalimpong to meet him and receive teachings, but there were too many obstacles. Being refugees, our ability to move about as we pleased was severely restricted. Also, my mother was quite sick. We spent two winters in a refugee camp. Then my sister Yangzom died, and not long after that, so did my mother. My father decided that we must now go on pilgrimage, first to Darjeeling, then to Kalimpong, to see His Holiness.

We made it to Darjeeling, but even though Kalimpong was only about thirty-five kilometers away we could not get there as we did not have the necessary permit and passport. We spent the entire summer of 1963 in Darjeeling. Then, that October, His Holiness came to Darjeeling at the request of Kyabje Chatral Rinpoche. Kyabje Chatral Rinpoche had built a statue of Guru Padmasambhava, approximately five feet tall, made of copper and gilded in gold, and he had asked His Holiness to consecrate it. His Holiness also gave an empowerment on Guru Padmasambhava. This was the first time I met His Holiness; it was also the first time I received teachings and empowerments from him. It seemed so auspicious that I could connect with Guru Padmasambhava, the gateway of the blessings of the vajrayana, through his living representative, His Holiness Dudjom Rinpoche. At least five hundred people attended this great event. Everyone waited patiently in line to receive empowerments and protection cords.

A few days later we left for central India to visit Bodhgaya and Varanasi, sacred places of Buddha Shakyamuni. Then, gradually, we traveled to Old Delhi with many Tibetan refugees. Eventually we joined a group headed by the renowned Sakya master Dzongsar Gona Rinpoche. At this time His Holiness Dudjom Rinpoche and his assistant, Kathok Öntrul Rinpoche, were traveling from Dharamsala. They were waiting in the Old Delhi station for the connecting train that would take them to their destination, which was Kalimpong. Kathok Öntrul Rinpoche was a friend of Dzongsar Gona Rinpoche's and went to visit him. When Dzongsar Gona Rinpoche learned His Holiness was in Old Delhi, he asked whether an audience might be possible. An audience was quickly arranged at the train station. We formed a line and one by one approached His Holiness. His Holiness gently placed his right hand on each person's crown chakra as a blessing. Shortly after this, we stopped at Tso Pema (Lotus Lake), which is a sacred place associated with Guru Padmasambhava and the site of a private monastery belonging to His Holiness. Around this time Dudjom Tulku had become the head of all the Nyingma schools. Shortly thereafter I enrolled in the Nyingma monastic school at Tso Pema. This school was eventually relocated to Dehra Dun.

In 1965 His Holiness the Dalai Lama organized a historic conference in which the leaders of the Nyingma, Kagyu, Sakya, and Gelug schools assembled and discussed how best to preserve and continue the ancient teachings of Tibet. As a result of this conference, in the autumn of 1967, the Central Institute of Higher Tibetan Studies was formed. His Holiness Dudjom Rinpoche sent telegrams to my brother, telling him to represent the Nyingma School. My brother complied and became one of the founding members of the Institute. The Institute taught Sanskrit, English, Hindi, and Tibetan languages, as well as Tibetan philosophy and culture. My father wanted me to study there; he said it would be good if we two brothers could be together. My brother also asked me to come. I became one of the first ten students at the Institute. And through my brother, I began to have more contact with His Holiness.

In 1969 His Holiness gave an empowerment and teachings on *The Eight Herukas—Embodiment of All the Sugatas* by the great tertön Nyangral Nyima Özer. Many masters and hundreds of monks, nuns, and lay practitioners were in attendance. At the conclusion of the ceremony, His Holiness asked one of his main attendants, an expert in the ritual arts, to take down the shrine that was erected for the purpose of the empowerment. As the shrine was elaborate, the attendant called for assistance, but there was so much commotion—people moving about and talking—he did not receive as much help as he wanted. Then some of the monks who at first came to his aid disappeared into the crowd. His Holiness was about to give a series of transmissions, but first the shrine needed to be taken down; he repeated his request to the attendant, this time adding, "Do it quickly." The attendant called for help but to no avail; he grew increasingly frustrated. Finally he lost his temper altogether and started hurling plates of tormas to the ground, one after another. Tormas are sacred objects not to be handled disrespectfully. I wondered how His Holiness would respond. When I turned to look, His Holiness was smiling and gently laughing.

The attendant, a close student of His Holiness and a well-known yogi from Bhutan, passed away recently amidst signs of realization. First, he announced he was going to rest, and he then secluded himself. He died shortly thereafter. When his body was discovered, it had begun to shrink, and lights appeared. After the cremation relics were found.

His Holiness was gentle and kind. Once he was visiting in Switzerland where I was recovering from tuberculosis in a sanitarium. I could not leave to see him and receive his blessing. I called the family that was hosting him on the phone instead, never expecting to be put through to him directly. I was surprised that he took time to talk with me. He told me not to worry, that I would be fine and that he would see me in India. Later, when I visited that family, I discovered that His Holiness had left dharma nectar medicine and protection cords for me.

In January 1978 His Holiness completed a major empowerment and transmission of the *Dudjom Tersar* cycle, which includes his own teaching as well as that of his previous incarnation, Dudjom Lingpa, near the holy Boudnath Stupa in Kathmandu, Nepal. I was fortunate enough to attend. Then I returned to India, first to Varanasi, then to Darjeeling to my father's house. My father had been in Nepal, practicing in Yangleshö and in the Asura caves, holy places where Guru Padmasambhava actualized Vajrakilaya and Yangdag Heruka. Afterward my father visited His Holiness. His Holiness wanted to do some work with me and asked whether that would be possible. My father said, "Whatever my son can do to help you would honor and delight me." Shortly thereafter His Holiness sent a messenger with a letter asking me to be abbot of Shedrub Döjo Ling, known in English as the Wish-Fulfilling Nyingma Institute. Although this seemed like an indication of an auspicious future connection, I did not think myself capable or worthy of helping His Holiness; nevertheless, I could not refuse the request of such a great master and quickly went to him in Nepal. As soon as I arrived in Kathmandu, I showed up at the door of his house in the late afternoon and asked for an audience. His attendants brought back his reply, "It's too late today, come tomorrow morning." The next day I returned and received his instructions.

I had the great privilege of being a close personal attendant and secretary to His Holiness from 1980-1983. One time in New York City at his Yeshe Nyingpo Center, when we were alone, he told me about the life of his father and, in great detail, about how he himself had taken birth. This was in December 1982. I tried my best to remember everything he told me, and I committed it to writing. Although I wanted to hear more, I did not ask.

In March 1983 we were in Santa Monica, California. His Holiness was about to take a walk, and his wife encouraged me to accompany him. We could not go very far, because there were many long and unfamiliar streets, so we stayed close to the house. His Holiness spoke once again about the life of his father and about his own birth—this time in even greater detail; in addition, he told me stories about other family members. Afterward, to the best of my ability, I wrote down everything he had said. I wanted to ask His Holiness to tell me even more and consulted his lama-disciples about

Guru Padmasambhava, Shantarakshita, Yeshe Tsogyal, and King Trisong Deutsen
From the Gonpa wall murals at Padma Samye Ling

whether that would be wise. Everyone agreed that I should not ask, for it would be inauspicious—to ask a master to recount his or her life might be a sign that the master did not have long to live.

Today I regret I did not ask His Holiness to at least write a short auto-biographical prayer. It has long been a Tibetan practice for students to make such a request of their masters. But there is no such prayer. Therefore, what he told me on those two occasions must serve as the foundation for this humble biographical sketch of His Holiness Dudjom Rinpoche, one of the great masters of Tibetan Buddhism and one of the most humble people in the world.

THE PRINCIPAL PURPOSE OF THIS INCARNATION

In the eighth century in Tibet, the great abbot Shantarakshita, Guru Padmasambhava, and King Trisong Deutsen united their intentions, built Samye Monastery, and established schools of academic Buddhism. They gathered smart, young Tibetan boys and taught them Sanskrit and other languages of neighboring Buddhist countries. They translated the Buddha's teachings, mainly from Sanskrit, and also from other languages. These translations were corrected and edited. They established academic (*bshad gra*) and meditation (*sgrub gra*) institutes, and gave empowerments and transmissions of the teachings.

Guru Padmasambhava and his chief disciple, Yeshe Tsogyal, hid teachings throughout Tibet. These teachings were intended for future times, to prevent upcoming disturbances and negative influences in Tibet and the world. Guru Padmasambhava prophesied that these teachings would be revealed by extraordinary individuals to whom they were entrusted. The first of these treasure revealers, or tertöns, was the eleventh-century master Sangye Lama, and they have been appearing ever since, even to the present day. Tertöns can be simple, ordinary men and women in the form of lay practitioners and householders or wandering yogis. They can be ordained monks and nuns or great scholars. Tertöns are sometimes childlike in their behavior or crazy and wild. Sometimes they are humble and low. Sometimes they are powerful and majestic such as the fifth Dalai Lama, who became the temporal and spiritual leader of all Tibet and the exemplar for all subsequent Dalai Lamas. Tertöns come to restrengthen the teachings of the Buddha Shakyamuni in general and of Guru Padmasambhava and Yeshe Tsogyal in particular. Tertöns also eliminate hardships and bring peace and harmony to living beings. Tertöns can have a salutary effect on the natural environment—they perform special ceremonies at the different geomantic energy points of the earth so that the four elements will be balanced, just as Guru Padmasambhava instructed in his teachings. Similarly, when tertöns remove termas from the ground or mountains, they perform ceremonies and replace what has been extracted with other blessed sacred objects. In this way, earth energy and harmony are preserved.

His Holiness Dudjom Rinpoche was a great tertön. He was the emanation of not one but of many great beings. In the terma teachings it is said that he was the body emanation of Drogben Khyeuchung Lotsawa (one of the twenty-five heart students of Guru Padmasambhava), the speech emanation of Yeshe Tsogyal, and the mind emanation of Guru Padmasambhava. In other terma teachings it says that Guru Padmasambhava and Yeshe Tsogyal reincarnated together in the form of His Holiness Dudjom Rinpoche, so that he was their actual presence—only the body was different. His Holiness was a householder, a family man, and lived a long life; he was recognized and revered as a master from the day he was born; he revealed many important and profound teachings, but he did not behave like someone great—he was humble and casual at all times; his bearing was that of an ordinary person. This is what Guru Padmasambhava meant when he predicted, centuries earlier, that His Holiness Dudjom Rinpoche would have the personality of a child.

His Holiness was known by many names. His birth name was Nyima Gyaltsen. His father, as instructed by the dakinis in a dream, gave him the name Yeshe Dorje. The great tertön Jedrung Thrinle Jampa Jungne composed a long-life prayer for him shortly after his birth and named him Jigdral Dechen Dorje Dragpo Tsal. Owing to his prowess in the sciences, he was named Tsojung Gyepai Langtso Ngönme Dawa Sarpa. Upon receiving upasaka vows, he was named Gyurme Gelek Chogle Namgyal. Upon receiving bodhichitta vows, he was named Gyalse Lodrö Drimed Phende Dawai Özer. His vajrayana empowerment name was Dorje Dütsal Drag. His Nyingthig empowerment name was Yenpa Lode. When Guru Padmasambhava and Yeshe Tsogyal empowered and enthroned him as a great tertön, they gave him the name Drodul Lingpa. And the name he was most commonly known by was Jigdral Yeshe Dorje.

His Holiness was born in 1904, fifty years before the tragic events in Tibet. Great tertöns often appear just prior to periods of great upheaval. Guru Padmasambhava wanted His Holiness to incarnate at this time to save and strengthen the religious and cultural traditions of Tibet, which were in danger of being destroyed as if by fire and flood.

In the 1950s the Communist Chinese invaded Tibet. The Tibetan people were forced to leave their country, and there was great anxiety regarding the future. His Holiness sang a beautiful song. He, too, was leaving his home-land; the destination was uncertain. The song includes this stanza: "I, the tiger, do not need a rich mansion. / The tiger's forest thickets are my rich mansion. / Anywhere I like, I parade my bold stripes, / Heading toward good spots in sandalwood forests." And it concluded like this: "I, the yogi do not need a family home. / All the yogi's good places are my family home. / Since the two aims are instantly realized, / Anywhere I go I like, heading out at ease." This song displayed His Holiness's fearless realization.

His Holiness arrived in India in the mid-1950s. Expatriate Tibetans flocked around him, and he always helped them. By example and through meditation and practice instruction, he not only preserved but actually restrengthened the lineage teachings, and he was responsible for a renaissance in Tibetan studies. He truly fulfilled the mandate of Guru Padmasambhava.

During the 1960s two separate and rival political parties, "United Tibet" (which represented central Tibet) and "Thirteen Ethnic Groups of Tibet" (which represented mainly eastern Tibet) were each seeking support from famous, titled individuals. "United Tibet" and "Thirteen Ethnic Groups of Tibet" asked His Holiness to join. He joined both. His Holiness had a very open mind! He was nonpartisan and a teacher to everyone. Ultimately his interest was in spiritual, not worldly, affairs.

Reflecting upon the life and legacy of His Holiness Dudjom Rinpoche, we witness six extraordinary activities that he performed during this most crucial time in Tibetan Buddhist history:

(1) His writings number twenty-five volumes and are among the most profound and influential in Tibetan Buddhist history. They include his own terma revelations, poetry, historical treatises, and commentaries on the terma revealed by past masters, the kama teachings, and philosophy. As an acknowledged master, teacher, and expositor of instrumental and vocal music, chanting, and lama dance, as well as of esoteric practices, such as tsa-lung, tummo, and trülkhor, he also composed works on the ritual arts and yoga.

(2) He gave the empowerments of and teachings on the *Treasury of Precious Treasures* (the complete collection of termas compiled by Jamgön Kongtrul Rinpoche) an unprecedented ten times, to countless thousands of people, including many great masters, khenpos, and tulkus, thus securing and strengthening this vital tradition for generations to come.

(3) He collected, compiled, and edited the complete kama teachings of the Nyingma School, many of which were scattered throughout Tibet and its environs and thus in danger of being lost. He edited the existing thirteen volumes, originally printed in the u-med *(dbu med)* short-hand script, and reprinted them in twenty volumes in the u-chen *(dbu chen)* block-type script. To these, he added thirty-eight more volumes and then published all fifty eight. He also gave empowerments and teachings on the complete kama teachings three times.

(4) He gave the transmission of all the Kangyur teachings, inspiring his students as to their importance, thus securing textual study and meditation practice based upon the foundational teachings of the Buddha.

(5) In the 1960s—the most difficult time in Tibetan history—he, along with other masters and academics, rekindled the Tibetan educational system by editing the course-books used by primary and secondary school children.

(6) He was unanimously proclaimed by all the Nyingma masters and devotees to be the head of the Nyingma School, the first ever in Tibetan Buddhist history. He served in this capacity from the time of his appointment in the early 1960s until his maha-parinirvana in 1987, uniting all the subschools of the Nyingmapa and invigorating the tradition as a whole.

His Holiness Dudjom Rinpoche incarnated principally to perform these six activities in order to ensure the continuance of Tibetan Buddhism long into the future, as well as to benefit countless beings.

DYING WITH FEARLESSNESS AND
LEAVING WITH HOLY MARKS AND SIGNS

In Buddhism death is part of nature's process. Buddha Shakyamuni taught that there are four stages to human existence: birth, aging, sickness, and death. These are continuous like a turning wheel, so following death, there is rebirth and then life again.

The rotation of death and life is reflected in the procession of the seasons. When winter comes, it does not mean there is no spring; in fact, winter is a certain sign that spring is coming. This is true also for night and day. Death and life are therefore two sides of a single coin.

In vajrayana Buddhism we practice life and death as path. The creation stage purifies the habitual patterns of life; the completion stage purifies the habitual patterns of death. When our habitual patterns are purified we realize both life and death are as a dream.

At this time we may perceive that life and death are opposite and have firm faith that they are real, but in fact they are fabrications of the mind. The *Lankavatara Sutra* says, "There are no solidly existing external appearances; everything is the display of your mind." In other words, your own body, all the objects that appear in the environment around you, all that occurs and space itself—all is mind. The *Avatamsaka Sutra* says, "The mind is an artist. The artist-mind makes aggregates and universes. All are drawings of the mind." Again, from the *Hevajra Tantra*: "Without the precious mind there are no beings and no buddhas." As the Buddha Shakyamuni taught, when you realize the true nature of the mind, or rigpa, you realize the true nature of everything, and you are beyond life and death.

The great yogi Milarepa said, "I was scared of death. I went to the mountains. I meditated on impermanence and death—now I have lost the fear of death." The great master Longchenpa, as he was about to enter the dharmakaya state, said to his disciples, "Samsara has no solid essence. Now I am going to let go of this magical body of impermanence. Listen carefully to my instructions. Sentient beings are travelers bound for a single destination. Some have already reached it. Some are reaching it this very moment. Others will reach it in the future. Recognize this fact. Life's experience is like daytime; the afterlife experience is tonight's dream. Tonight's dream of afterlife is fast approaching—become familiar with the true nature of your mind this instant!" Longchenpa continued, "Every gathering ends in dispersion. I will not stay. I go now to the land of liberation. This traveler's time has come; he takes the road. My joy in departing is greater than the merchant who obtained the wish-fulfilling jewel from the ocean, greater than Indra defeating the asuras in battle, greater even than profound meditative experience. I, Padma Ledreltsal, will not stay; I go to the fortress of immortality, great blissfulness."

According to the Buddha's teaching, this body is rented from the four elements—the flesh, from earth; the blood and other liquids, from water; the heat or warmth, from fire; the breath, from air/wind. These elements will not last unless they are refined into their essences, the culmination of which is called the "rainbow body." Mind, however, does last, and it will continue from life to life, carrying with it the habitual patterns of karma until at last its true nature is realized.

Death is coming. Everyone should be prepared. Good practitioners have nothing to worry about; for ordinary people the most important thing is to not become ensnared in hope and fear. Let there be no anxiety. Rebuild your courage. Think, "Death is everyone's experience. It is natural, inevitable, and now it is approaching me." Bring to mind and celebrate the good deeds you have done in life. If you committed bad deeds, mentally ask for forgiveness, purify them with practices such as Vajrasattva, and then let them go forever. Think, "May my illness and death substitute for all others' illness and death."

With regard to possessions, if you have already distributed them, that is excellent. If not, make mental offerings to the three jewels, Buddha Amitabha, or to whomever or whatever you believe in. Pray, "May these objects bring benefit to those who use them, and may they never become the cause of quarreling and fighting." If possible, ask your friends and family to help you. Good thoughts at the time of death help ensure a smooth transition to the first stage of the bardo. When the bardo is good, all the processes that lead to the next birth will be good.

According to the Dzogchen teachings, the good practitioner, upon dying, merges his or her rigpa into the space of dharmadhatu. Such practitioners can leave the body in a variety of ways, of which three will be mentioned. Some leave the body as a heap of rainbow light or leave it as a heap of one of three elements—fire, water, or air. Others, utterly unconcerned, leave the body anywhere, in the manner of an animal. Still others make an announcement, give pith instructions and advice to their disciples, and leave their bodies as precious relics for generations to come. His Holiness Dudjom Rinpoche chose the third way.

The body is the product of past karma. Even good practitioners experience physical difficulties. It is said that for the yogi, the body is bondage—it prevents the blazing power of rigpa from manifesting. The moment the body and rigpa separate, the Dzogchen yogi attains the youthful vase body, or Samantabhadra state. This is not death—it is liberation.

His Holiness Dudjom Rinpoche entered mahaparinirvana on January 17, 1987, at his home in Dordogne, in southern France. There were many signs of his great realization—visual, auditory, olfactory, and tactile. The visual signs were that his complexion remained bright and clear, just as a living person; also, rainbows and spheres of light appeared. The auditory signs were beautiful sounds heard in and around the home. The olfactory signs were beautiful fragrances, also within and outside his home. His Holiness's body was flexible and soft to the touch, without a trace of rigidity—this was the tactile sign.

The Dzogchen tantra *Blazing Relics of Buddha-Body* describes signs of realization observable to others when a great master leaves the body, as well as the meaning of those signs. When a circle of light surrounded by rings appears after death, that individual has reached the ultimate state. When a light goes straight up, it indicates that the individual has instantly reached enlightenment without having to experience the bardo. When beams of light appear, it means the individual is reaching enlightenment at the end of the bardo. That same tantra teaches that when a sound comes from the eastern direction, the practitioner has achieved enlightenment in the vajra family; from the south, in the ratna family; from the west, in the padma family; from the north, in the karma family; and from above, in the buddha family. Furthermore, the complexion of one who has merged the child and mother clear-light luminosity states remains bright; even if the body is left for as long as twenty-five days, it will remain fresh. And fragrances are emitted, more pleasant than camphor, saffron, and sandalwood.

Before His Holiness's *kudung* was embalmed, it was observed by lama-disciples to be both getting smaller and becoming less dense, a process called *ö-du-zhu* (*'od du zhu*), which may be translated as "melting away" or "melting into light," another sign of great Dzogchen realization. At the same time the kudung was being embalmed in France, preparations were being made to receive it at his monastery in Kathmandu, Nepal, known as Orgyen Dongak Chökhorling.

His Holiness's kudung was flown to Kathmandu Airport. The monastery arranged a great procession. Great teachers, monks, and devotees from all the neighboring monasteries lined the streets and offered their devotion. According to the varying customs of the people, there were beautiful displays of singing and dancing. Then the kudung was flown to Bhutan, where it received a similar reception. After this it was returned to Nepal.

His Holiness's kudung was taken to his monastery and placed in a stupa built and consecrated under the close supervision of Kyabje Chatral Rinpoche. (His Holiness's face is visible from the stupa.) Spheres of light appeared as this took place, not only inside and outside the monastery but also around neighboring buildings as well. People in these buildings mistook these spheres of lights for stains and tried to wipe them off windows. Some people saw buddhas such as Vajrasattva and Guru Padmasambhava within spheres of light; others saw beautiful landscapes. A nun named Ani Tamdrin, known to be very skeptical regarding visions, actually saw the holy lake Tso Pema and His Holiness together within a sphere of light and was heard rejoicing over it. The great master Kyabje Chatral Rinpoche saw blue Vajrasattva. Many people witnessed and were inspired by these occurrences, not only his devotees but even those who did not know the dharma. For the latter, a profound and everlasting connection was made.

THE BENEFITS OF WRITING A GREAT MASTER'S LIFE STORY

The *Avatamsaka Sutra* says, "Whoever offers melodious-sounding prayers to Noble Ones expressing their enlightened qualities will greatly benefit." The great master Saraha said, "In order to reach enlightenment you must accumulate the two merits and receive the lama's blessings through devotion—there is no other method." Saraha also said, "Whoever receives the blessings of the lama will reach the heart of enlightenment; it is like discovering a treasure in the palm of your hand." The Buddha Shakyamuni said, "All the one thousand buddhas of this Fortunate Aeon attained enlightenment by contacting a qualified teacher."

The student who connects with a qualified teacher will receive all the qualities of that teacher. For diligent and enthusiastic students the qualified teacher is a torch that dispels all darkness and leads them swiftly and smoothly to the shore of enlightenment. The qualified teacher is extremely hard to find. Once you find such a one you should maintain contact with him or her with appreciation, courage, and commitment. This will bring you every spiritual reward you are seeking.

Buddha Shakyamuni, Guru Padmasambhava, and other masters stated again and again that whoever writes of the qualities and activities of great teachers will truly benefit; they also said such writings will inspire those who read them. As long as books last, this will be so. And the invisible benefits will accrue far beyond even this. Trust in these words.

In the tantras it is said, "The lama is the embodiment of all the buddhas, the holder of the secret vajrayana, and the root of the three jewels. I bow down to the great teacher." The body of the lama is the sangha; the speech of the lama is the dharma; the mind of the lama is the buddha. The *Chakrasamvara Tantra* says, "The lama is buddha, dharma, and sangha, as well as lord of the mandala; therefore, the lama is Vajradhara."

Again, it says, "Through the kindness of the lama great blissfulness is bestowed instantly in the manner of a wish-fulfilling jewel. Therefore, I bow down to the lotus feet of the vajra masters." Reflecting on these words, I wrote this book for present and future devotees of His Holiness Dudjom Rinpoche, for friends of the dharma, and for myself, as a support for our devotion.

How This Book Was Conceived and Supported

His Holiness Dudjom Rinpoche, the regent of Guru Padmasambhava and all the kama and terma masters, was a beacon of hope for the Tibetan people. Many great and famous lineage holders were taught and inspired by this extraordinary master, but so far it seems no one has written a major biographical work on him. His Holiness spontaneously taught me a brief version of his life story. He was, I believe, indirectly giving me permission to compose and publish it. This work is the product of everything His Holiness told me, and also what I learned about him from my vajra brothers and sisters.

Writers can conceive and execute biographies from a variety of perspectives—historical, political, psychological, aesthetic, etc.—which can be of their own or others' choosing. I chose to write a biography of His Holiness from the religious perspective; it focuses upon his vast, meritorious spiritual activities on behalf of the Buddhadharma, the Tibetan people, and all living beings. While composing this work, I remained faithful to the facts regarding His Holiness's life and work and tried to avoid imposing my likes and dislikes. Still, this book is far from perfect. I welcome suggestions from the great lineage holders of His Holiness, some of whom had close contact with him for longer periods than I, as to how this book may be corrected, improved, and expanded.

Tibetan Buddhist books are composed of three sections—beginning, main body, and conclusion. The beginning section is always based upon bodhichitta, that is, the commitment to attain enlightenment for the benefit of all beings, and devotion, also known as "praising the noble ones of the past." The conclusion is likewise based upon bodhichitta and devotion; it includes prayers that the book will bring to all beings peace, happiness, and ultimately the full awakening of buddhahood. The main body of the book treats the subject under consideration, in this case the life story of His Holiness Dudjom Rinpoche. The prose style of writers of Tibetan Buddhist books is straightforward; some writers compose poetic verses and then insert them either before or after each section of prose. The verses are intended to condense and illuminate the meaning of the prose section. I followed the latter way by writing some offering verses to this great teacher, according to my capabilities.

I will explain the title of this biography. Shortly after His Holiness was conceived, wisdom dakinis appeared in a dream to his father, Khengen Tulku. They announced he was to have a son and gave him a ritual mirror and a dorje, saying, "These are his name." Khengen Tulku interpreted these objects to mean the name "Yeshe Dorje." *Yeshe* (wisdom) is no other than dharmakaya, the ineffable, infinite, empty essence of the true nature, and *Dorje* (indestructible) is sambhogakaya—the true nature's fertility, abundance, and richness. Since Yeshe Dorje was His Holiness's name, and also describes his realization, I thought it would be auspicious to use it in the title. As mentioned previously, Jedrung Thrinle Jampa Jungne had given him the name Jigdral Dechen Dorje, and His Holiness joined Jigdral to the name his father had given him. *Jigdral* means "fearless," one who embodies the four fearless states. This characterizes both the dharmakaya quality of his realization and his ceaseless rupakaya activity on behalf of all beings. To this I added "light," which symbolizes the brilliant sunlike quality of his achievement that shines throughout samsara and the buddha fields and the beacon-like aspect of his activity that guides sentient beings everywhere to the clear path of enlightenment. In this way *Light of Fearless Indestructible Wisdom* represents the life and legacy of His Holiness Dudjom Rinpoche.

To symbolize the eleven bhumis of the Mahayana path, I divided this biography into eleven chapters, each one introduced with the phrase *Heap of Lightbeams*. According to the Mahayana teaching, one begins the path with joy and devotion, proceeds with courage and commitment, develops bodhichitta, and in this way traverses the ten bhumis and reaches the eleventh, buddhahood.

The first chapter names and describes His Holiness's previous incarnations; it is based upon a work he himself composed, *Prayer to the Successive Incarnations, Called Garland of Pearls*. In that work His Holiness lists seventeen masters of the past and two masters of the future. The two future incarnations will be the King of Shambhala, Rigden Dorje Nönpo, who will defeat the forces that oppose peace and happiness, and Möpa Thaye, the last of the one thousand buddhas of this Fortunate Aeon. Due to constraints of time, I have focused on eight of his previous incarnations. For information on the others, the interested reader may consult His Holiness's collected works, as well as other Tibetan Buddhist histories.

The second chapter tells briefly about His Holiness's father, mother, and birthplace. His father, Khengen Tulku, was a renowned incarnate lama in upper Pema Kö. Khengen Tulku descended from the royal clan of the Tibetan dharma monarchy. His Holiness's mother descended from the famous fifteenth-century tertön Ratna Lingpa, whose teachings spread to and are widely practiced by all the Nyingma schools, as well as the Kagyu.

The third chapter pertains to the birth of His Holiness, which occurred on the tenth day of the sixth month of the Tibetan lunar calendar, just as the sunlight was reaching the rooftops of village homes—the same day and time that Guru Padmasambhava was born 2,440 years earlier. In Tibetan Buddhist culture, when a baby is born ceremonies are performed to harmonize his or her as well as the family's elements. To that end His Holiness's mother invited two ngagpas to the house shortly after his birth. They performed ceremonies and named him Nyima Gyaltsen. *Nyima* means "Sunday" (the day His Holiness was born), or "sun," and *Gyaltsen* means "victorious."

The fourth chapter deals with the recognition and enthronement of His Holiness shortly after his birth by the renowned disciples of his previous incarnation, Dudjom Lingpa.

The fifth chapter describes his education. His Holiness Dudjom Rinpoche was born enlightened; still, he followed the tradition of spiritual education. He studied, contemplated, and meditated upon all the Buddha's teachings, up to and including the ninth yana, Dzogchen. With joy and devotion he connected and studied with many great teachers. Some of these teachers received teachings in turn from him. By carefully observing and assimilating everything they taught, formally and informally, he became supremely qualified to represent and uphold the Nyingma lineage and Tibetan Buddhism. In this chapter I have listed only those teachers His Holiness himself cited.

The sixth chapter tells of his principal beneficial activities—maintaining the lineage teachings and helping beings. His Holiness traveled all over southern and central Tibet, India, Nepal, Bhutan, Sikkim, Southeast Asia, and the West giving transmissions, empowerments, instructions, encouragement, and inspiration.

The seventh chapter focuses upon his terma revelations. According to the teachings, there are earth, sky, pure vision, and mind termas. His Holiness revealed mostly mind termas. Guru Padmasambhava and Yeshe Tsogyal said, "So precious is this teaching, it will not be hidden in any common way, but sealed in the heart of the one with pure wisdom mind and good fortune who is no different from us." His Holiness also discovered earth termas. I was fortunate to be present at an audience in which he displayed phurbas and other terma ritual objects that he had revealed. But His Holiness was quiet about these matters. Neither I nor any of his disciples with whom I was acquainted ever heard him speak about his revelations, nor about any of his extraordinary activities, visions, and realizations. He kept his qualities secret, like stones buried in an ocean bed.

Guru Padmasambhava predicted that His Holiness would reveal new termas and restrengthen ancient ones. The eighth chapter describes his work in the latter sphere. His Holiness collected, edited, in many instances corrected, and propagated the teachings of great tertöns, such as Pema Lingpa, Dorje Lingpa, and Yarje Orgyen Lingpa, among others. As mentioned above, he also revitalized the kama tradition.

When His Holiness Dudjom Rinpoche completed his work, he wanted to enter mahaparinirvana, but owing to the request of his wisdom consort, Sangyum Kuzhok, as well as family members and disciples, he extended his life for two and a half years, remaining in deep dharmakaya meditation. This is the topic of the ninth chapter. Khenchen Palden Sherab Rinpoche, who had an opportunity to visit him in France during this time, observed, "When he saw me he smiled and said, 'Hello, Khenpo, how are you?'—not much more than that." Whoever approached him would be warmly welcomed. He received questions, answering them simply and directly, in few words. He had achieved the state known as "phenomena exhausted in the true nature of dharmata." In this state everything is primordially pure—good and bad, nirvana and samsara: everything is resolved as a single wisdom. His Holiness must have had many astounding visions during this time and experienced different states of samadhi and pure lands, but he never discussed them. Externally he appeared joyful, alert, relaxed, and open-minded. Occasionally he would say, "This traveler has been lingering for a long time; he is long overdue at the Glorious Copper-Color Mountain." Whenever he saw an image of Guru Padmasambhava, he picked it up and touched it to his crown chakra.

The tenth chapter pertains to his mahaparinirvana. Representatives of countries with disciples devoted to him—Bhutan, Nepal, Sikkim, and Ladakh—pleaded to have his kudung displayed in their lands. Owing to time constraints, it went only to Bhutan, where it was flown by Royal Bhutan Airlines, then back to Nepal. This was the first time in Tibetan Buddhist history that a great master's kudung was honored in different countries. Hundreds of thousands of devotees expressed their devotion and received his blessings. In this way His Holiness Dudjom Rinpoche, who transcended duality, displayed the same power in death as he did in life.

Finally, the eleventh chapter represents his unimpeded enlightened activity. It is a partial list of his disciples all over the world who by maintaining and transmitting his teaching ensure that it continues long into the future. I encourage those who know of other disciples to add their names to this list.

Many people supported this project. The Western nun Jomo Lorraine devotedly kept many advertising brochures of His Holiness's dharma activities, as well as other information pertaining to him. She generously made these available to me and always encouraged me to write. I engage in dharma activities, such as teaching, meditation, and monastic and administrative work, and at times can be quite busy. But this never stopped me; I wanted to write this biography with courage and commitment as an offering to this great teacher and as a gift to practitioners. The Tibetan version was completed with the assistance of Philippe Turrenne, Nancy Roberts, and Alex Chernoguzov and published in India through the sponsorship of Orgyen Chötso in 2004 to celebrate the one hundredth anniversary of His Holiness's birth. Generous support for this effort was also contributed by Les and Katherine Levine. Celia Barnes helped during the early stages of my translating the Tibetan prose into English. Carl Stuendel and I juggled our respective schedules for years to meet almost daily at the Shantarakshita Library at Padma Samye Ling to work on the prose translation, an extensive elaboration of the footnotes, and the Glossary. Without his commitment and insistence this project might not have been completed. Toy-Fung Tung and Marie-Louise Friquegnon helped me translate the verses into beautiful English poetry. I want to thank both of them for years of devotion and joyful effort. Nancy Roberts helped with the name and title appendices and checked for consistency of Tibetan text titles, proper names, and place names throughout the text. She also offered great support to Carl and me. Richard Steinberg helped me refine the introduction. Arthur Mandelbaum did the first translation of His Holiness's songs and helped compile a first list of footnotes. Philippe Turrenne also helped with the first compilation of the footnotes. Connie Musselwhite, Tim Tavis, and Jane Gilbert helped with proofreading and editing. To all the staff at Snow Lion, I offer my thanks, and in particular to Sudé Walters for her editorial scrutiny.

I want to thank His Holiness's wife, wisdom dakini Dudjom Sangyum Kuzhok Rigdzin Wangmo, who gave her blessings and support for this book. She provided much information, as well as the beautiful photographs, and kindly wrote the foreword. I also want to thank Jomo Lorraine, Laia Pema Tsultrim, and Pema Dragpa for their administrative work so that I could concentrate on this project. The blessings of my father, Lama Chimed, and my brother, Khenchen Palden Sherab Rinpoche, were great sources of inspiration.

I dedicate the merit of this work to my late father and teacher, the hidden yogi Lama Gyalchog, to my mother, Pema Lhadze, who was so peaceful, quiet, and kind, and to my beloved sisters and playmates, Yangzom and Ting Ting Karmo—we couldn't spend much time together due to the hardships of our journey to India. I dedicate the merit to the late Bill Hinman (Pema Drimed), who was a tremendous force behind the realization of Palden Padma Samye Ling, as well as to all the members and friends of the sangha —those living and those who have passed away—who through their joyful support have established monuments to peace and the three jewels on behalf of Padmasambhava Buddhist Centers worldwide. I dedicate the merit to present and future dharma practitioners and to all beings. Finally, may this small deed help to strengthen and spread the Buddhadharma and its message of universal love and compassion.

SPELLING AND OTHER CONVENTIONS

Throughout the text the honorific titles Kyabje (*skyabs rje*) and His Holiness are used to refer to Dudjom Rinpoche, Jigdral Yeshe Dorje. *Kyabje* means "lord protector," "lord of refuge," and this Tibetan term is translated into English as "His Holiness."

The Sanskrit equivalent of the Tibetan *Yeshe* is *Jnana*, which means "wisdom" in English. *Jnana* is occasionally used in this biography to refer to His Holiness. The verses sometimes call him "Terchen Lord" and "Terchen Lama."

The biographer, Khenpo Tsewang Dongyal, speaks of himself as "the author of this biography."

Shakyamuni Buddha is considered to be the fourth buddha of one thousand that will appear in this Fortunate Aeon. In this biography the expression "second buddha" is used as an honorific epithet, almost always referring to Guru Padmasambhava. It is never used to refer to the second of the one thousand buddhas.

The abbreviation TRE is used in conjunction with a date to designate the number of years elapsed since the inception of the Yarlung dynasty in 127 BCE, known as the Tibetan Royal Era.

The English spelling of personal names and places throughout the text is based on a conventional phonetic transcription that attempts to approximate the Tibetan pronunciation. When such a spelling is at odds with one commonly given for certain teachers well known in the West, the well-known spelling is used, e.g., Chatral instead of Jadral (*bya bral*), Tulku Thondup instead of Trulku Döndrub (*sprul sku don grub*), and Patrul instead of Paltrul (*dpal sprul*). The Wylie spelling for these names can be found in the Index of Personal and Place Names.

For the most part Wylie spellings (*italicized and enclosed within parentheses*) for names, titles, and technical terms are given only in the endnotes, appendices, and Glossary. The abbreviations Tib. (Tibetan) and Skt. (Sanskrit) are used only when terms from both languages are presented together.

LIGHT OF FEARLESS
INDESTRUCTIBLE WISDOM

His Holiness Dudjom Rinpoche

Introductory Verses:

*homage to the masters of the Nyingma lineage
and a pledge to bring this biography to completion*

Homage, Lord Lama, your compassion is infinite.
Please hold me with your great kindness.
Bestow all the blessings of your supreme body, speech, and mind.

1

In boundless pure lands filling all ten directions,
Magic clouds arise, play of the three kayas,
Nirmanakaya source of benefits for beings:
Supreme lord lama, may I be protected by you.

2

Jigdral, unmoving from the dharmakaya,
Yeshe, compassion beyond all times and directions,
Dorje,[1] powerful sign pointing to the perfect path:
Three lineages'[2] lama, at your feet I bow.

3

Vast from the beginning, peaceful, uncontrived,
Unchanging, beyond decrease, increase, thought and words,
Kuntuzangpo's wisdom passes from heart to heart.
Buddhas, speaking mind to mind, to you I bow.

4

From innate clear light, spontaneous and ceaseless,
Blazing forth with the power of compassion,
Great secret symbols awaken lucky ones.
Vidyadharas, speaking through signs, to you I bow.

5

Perfecting the boundless two aims, as befits
The wishes and talents of good practitioners,
Empowerments, pith advice, pass from mouth to ear.
Lineage masters of words, to you I bow.

6

Seeing everything clearly for what it is,
Embodiment of peace, Shakyamuni, you
Love infinitely the six realms as your own child:
A friend even to those who know you not. Homage!

7

Only body of the buddhas' three secrets, abounding in love, power, and
    wisdom; [3]
Only safeguard of endless beings, their great help in countless forms,
    wrathful and peaceful;
Only refuge in the present, future, and bardo: Padma Jung,[4] lord of
    compassion.
Only putting my trust in you: mind, heart, and chest,[5] I clasp you to
    me and none other.

8

Body, sun's bright dawn, glorified by major and minor marks;[6]
Speech, in Brahma's tones, rousing all beings from dark ignorance;[7]
Mind, vast all-knowing light of absolute and relative truth:
Manjushri, please guard me until I attain enlightenment.

9

Yeshe Tsogyal,[8] wisdom's beauty of major and minor marks,
Lake-born essence of all the buddhas and bodhisattvas,
Noble queen of the buddhas' constant spontaneous deeds,
Swift heroine, fending off fear, mother, I remember you.

10

Enlightened within wisdom's uncontrived body,
Ever young, beyond birth and death, vajra rainbow,
Filling skies with countless thousands of light displays:
Primordial Vimalamitra,[9] reign supreme!

11

Great scholar of the Madhyamaka and Mind-Only schools,[10]
Great siddha who lived for nine hundred years,
Great compassion's lamp of stainless teachings,
Great bodhisattva Shiwatso,[11] I pay homage to you.

12

Through great wisdom, ranking with scholars and siddhas,
Through great courage, perfecting the Buddha's teachings,
Through great power, holding lands in four directions,
Great King Trisong Deutsen,[12] I pay homage to you.

13

Lovely, lovely Tibet, where Buddha's stainless teachings were brought
and revered without dissension by great aryas of the past;
Most sublime siddhas: scholars such as Sambhota,[13] Vairo, [14] Ka,[15]
Chok,[16] Zhang,[17] So,[18] Zur,[19] Nub,[20] Nyak,[21] Rong, [22] Long,[23] Lochen
Chöpal,[24] and Mipham;[25]
Most sublime scholars: siddhas like Nyang Ral,[26] Chöwang,[27] the five
Lingpas,[28] and Thang Gyal,[29] Jatsön,[30] Terdak Ling,[31] Tsasum Ling,[32]
Jigme Ling;[33]
Great, great, scholars, siddhas: Patrul,[34] Khyen,[35] Kong,[36] Chog Ling,[37]
Dudjom Ling,[38] and all mind-lineage lamas: please bestow your
wisdom. Che!

14

Upholder of Buddha's stainless doctrine around the world, through
    teaching, practice, and deeds,
The scholar well versed in three unerring modes of thought,
    Khenchen, glory of Prajna; and
The scholar rich in realization, crown jewel of true speech, Thubten,
    joy of Virya; and
The great hidden yogi, Pema Shila: in such teachers, I place faith and
    devotion. [39]

15

Essence of the buddhas of the three times,
Great captain,[40] leading beings to freedom,
Terchen lord of three dharma kindnesses,
Padma's[41] regent, Dudjom Drodul Lingpa.[42]

16

Hero-conqueror of four demon evils,
Treasure holder of ocean's depths[43] of wisdom,
Great teacher of the sure, secret vajra path,
Lord Lama, to your body, speech, mind, I bow.

17

Inconceivable deeds of the terchen lama,
Such as they were, how can a child's mind hold them?
Yet for those like me, now and in the future,
I write this, drawing devotion from devotion.[44]

18

Fierce, fierce, fearsome formidable hero's body, great and grand, grue-
somely adorned, howling "ha ha" through bare fangs, dread
guardian of Buddha's doctrine: Mahakala.

Crack, crack, crackling blasts of fiery winds whipping white clouds into
swirling cyclones, richly to robe Kunzangma, lady guardian of
samaya keepers: Ralchigma.

Black, black, boiling tides of poison blood, spewing, sputtering, froth-
ing, foaming, all around the victor who time after time relishes
crushing dharma foes: Rahula.

Crush, crush, smashing the ten discordant spheres[45]—flesh and
bones—quickly, quickly safeguarding the four actions of male and
female yogis: Dorje Lekpa.

Here, now, guard us!

19

The lineage lama's heart, a wish-granting jewel,
Keep always as your treasured crown ornament.
Swiftly, to benefit beings and teachings,
Now lend your aid, all you vajra protectors, please!

20

Abiding by precepts of Padma Buddha[46]
Amidst Tibet's twenty-one holy glaciers,
Dokham Zegyal, famed as Mayo Gapa,[47]
O sacred guardian, think once more of me.

The author of this biography greets you with this lineage invocation
and now presents the life story of the embodiment of the victorious ones of
the three times, the regent of Guru Padmasambhava, the crown jewel of all
the scholars and siddhas of this time, Vidyadhara, Lama, and great tertön
Dudjom Jigdral Yeshe Dorje. Enlightened countless aeons ago, he has continuously emanated rupakayas in response to the needs of beings.

Thangka of some of the previous and future reincarnations
of His Holiness Dudjom Rinpoche

THE FIRST HEAP OF LIGHTBEAMS:

Kyabje Dudjom's previous incarnations

Though his past praiseworthy lifetimes are many, these are the names of a few: Vidyadhara Nuden Dorje; Shariputra, endowed with supreme wisdom powers; Trignadzin, minister of dharma to King Indrabhuti; Mahasiddha Saraha; Khyeuchung Lotsawa (of the Drogben clan); Drogön Chögyal Phagpa; great tertön Dudul Dorje; and Tragtung Dudjom Lingpa. To plant the seed of devotion, I will elaborate on these examples taken from the more complete account given in *Prayer to the Successive Incarnations, Called Garland of Pearls* written by His Holiness himself.

Aeons ago in a world known as Nampar Gyenpa, there lived a universal monarch named Yulkhor Sung who had 1,002 sons. He observed their remarkable characteristics and knew that each of them was destined to become a fully awakened protector of beings. He wondered, "Which of my sons will accomplish this first?" and sought out **Vidyadhara Nuden Dorje** for the answer.

To oblige the king, Nuden Dorje opened the mandala of the great secret teachings and undertook a seven-day practice ritual. He then wrote down the names of each prince and put them in a jeweled vase decorated with beautiful silks, jewels, and flowers, which he set on a lotus with many varieties of offerings. He summoned the king, queens, and all the princes to receive empowerment. At that time he began to pull the names from the vase and the order in which they were drawn indicated the order in which they would become the 1,002 buddhas of the Fortunate Aeon.[48] Because Nuden Dorje gave them empowerment and instruction and prophesied their awakening, he is regarded as their dharma father.

Shariputra, endowed with the abilities of supreme wisdom, was born in the Indian kingdom of Magadha, in the Brahmin village of Nalada,[49] where the world's first great monastic university, Nalanda, would later be established. His father, Kargyal, was a Brahmin and scholar, and his mother, Sharika, was exceptionally wise, quick, and bright. Hence they gave him the names Nyegyal, "the one dear to Gyal," and Shariputra, "Sharika's son." He became an expert on Brahmin ritual and philosophy and soon had a following of two hundred and fifty students.

In the nearby village of Shingthagchen lived a very wealthy Brahmin who was the teacher of the king of Magadha. He had a son, Maudgalyanaputra, who became a great scholar and also had about two hundred fifty Brahmin students. The moment Maudgalyanaputra and Shariputra met, they became the best of friends. They gave up their homes to become wandering ascetics, making a commitment to each other that whoever first received the nectar of realization would immediately share it with the other. Though they were great teachers, they sought deeper understanding. They went to many teachers but weren't satisfied.

Around that time the Thus-Gone Teacher, Subduer of Enmity, arrived at Rajgri, the capital of Magadha, accompanied by his retinue of monks, and stayed in the park called Bamboo Garden of the Kalanda Bird. Able to see Shariputra's and Maudgalyanaputra's readiness for enlightenment, Buddha thought, "Who shall inspire them? Shall I or a disciple?" Instantly he knew it would be one of his disciples. He thought, "By what means shall they be inspired? With a spoken teaching or by a mode of conduct?" Immediately he knew it would be by a mode of conduct. Among all his students, the arhat Tathul[50] was renowned for his excellent conduct. Buddha spoke with him and asked him to keep Shariputra in his thoughts.

The next day Tathul went to town to beg for his lunch. As his manner of walking and wearing his robes and his entire deportment were peaceful, gentle, and soothing, Shariputra, seeing him, generated a strong faith and went to ask him, "Who is your teacher? For what purpose did you take ordination?" Pleased with his response, he continued, "What is the teaching of that teacher?" Tathul said, "'Everything that arises, arises from a cause. To prevent the result, eliminate the cause.' That was taught by the Tathagata, who since he teaches that, is the Great Sage." As Tathul spoke, Nyegyal Shariputra perceived all dharmas with the stainless eye of dharma.[51] He asked, "Where is this teacher now?" Tathul replied, "He is here, right now, at the Garden of the Kalanda Bird."

Shariputra immediately went to see Maudgalyanaputra. When his friend saw him he said, "Your complexion is bright and you look so happy. You must have received the nectar. Share it with me." Shariputra repeated what Tathul had told him and in that moment Maudgalyanaputra obtained the same realization.

Together they went to Buddha, requested full ordination as monks, and at the moment of taking vows, both attained the realization of arhat. Among Buddha's disciples they became supreme.

Trignadzin was the principal minister of dharma to King Indrabhuti. This king became the adoptive father of Padmasambhava, and this is how it happened.

Indrabhuti had sailed homeward after completing his quest for the wish-fulfilling jewel in the ocean's depths. As Trignadzin was approaching in a small boat to welcome him, the king beheld across the bay magnificent rainbows and flocks of birds circling and heard the beautiful warble of their songs. He called out, "What is that over there?" Trignadzin, who had from his vantage been able to discover more of this wonder, shouted excitedly, "It's a beautiful, remarkable boy sitting on a lotus. I think we should invite him to the palace. This is surely the son you've desired."

Trignadzin, in his role as minister, supported all the king's activities on behalf of his subjects. He was the first to see Padmasambhava and the one who suggested that Indrabhuti adopt Guru Padmasambhava as a son.

The mahasiddha **Saraha** was born into a Brahmin family. He was the second abbot of Nalanda Monastic University, whose curriculum and facilities he stabilized and expanded. It was he who ordained Nagarjuna.[52] Later, after turning over the position of abbot to the glorious protector Nagarjuna, he entered into retreat and commenced crazy wisdom activities. He took a consort, a young woman of the lowest caste whose color was as dark as the blue lotus. He sang, "Until today I never was a monk, but from today I am. The glorious heruka is the monk supreme." Thus he sang and from then on spontaneously continued to sing many mahamudra vajra dohas[53] that introduced naked fresh awareness. These became the basis of his instruction to numerous followers. He achieved the glorious state of Vajradhara.

Khyeuchung Lotsawa was born into the Tibetan Drog clan in the late eighth century CE. This was a glorious time when beings existed whose realization and splendid activity made them indistinguishable from the buddhas. Among such exalted masters were Guru Padmasambhava, Shantarakshita, King Trisong Deutsen, Dzogchen master Vimalamitra, master translator Vairochana, and Yeshe Tsogyal, along with many other skillful translators and Indian masters. They began the process of establishing the Buddhadharma in Tibet, constructing Samye Monastery and filling it with objects of veneration. Thus were Samye's inner and outer aspects completed. Flawlessly, they translated all the Buddha's teachings and commentaries and then began to give and practice those teachings.

Soon the valleys of Tibet would be filled with great, realized male and female yogis, and Khyeuchung Lotsawa would be counted among them. Even as a child he exhibited profound knowledge and wisdom. He was invited to join the group of translators, and soon began rendering the dharma into the Tibetan language, thus gaining the epithet Khyeuchung Lotsawa, "child translator." From Guru Padmasambhava, Acharya Shantarakshita, Vimalamitra, and many other great teachers, he received instruction, which included the teachings of hinayana, mahayana, and the outer and inner tantras. As a sign of his accomplishment he could summon flying birds by directing his gaze and pointing his finger at them.[54] He remained a white-robed ngagpa for the rest of his life.

Drogön Chögyal Phagpa was born in the Khon clan in 1235 CE. His father, Zangtsa Sönam Gyaltsen, was the younger brother of the great master Sakya Pandita. His mother was Machik Kunga Gyenkyi. Around the age of ten, he traveled to Mongolia as an attendant to Sakya Pandita, whom Genghis Khan had invited to be his teacher. He studied all fields of knowledge, particularly Buddhist teachings and philosophy, under the tutelage of his uncle and took novice monk ordination from him, receiving the name Lodrö Gyaltsen Palzangpo.

At age nineteen he himself became the royal teacher of Kublai Khan and bestowed extensive empowerments upon him. In gratitude he was offered many treasures including all the regions of Tibet. Kublai Khan said, "I would like to convert all the Tibetan schools to your school, the Sakya." Phagpa replied, "Please leave everything just as it is." As a result a conversion did not occur.

Around the age of forty-one, he gathered monks, about a hundred thousand in all, from the different schools of Tibetan Buddhism at Tsang Chumig. In addition to the teachings he gave, he conducted a great offering ceremony presenting each monk with gifts. Having completed boundless beneficial activities for sentient beings, in 1280 CE he passed beyond this world.

Rigdzin **Dudul Dorje** was born in the Ngulphu Nang district of the Kingdom of Derge in eastern Tibet to his parents, Ludrub and Boluma. Having first studied reading and writing with his father, Ludrub, an expert physician, he served many teachers regardless of their sectarian affiliation. Taking their teachings to heart, he developed pure perception, expanded his realization, and completed the yoga of the channels, winds, and essential nuclei. Once, in a dream, he experienced spending twenty-eight days in the Glorious Copper-Color Mountain. While there, he was graced to receive from Guru Padmasambhava and Yeshe Tsogyal teachings, empowerments, and prophecies regarding his future discovery of terma.

At age twenty-nine, with the assistance of his consort, Rigden Padma Kyi, on the rocky mountain Yutso Rinchen Drag he discovered his *khajang*. Soon after, he revealed the *Quintessence of All Dharma Realizations* cycle of teachings from the hidden cave of Dongchu Dechen Sangphug at Puwo in southern Tibet near Pema Kö. This was his principal terma and he subsequently revealed its subsidiary branches along with ritual objects and relics from many regions of Tibet. Transmitting these to the disciples predicted by Guru Padmasambhava and Yeshe Tsogyal, he completed limitless beneficial activities on behalf of the teachings and living beings. In the Water Mouse year, at age fifty-eight in 1672, when he had fulfilled his activities, he departed for Pema Öd, Land of Lotus Light, amidst sounds, lights, and a rain of flowers. His body dissolved into light, shrinking to a mere cubit in height, and when it was cremated many relics of the dhyani buddhas, called *ringsel*, remained in the cremation ashes.

Terchen **Dudjom Lingpa** was born on the tenth day of the miracle month[55] in the Wood Sheep year of the fourteenth *rabjung*,[56] 1835, in the Golok area of Tibet. At his birth, his father and mother, Aten of the Nub clan and Mutsawo Dzog, witnessed wonderful indications. From his birth until the age of three, family members could at times see dakas and dakinis protecting him. When he was still very young, a dakini invited him to the Medicine Buddha Pure Land. There the Medicine Buddha gave him empowerments and teachings and appointed him as his regent. As a child, he often amazed his playmates with some display of miraculous powers, for instance, on one occasion crossing without difficulty a wide, roiling river.

When still only ten years old, he met his karmically connected guru, Lama Jamyang, who gradually conferred upon him the ngöndro teachings and the initiations and transmissions of the terma cycle of Dudul Dorje. He practiced Dorje Drolö[57] and achieved signs of accomplishment: he directly perceived Guru Padmasambhava and from him received pith instruction on Dzogchen along with predictions and advice. In addition, he had visionary encounters with, among others, Black Tröma,[58] Saraha, the eight vidyadharas, several Indian masters and translators, the twenty-five disciples of Guru Rinpoche, and the omniscient Longchenpa. As a result of discerning the illusory wisdom body of these awakened beings, his inner wisdom blazed without partiality, his realization merged with the vast expanse, and terma sprang from his wisdom-mind. As instructed by Guru Rinpoche and Yeshe Tsogyal, at age twenty-five on the tenth day of the *Chutö* month of the Earth Sheep year, he revealed his first terma from the rocky mountain Margyi Bater Drag. Thereafter, from numerous locations, as well as from his wisdom-mind, he revealed teachings and practices of the three roots and the dharma protectors. After transcribing them, he transmitted the nectar of these teachings, which would ripen and liberate beings, particularly the disciples predicted by Guru Padmasambhava.

Seeing that he had fulfilled the physical activities of that lifetime, he said to all his heart disciples, "Very soon now foreign barbarian armies will begin to flood the dharma land. Therefore there will be little peace or happiness. With prayers to Padmasambhava, quickly make ready to go to the hidden land of the Guru, Pema Kö. I will go there too. In fact this old man will arrive there before you do." Thus he said, and on the eighth day of the eleventh month in the Water Rabbit year, 1903 CE, at the age of sixty-nine, he entered the glorious lotus palace without any sickness or discomfort, displaying amazing signs such as sounds, lights, and a rain of flowers. His body was transformed into light, leaving a form the size of an eight-year-old boy. After the cremation took place, five-colored ringsel of many sizes were found in the ashes.

21

    Where Ze Tsang's[59] son, great guide of beings,
    Fulfilled the twelve great deeds,[60] that place is
    Holy India, north of which,
    Leagues away, lie Tibet's cool lands.

22

    High peaks, pristine source of all rivers,
    Massive rocky domes, adorned with snow:
    No sweet tree, nor healing herb is missing
    There in lush valleys, green with streams, lakes, brooks.

23

    Wild and tame beasts move leisurely,
    Bright, beautiful birds soar in delight,
    Fruits, wheat, barley, peas, richly abound
    In this peaceful, far land, praised by all.

24

    Most people there are mild mannered.
    Practicing virtue, peace loving,
    Respecting elders, kind to others,
    They live in ease and happiness.

25

    Here and in other places not mentioned,
    To bring the two benefits to all beings,
    Over lakes of lucky disciples' minds,
    However many, you rose, tulku,[61] new moon.

26

    By burning the dried dung of grasping
    And reaching your own spiritual goals,
    To all beings, mired in suffering,
    You came, as needed, to be their guide.

27

    Dharmakaya father of one thousand buddhas,
    Nuden Dorje, light of samsara and nirvana;
    With your sharp, swift, unique self-reliant wisdom,
    You were renowned as Shariputra, second buddha.[62]

28

    Virtues flourished under your skillful rule,
    As Trignadzin, friend of two benefits.
    You burned duality's veil with wisdom's fire,
    As Saraha, grandfather of great siddhas.

29

    Birds, drawn by your compassion, perched on your fingers,
    When you were Khyeuchung Lotsa, the Guru's equal.
    To Kublai Khan, great lord of armies and wealth, you
    Were Chögyal Phag, his protector and crown jewel.

30

    Lord of all termas and dharma wealth,
    Dudul Dorje, king of treasure finders;
    Your crazy wisdom crushed duality's law,
    As blood-drinking heruka, Dudjom Lingpa.

31

    Many nirmanakaya steps you danced
    On the stage of practitioners' deep love.
    However many countless forms you took,
    Always, to great aryas, you were the guide.

This concludes the first heap of lightbeams, briefly exhibiting a few of his previous incarnations, a garland of white lotus flowers.

Pema Kö

IAN BAKER

THE SECOND HEAP OF LIGHTBEAMS:

a brief account in Kyabje's own words
of his birthplace and parents

Dudjom Lingpa, my former incarnation, always had thoughts of
going to Pema Kö in southern Tibet. A daughter of King Kanam
Depa entered the dharma, becoming a nun and taking the name
Ani Nangsal. She distinguished herself in the dharma and was
renowned for her administrative activities. Dudjom Lingpa wrote
a letter to her, saying that he was planning to come to Pema Kö.
Upon receipt of this letter, Ani Nangsal was elated. She replied, "If
you come here, I'll provide lodging, food, and clothes without fail
for about one thousand of your students." Along with the letter,
enfolded in a white scarf, she sent her own golden ring.

Years later Gyurme Ngedön Wangpo, Dudjom Lingpa's
disciple, informed me he was there when the letter arrived. "He was
very happy to receive the letter and the present. Immediately he
tried the ring on his index finger, but it didn't fit. He slipped it onto
his ring finger, and it seemed as if it were made for him. He was
quite pleased. Looking at it often, he'd show it to others, saying,
'This ring is a gift from Ani Nangsal, daughter of Kanam Depa.
Isn't it beautiful?' It was said that if the situation and circumstances
had been perfect, she would have become his wife and that this
would have resulted in a great deal of benefit for the dharma and
for beings, including the opening of the hidden valley of Pema Kö,
but that due to unfavorable circumstances, it never came to be."

Dudjom Rinpoche's father's former reincarnation—
Japhur Lama—soars across the river gorge

King Kanam Depa's son, Khengen Tulku, was my father, and his monastery was located in the upper valley of Pema Kö near Lhotod Kha. He was a reincarnation of Kathok Gyalse Sönam Deutsen's[63] son[64] who in that former lifetime had been told by a dakini to go to Pema Kö. Following her instruction, he left his home in Kham, made his way over the mountain pass of Je Shong in Puwo, then down into Pema Kö. Traveling on, he arrived at a large river but didn't have the money to ride the rattan hoop suspended from a rope spanning the gorge. The toll-collectors wouldn't make an exception. Perturbed, he decided on an alternate route. Using his shawl for wings, he flew like a bird to the other side. The toll collectors, astonished by this herukan display, called him Japhur Lama, "Soaring Bird" Lama, and beseeched him, "Please be our teacher. Stay here in this area. We'll provide for all your needs." The lama accepted their request, and thus they became his first disciples in Pema Kö. They offered him the entire mountain, the valley of Lha Dzong, and Khang Kheng, which he also accepted. At Khang Kheng he established a monastery and worked for the welfare of all the villagers, and this became his principal seat.

So much for my father's former incarnation. As for my father himself, although he wasn't a monk, he wasn't married. He was living at his monastery at Khang Kheng and performing beneficial activities. Once again a dakini, and also Lama Chabdo Phagpa Lha, told him to go to the Terkong Nang area, where he would meet a karmically connected dakini, establish a monastery, and have a very special son who would benefit the dharma and sentient beings greatly. Following their instructions, he eventually arrived there and found the area populated by about thirteen large families and fifteen or sixteen retinue families. Among the large families was one that had emigrated from eastern Bhutan and was descended from the great Nyingma tertön, Ratna Lingpa. Khengen Tulku asked that family to host him, and with great joy and respect they

Map with arrow pointing to location of Pema Kö in southeastern Tibet

agreed. This family had a young sixteen-year-old daughter named Namgyal Drolma. He slept with her that night and many beautiful signs and indications came. In the early morning he told the daughter's parents, "I want to stay in this area and build a monastery near the mountain, but I'll need your help. I'd also like your daughter to be my wife." The parents joyously agreed.

They sought out a perfect location for the monastery and found a beautiful site about three miles from the village. In that area, however, there were no stones, and everyone said, "If the temple is not built of stone, it won't last long." The lama prayed to the three roots and especially to Guru Padmasambhava, performed many ganachakras and made many offerings to the local land deities. He had auspicious dreams that night. Early in the morning he told his students and dharma patrons, "Today I'm going to reveal a treasury of stones, but I'll need the assistance of a man named 'Stone.'" Everyone was trying to think of someone with that name. Someone remembered a very good craftsman from Puwo named Dorje Dragpa, and there was general agreement that he must be the man.[65] They located this man, and then all of them accompanied the teacher to the selected location where they did fire puja[66] and dharmapala offerings. Lama Khengen Tulku said to Dorje Dragpa, "Dig in the dirt." Dorje struck with his pick, and when he did, many stones of different sizes emerged looking like they'd been prepared by a mason. With them they were able to complete the construction of the monastery.

Approximately two thousand years ago the Tibetan king Drigum Tsenpo was assassinated by his minister Longam. The king's three sons— Jatri, Shatri, and Nyatri—fled. Jatri settled in the Puwo area and ruled as king.[67] He and his descendants later came to be known as the Kanam Depa clan. They ruled Tibet's southern-most regions, centered in Puwo but including Pema Kö and other valleys, for almost two thousand years. They subdued outlaws and extended their loving protection to the weak, thereby gaining a very special place in Tibetan history. They were dharma patrons mainly for the Nyingma and Kagyu schools of Tibetan Buddhism and in particular for the great Nyingma tertöns Dudul Dorje, Taksham Nuden Dorje,[68] and Tsasum Lingpa. Accounts of these tertöns can be found in their own biographies.

32

Heaven's bright splendor, this son of gods,
Brought Tibet's red-faced race[69] good fortune.
From this first great king, Nyatri Tsenpo,[70]
Came a fearless line, jewels of the earth.

33

More fierce and brave than tiger, leopard, and bear,
The majestic lion, King Drigum Tsenpo,[71]
With his three young cubs, Jatri, Shatri, Nyatri:
Crown jewels of all of Tibet's kings and subjects.

34

Because of Minister Longam's misdeeds,
Jatri's thousand lights shone over Puwo,
Bringing the good to bloom, uprooting the bad,
And the Kanam Depas' fame spread everywhere.

35

Rich in worldly wealth, power, and lineage,
Rich in inner visions, realization, wisdom,
Khengen Tulku, a divine clan's heir, named also
"Rigdzin Jampal Norbu," was the blessed one's father.

36

From Langdro Lotsa's[72] wise, magic dance,
Came Ratna Ling, secret path tertön.
From that line's sheltering wish-fulfilling tree,
Also bloomed the smiling fruit, Namgyal Drolma.

37

Firmly rooted in loving compassion,
Honest, good natured, generous, fine limbed,
Beautiful, a fresh flower in full bloom:
Sublime woman, sublime tulku's mother.

38

> From this majestic throne of high lineage,
> Ennobled by all the world's wealth and blessings,
> From a mother and father, perfect in every way,
> Came Padmasambhava's regent,[73] to subdue dark times.

This brief explanation of his parents and his birthplace, as the gracious teacher himself presented it, concludes the second heap of lightbeams.

His Holiness Dudjom Rinpoche
From the Gonpa wall murals at Padma Samye Ling

THE THIRD HEAP OF LIGHTBEAMS:

as predicted by the second buddha, Guru Padmasambhava,
His Holiness takes birth in the royal clan of Kanam Depa

The great tertön Orgyen Dechen Lingpa revealed terma of Padmasambhava that stated, "Southeast of Samye, beyond the Nine-Glacier Mountain
Range, is the secret hidden land of Vajravarahi, a valley where an emanation of Drogben Khyeuchung Lotsawa will be born in the royal clan. His
name will be Jnana.[74] He will be a yogi, brimming with wisdom and in
conduct as spontaneous as a child. He will reveal new terma and preserve
the ancient terma teachings. Whoever is connected to him will be led to the
Glorious Copper-Color Mountain."

At the age of forty, on the twenty-fifth day of the midsummer month,
Dudjom Lingpa and the great Queen of Space, Ekajati, had discussions
about his former and future lives. She told him, "Your emanations will
come, and they will spread the dharma throughout the countries of southern Tibet and the Mön region."[75] This is recorded in *Clear Mirror Explaining
the Secret Visions*, which is a section of *Net of Wisdom Visions*.

And consider these citations from Dudjom Rinpoche's own revealed
treasures. In *Vajra Subduer of Demons, Crazy Wrathful Blood-Drinker Pema*
Padmasambhava states, "This magical being who is my emanation . . ."; and
in *Vajrakilaya, the Razor That Destroys on Contact* Yeshe Tsogyal says, "In the
mind-stream of the fortunate one who is no different from me . . ." Thus,
vajra predictions repeatedly announced the arrival of Lord Terchen Lama.

The natural beauties that appeared on the day of
His Holiness Dudjom Rinpoche's birth in Pema Kö

Terkong Nang is a land of medicine and healing, a part of the secret land of Pema Kö, which was blessed by Guru Padmasambhava, Yeshe Tsogyal, and other great masters. Jatri Tsenpo, whose ancestors were descended from heavenly beings of the sky-of-clear-light, came and ruled Puwo Valley and gave birth to the Kanam Depa clan. Khengen Tulku Jampal Norbu Wangyal, a member of this stainless dynasty, was His Holiness's father. His mother, who possessed all the characteristics of a dakini, was Namgyal Drolma. She came from the clan of the great vidyadhara Ratna Lingpa. It was here in Terkong Nang that His Holiness was born in the year 2444 as dated from Buddha's parinirvana; 2440, dated from the birth of Guru Padmasambhava; 2031, Wood Dragon year, dated from the inception of the Tibetan monarchy,[76] and 1904 in Western calendars.[77] He was born on the tenth day of the sixth month, which is also the birthday of Guru Padmasambhava, on a Sunday, just as the sun's first rays were touching the village. There were beautiful signs and omens and the birth was without pain for his mother. In Kyabje's own words:

> Because he was at the family house in Puwo, my father, Khengen Tulku, wasn't there at the time of my birth. My mother invited two local ngagpas, Dongak and Bu Thinley, renowned in Gezhing village, to do birthday ceremonies. Since I was born on Sunday, they named me Nyima[78] Gyaltsen. Soon after, Khengen Tulku came back from the Kanam family home. Mother gave him all the details, which included telling him, "I invited Ngagpa Dongak and he gave our son the name Nyima Gyaltsen." Khengen Tulku said, "That's a beautiful name, but I received a name for this baby from a dakini long before he was born. I had a dream in which a beautiful woman came to me and said, 'You will have a son and give this name to that boy.' She handed me a mirror with a golden dorje standing upright and put it in the fold of my chuba. The mirror symbolized wisdom and the vajra indestructibility, and so I will give him the name Yeshe Dorje." That's how I got the name Yeshe Dorje. When I was small the villagers used to call me Tulku Yeshe.

*Insignia of His Holiness
Dudjom Rinpoche*

39

Orgyen Dorje Chang [79] and Shantarakshita, along with
Vimalamitra, Vairochana, Trisong,[80] Karchen Za,[81]
Scholars and siddhas, like unto the Buddha, beyond number,
Again, again, blessed the land of Tibet. So it is known.

40

A wild demoness, sleeping on her back,[82] seems to be
Cradling, in the pistil core of her lotus heart,
Samye, revered in samsara and nirvana,
From whence Buddha's teachings brightly shone out of Tibet.

41

From Samye, many leagues to the east,
Across nine cosmic glacial mountains,
Lies Pema Kö, the place known as holy land:
Perfect unmade image of Phagmo's[83] body.

42

Mountain tops, like pillars of the sky,
Wear lovely turbans of pure white snow.
Billowing clouds and silken mist drape
Forests in sumptuous finery.

43

    Here, all the trees' branches join hands,
    Heads swaying with joy in fresh breezes,
    As bamboo canopies let peek through
    Bright sparkling sunlight and blue sky.

44

    Lovely flowers of diverse colors,
    Forms delighting the eye, beyond words;
    Shapely songbirds singing sweetly,
    A gandharva's[84] feast for the ear.

45

    Always dining on a blue-green repast,
    Large and small hoofed beasts frolic in this place.
    Clear, cool waters of rivers, streams, and brooks
    Run together, chattering with laughter.

46

    Animals, birds, whole flocks, together recite
    The six syllables, [85] calling the lama,[86] and so on.
    Rather than sleeping at dawn, they chant sweetly,
    Again, again, famous for their deep meditation.

47

    At the moment they pass away,
    Still meditating,[87] rainbows and relics come,
    Filling all hearts with such wonder
    That even sun and moon seem to pause and stare.

48

    Apples, grapes, pears, bananas, many other
    Kinds of fruits, all rich in taste and colors,
    Crops of rice, barley, wheat, wild grains, untended,
    Always grow. When is it not harvest time?

The Tsangpo (Brahmaputra) River Gorge in Pema Kö

49

There, people rich in gentleness and peace,
Always do good deeds, again and again.
Heaven's realm put on earth, that place was
Blessed by the second buddha,[88] as all know.

50

When the twelve-months' wheel turned the chariot of the Wood
    Dragon year toward summer's drums,
And Sunday ruled over the planetary circle of Monday, Tuesday
    and so on,
When dawn's light rose on the fortunate king of days, the tenth day of
    the Monkey month,
Jigdral Yeshe Dorje's sun filled samsara and nirvana to benefit beings.[89]

51

At that time, from all directions without cease,
Rainbow scarves and sweet fragrances filled the air.
Music, and so on, touched upon the senses.
Charged with joy, all said, "The supreme tulku comes."

52

In south Pema Kö's garden, rich in healing plants,
From direct descendants of the god realm,
Into the powerful clan of king of Kanam,
The great protector of beings took birth.

53

Past wishes, past bodhichitta, now ripe,
Best of the best, beyond all men, great arya,
Young boy, "Young Lotsa's"[90] incarnate form,
These times' dark times comes to conquer with light.

This brief story of how His Holiness Dudjom Rinpoche Jigdral Yeshe
Dorje took birth in the royal clan just as Guru Padmasambhava had predicted concludes the third heap of lightbeams.

The young Dudjom tulku greets his disciples

THE FOURTH HEAP OF LIGHTBEAMS:

early signs, recognition as the reincarnation of
Dudjom Lingpa, and Kyabje Dudjom's enthronement

Kyabje said:

When I was two or three years old, a Gelugpa lama named Tsewang, having quit the Khyungpo area due to disturbances there, arrived with about ten monks and thirteen families. I often joined them in their ceremonies, and after a while had memorized the prayers. During that time the ngagpas of Terkong Nang assembled for a drubchen based on *The Gathering of All Dzogchen Objects of Refuge*, and the Gelugpa monks participated alongside their Nyingma brothers. On the final day of accomplishment I was urged to give the empowerment, and I did so even though I couldn't read the text. Very happy, they exclaimed, "How wonderful!"

When as a toddler he first began to speak, it was the Golok dialect of Tibetan he used. In addition to this being the dialect spoken by Dudjom Lingpa, he'd repeat the names of that teacher's students and exclaim, "I am Dudjom Lingpa." These signs persuaded the villagers to believe that he was who he claimed to be.

That great lama had told his students, "Now bad times are coming for Tibet. It is time to go to Pema Kö. Those of you who are able, go there, and I, an old man, will follow you." At other times he told them, "I, an old man, will get to Pema Kö before you do." Because of his admonition, several students, led by Ling Lama Chöjor Gyatso, began the journey. Not long after their departure, he passed away. When the news caught up with those on the road, they decided to slow their pace in order to do pilgrimage.

In preparation for his cremation, the body was placed inside a cremation mandala house in meditation posture facing eastward. Suddenly and on its own, his face turned to the southwest in the direction of Pema Kö. Everyone who witnessed this event thought, "Pema Kö will be the place of his reincarnation."

When Ling Lama Chöjor Gyatso with the group of disciples arrived in the northern part of Pema Kö, they learned that the great teacher and tertön Jedrung Thrinle Jampa Jungne was residing in the nearby valley of Chidrug Nang. The travelers went to see him and receive blessings and asked, "Could you please identify the reincarnation of our teacher, Dudjom Lingpa?" Jedrung Rinpoche told them precisely the names of the parents and the birthplace of the teacher and added, "Your tulku is already there. Quickly go to him, take care of the new tulku and offer him knowledge." He wrote a beautiful poem, a long-life prayer named Jigdral Dechen Dorje Dragpo Tsal, and sent it, a white scarf, and items representing the Buddha's body, speech, and mind—statues, texts, and ritual objects—as offerings. (As an aside Kyabje told the author of this biography, "I kept the name received from the dakini and added 'Jigdral,' which I received from Jedrung Rinpoche. And so my name became Jigdral Yeshe Dorje.")

The students were overjoyed to hear this, and they departed for Terkong Nang in high spirits. A few days before their arrival, the young Dudjom tulku told his parents, "We are going to have very important guests, please prepare the rooms and make other preparations." The parents weren't expecting anyone, so they neglected his request. The next day the young tulku again insisted that they make preparations. They thought that since he was not an ordinary child, maybe visitors were coming. They made preparations. By midafternoon some nomadic monks and nuns were seen approaching the house. When they came closer, the young tulku ran toward them and in the Golok dialect called out the names of some of them, saying, "How are you? Are you well? It took a long time for you to get here," and so forth. They were awestruck. If there had been any lingering doubts about who this was, they vanished instantly.

The enthronement of His Holiness Dudjom Rinpoche

Upon the throne of their devotion and confidence, a lion's throne of the nine yanas, Vidyadhara Phugtrul Gyurme Ngedön Wangpo, Ling Lama Orgyen Chöjor Gyatso, and all the other chief disciples presented him with the offerings from Jedrung Thrinley Jampa Jungne. Tears fell like rain from their eyes, and they touched their heads to the little feet of the tulku. Thus was he enthroned.

54

    Rooted in courage, confidence, and faith; rich in leaves and stems of
        realization;
    Lineage holders and former disciples, lotuses, blooming with deep joy:
    Instantly touched by the sun of the tulku's face and the rays of his
        smiling voice,
    From heavenly vistas of their faces, poured out tears, streaming with
        happiness.

55

    At that moment, necks of living flutes
    Swelled tight with songs praising the two aims.
    On the mirror surface of faces
    Mandala offerings of tears were heaped.

56

    From the ocean's depths of mind,
    Waves of deep joy surge again, again,
    While vines of bodies bow low,
    As eyes glimpse the supreme tulku's face.

57

    The sun, the moon, and Dzambu's[91] gold,
    The lion, king of beasts,
    Who needs to be told what these are?
    Such things are known by everyone.

58

    Just so, the aryas of the three realms knew
    The crown jewel of samsara and nirvana,
    This young boy, Khyeuchung Lotsa's emanation,
    Through his manifest traits and true nature.

59

As these amazing events were taking place,
Buddhas and their heirs, seated in the ten directions,
Padma yab yum,[92] enthroned in Copper-Glory Mountain,
Seemed to smile, strew blossoms, and be seated nearby.

This brief account describing his reunion with his former students, the extraordinary signs convincing them that he was Dudjom Lingpa's reincarnation, and his enthronement concludes the fourth heap of lightbeams.

His Holiness's first teaching at the age of seven
on the Guide to the Bodhisattva's Way of Life

The Fifth Heap of Lightbeams:

Kyabje's exposure from an early age to the great teachers who bestowed the teachings, empowerments, and instructions

H.H. Dudjom Rinpoche said:

Ling Lama Chöjor Gyatso in the early part of his life was a student of Patrul Rinpoche and later a student of Dudjom Lingpa. He was a highly accomplished Dzogchen master. In compliance with his directive, Lama Pema Samphel, also a student of the former Dudjom and of Ling Lama, began to teach me how to read. He was serene, humble, and very gentle; no matter what I did, he saw it as beautiful due to his great devotion. He never said a cross word. Whenever we traveled a short distance together, I rode on his shoulders with my legs stretched over his chest. In brief, he always acted as if he were my student, rather than my teacher. Therefore, my reading didn't improve. Ling Lama Chöjor Gyatso saw this situation and scolded Lama Pema, and me in particular, saying, "Without education or realization, retaining the title of tulku and climbing up on a throne won't benefit the teaching or sentient beings. Just the opposite—it will do harm." Out of great concern he made this and similar strong statements.

Then he did divinations to determine who would be the best teacher for me. In accordance with the divination he appointed Lama Khedrub, another disciple of the former Dudjom. He was a great Black Tröma yogi who had practiced in the 108 cemeteries.

Lama Khedrub was nothing like Lama Pema Samphel. He was extremely wrathful, short tempered, and often scolded or yelled at me. To supervise my reading, he sat beside me holding a switch. Depending on the infraction, he struck me either with the thin or thick end of it—thin for little mistakes, thick for big ones. Using this technique, he taught me to read *The Gathering of All Dzogchen Objects of Refuge*. He was very strict and gave very little leisure time.

Then one day Lama Khedrub told me, "Tomorrow I don't have time to stay with you. I have some sewing to do. Tulku, you must study strongly because the day after tomorrow I'm going to give you a test." The next day Lama Khedrub and a nun, both of whom were expert tailors, were busy sewing from late morning until evening, and I had a great holiday, making noises like I was reading, but really looking around, playing with my hands, and just pretending to read. In the evening Lama Khedrub came by and said, "Tomorrow, if you don't pass the test, I'm going to beat you hard."

The following day he came with the switch as he said he would, and asked me to start reading from the beginning of *The Gathering of All Dzogchen Objects of Refuge*. I was really scared. In a state of dread I began reading and then recited mantras in their entirety even though the text gave only the first word of each.[93] He had not taught me that. Lama Khedrub was so amazed that he dropped the switch, covered his face with his hand and, for a short time, cried. Then he said, "You don't have to read anymore today. Take a break." Lama Khedrub reported this event to Ling Lama Rinpoche, who exclaimed, "These are definitely the signs of a great tulku. What other explanation is there?" Because of the kindness of Lama Khedrub, I was able to read very well by the age of five or thereabouts.

One day Ling Lama asked to see me. I went and he said, "When you were Dudjom Lingpa, your son, Dodrub Tenpai Nyima, gave public teachings on Shantideva's *A Guide to the Bodhisattva's Way of Life* when he was eight years old. It's only right that the father should give this teaching at the age of seven and no later than seven and a half. Yes, by then you must teach the first four chapters, and so you'd better start studying."

I did. Every day. When I reached age seven and a half, they made a big throne and asked me to sit there. The disciples gathered with Ling Lama seated in the foremost position. They chanted the *Tashi Gyepa* and Seven-Line Prayer, lineage prayers, and the seven-branch accumulation, made the mandala offering and request for teachings, and then I gave the teachings on those four chapters. When I'd finished, Ling Lama was very pleased. Immediately, he handed me a conch shell and said, "Tulku, take this outside and blow it one time in each of the four directions." Being a child, that sounded like great fun. I took it outside and quickly blew it in the eastern direction. I didn't know how to produce a good sound and, instead, made a series of small bumpy noises. I blew it in the southern direction and a beautiful sound emerged. When I blew to the west, an even lovelier, louder sound arose almost of its own accord. In the north I blew, but the sound was so negligible it seemed as if my mouth was tired and my breath small.

I came back into the temple and offered him the conch, which he happily accepted, saying, "Tulku, you did well. You won't do beneficial activities in the eastern direction, but that's all right because your former incarnation did. And you won't be doing such activities in the northern direction either, but that's also all right, because in the western and southern directions your activities will be of great benefit." He appeared to be very happy.

His Holiness blows the conch in the four directions

60[94]

   Firmly rooted in faith, this tree trunk, lush with leaves of good aspira-
      tions,
   In perfect joy and devotion, with strong-limbed shoulders branching
      right and left:
   There, the matchless tulku perched his lotus feet, when along the plains
      and valleys of relative truth
   Teacher and student now and then would roam, viewing the magic
      play of interdependent causes.

61

   Padma was spiritually adept,
   Yet, before you, small holy child,
   He was more a child than the child,
   And so honor was paid, child to child.

62

   Great god-realm's deep drum of knowledge:
   When signaled by the beating stick,
   Unrehearsed enfolded mantra sounds
   Clearly rolled out, to the teacher's wonder.

63

   Right then and there, right in that place
   The teacher, adept at teaching,
   Lama Khedrub, schooled beyond school,
   Let pour down tears of pouring rain.

64

As Indra and Brahma once beseeched Buddha, wise and learned Lama
    Chöjor beseeched
You, matchless guide, Padma's regent now, Nuden Dorje in the past,
    Möpa[95] to come.
Then, enthroned upon the three vehicles of true speech,[96] upheld by
    lions of four fearless states and four attractions,[97]
You, untiring in the world, soothed the four classes of gods and men,[98]
    with the dharma jewel of the six paramitas.

65

Then, Chöjor Gyatso, awash
In waves of joy gathering into
A smile that lit up his face,
Handed Terchen Tulku a conch.

66

"E Ma! Unrivaled tulku, bodhisattva,
With lotus steps, kindly come outdoors,
Take this good, sweet-sounding dharma conch,
And blow once in each of the four directions."

67

Sounds, sounds, resonating in the chambers of a right-spiraled conch,
Lovely, lovely, earrings floating to the four damsel-directions:
True, true, they told of your future deeds beyond thought,
Clear, clear, they gathered to show truth through magic signs.

68

When Lama Chöjor the sage
Explained the signs perfectly
To everyone's satisfaction,
Heart blooms of devotion opened.

From many great teachers he continued to receive the general and extraordinary teachings of the Buddha, as well as instructions on all the arts and sciences. As soon as they were given, he contemplated and analyzed them and straightaway gained realization. What follows is a summary of his principal teachers and the teachings they bestowed. Primarily they were the teachings of the Nyingma tradition of Tibetan Buddhism: empowerments, transmissions, and pith instructions[99] of the kama and terma lineages in their entirety. These teachings also provided a thorough training in ceremonial protocols, mainly according to the Minling tradition. Ceremonial protocols include the use of ritual objects, the preparation of tormas and mandalas, and a thorough knowledge of melodies appropriate for the sadhanas.

1. From **Ling Lama Orgyen Chöjor Gyatso** he received the empowerments, transmissions, and teachings of three great tertöns: Karma Lingpa, Rigdzin Longsal Nyingpo,[100] and Dudjom Lingpa. He received detailed instructions and teaching on *Definitive Distinctions among the Three Vows* of Ngari Pandita Pema Wangyal[101] according to the oral instructions of Patrul Rinpoche.

He received introductions to and practice instructions on the following ngöndros: Longchen Nyingthig, Dudjom Tersar, and Black Tröma. After completing the Nyingthig ngöndro, he was directed to start the Dudjom Tersar ngöndro, and after that, the Black Tröma ngöndro. He was told he could do short prostrations in the last two ngöndros, and he did over two hundred thousand for each. Upon completion of these practices, he received the six bardo teachings for six months, and following that, he received instruction on *khorde rushen*,[102] starting with the hell realms and concluding with the god realms. H.H. Dudjom Rinpoche said:

> After each session Ling Lama used to chant the *Heart Sutra* one time and then say, "Now meditate," and all his students meditated with him. This great teacher led me to the path, cultivated in me the wisdom generating disciplines of study and contemplation, and nourished me with his kindness. About him it can truly be said, "his kindness was unrepayable."

2. Phugtrul Gyurme Ngedön Wangpo. In Dudjom Rinpoche's own words:

> Phugtrul Gyurme Ngedön Wangpo was Vajrapani incarnate. From him I received empowerments, transmissions, and pith instructions on the following teachings:
> - The entire *Treasury of Precious Treasures*[103] by Jamgön Kongtrul
> - *Collected Sadhanas of the Excellent Wish-Fulfilling Vase* and the complete cycle of *Minling Tersar*, both by Orgyen Terdak Lingpa
> - *Cycle of Teachings of the Seven Entrusted Transmissions* of Lord Khyentse[104]
> - The *Dudjom Tersar* cycle
> - All the existing teachings of Longchenpa in general and the *Seven Treasures* in particular
> - The teachings of Patrul Rinpoche
> - The *Four Medical Tantras* and their commentaries.[105]

He gave detailed explanations on how to make mandalas and how to perform empowerments, fire puja, and all the other rituals, mudras, and activities of the vajra master.

When I received the teachings on *Treasury of Precious Treasures,* he jokingly told me, "This represents the activity of the two great Jamgöns,[106] and among all their disciples I've given this teaching five times, which is a record, but you'll give it ten times." On another occasion he said, "You are unmistakably the incarnation of the great dharma king, my teacher, Dudjom Lingpa. Great Tertön, you've changed your old body into this youthful form, but regarding your realization, nothing has changed. All I can do is offer you the lineage blessings of words." At yet another time he said, "The wealth of instructions of all the great ancestral teachers as a great mandala I now present to their heir. I have completed my responsibility and fulfilled the wishes of my root teacher, Dudjom Lingpa. You, noble one, practice these teachings and gain realization. Use it to help other beings."

And thus he honored H.H. Dudjom Rinpoche, calling him the vajra regent of all the great masters, including Phugtrul Gyurme Ngedön Wangpo himself.

3. Dudjom Namkhai Dorje[107] (Jedrung Thrinle Jampa Jungne) was the reincarnation of Langdro Lotsawa. From this great teacher he received the empowerment, transmission, and pith instructions for Jamgön Kongtrul's *Treasury of Pith Instructions*, which is the essential set of instructions on the eight practice lineages of Tibetan Buddhism. He received detailed explanations and pith instructions on Chogyur Lingpa's terma *Gradual Path of the Essence of Wisdom*[108] along with its commentary by Jamgön Kongtrul. In addition he received the secret and sealed section of *Treasury of Precious Treasures*, all Dudjom Namkhai Dorje's own terma teachings, and other miscellaneous teachings.

At around the age of nineteen, His Holiness gave extensive teachings on *Treasury of Precious Treasures* at Kongpo Dragsum Do, and afterward went to see Jedrung Rinpoche, to let him know he'd done this. The teacher was happy to hear it, praised him, and invited him to attend some teachings he was giving to his students. His Holiness accepted and at the conclusion of the cycle of instruction presented handmade, folded-paper flowers and birds as an offering to Rinpoche, who received them with delight. His Holiness made a decision to stay on with him for a longer period in order to study and receive teachings; not long afterward Jedrung Rinpoche passed away.

4. From **Gyurme Phende Özer**, the regent of the coming sixth buddha, Senge Rabsal,[109] he received the complete upasaka vows. He received the empowerments, transmissions, and pith instructions for the Nyingma kama in general and in particular for *Secret Essence Tantra—The Net of Magical Illusions*, *The Sutra Which Gathers All Intentions*, and the semde tantras.[110]

He received the empowerments, transmissions, and pith instructions for these terma teachings:
- *The Eight Herukas—Embodiment of All the Sugatas* of the great tertön Nyang-ral Nyima Özer
- *Embodiment of the Total Realization of the Lama* of Sangye Lingpa
- *Minling Tersar*
- *Root Sadhanas of the Longchen Nyingthig* of Jigme Lingpa.

Furthermore, he received the Vajrakilaya[111] teachings according to the tantra tradition. He also received systematic instructions on *Secret Essence Tantra—The Net of Magical Illusions*. In addition, he received Longchenpa's *Seven Treasures* and the *Trilogy of Relaxation and Ease*. Further teachings included *Definitive Distinctions among the Three Vows* by Ngari Pandita, *Treasury of Qualities* by Jigme Lingpa, *Treasury of All-Encompassing Knowledge* by Jamgön Kongtrul, and numerous transmissions on many other teachings. His Holiness said:

> Though he was giving these teachings to many renowned teachers, khenpos, and tulkus, he pointed to me specifically and said, "Now I have completed most of the kama and terma teachings, including the empowerments, transmissions, and pith instructions, and from now on, you must take full responsibility for the Nyingma lineage by preserving all its texts and spreading these teachings." Subsequently, he enjoined me over and over with words such as these.

Thus, H.H. Dudjom Rinpoche was acknowledged to be the Lord of the Nyingma School at the age of twenty.

5. From **Orgyen Namdröl Gyatso,** who achieved high realization through practice of the two stages and was renowned as a dharma lord of the vajrayana, he received the great empowerment for *The Eight Herukas— Embodiment of All the Sugatas* within the elaborate mandala and extended ceremony. In addition he was given the empowerments, transmissions, and pith instructions for great tertön Guru Chökyi Wangchuk's *Kilaya Sword*

and for *Concentrated Compassion.*

He received bodhichitta vows according to the Madhyamaka lineage of Nagarjuna. He received explanations of various philosophical texts, most of the tantras of *Hundreds of Thousands of Nyingma Tantras,* and many other pith instructions. The instructions he received included a thorough training in ceremonial procedure and paraphernalia and the preparation of dharma nectar medicine.

6. The great Khampa tertön **Zilnön Namkhai Dorje,** the reincarnation of the great translator Vairochana and Nanam Dorje Dudjom,[112] gave him his long-life terma, *Long-Life Sadhana of the Vital Force of Immortality,* along with all the rest of his terma. He pointed out the nature of mind. His Holiness was twenty-one and he'd been staying at Orgyen Mindröling Monastery in central Tibet. In his own words:

> On an impulse I went to see Tertön Zilnön Namkhai Dorje, and he received me with a joyful face. After a while he said, "I am old now, and I don't know how long I have to live, but seeing you, I know that I will be able to pass the dharma treasures I hold to their rightful heir." He predicted future events and gave me detailed advice. He said, "My terma teaching predicted you, and you will be of great benefit to the Nyingma School." Then I requested, "Please, would you transcribe the activity sections of the Vajrakilaya teachings from the yellow paper scrolls you've discovered?" He replied, "We'll see about that, but understand that now I've transferred my terma teachings to you, and it's up to you to decide what you'll do with them."
>
> Then he bestowed Jamgön Kongtrul's secret empowerment of Dorje Drolö. He looked at me with eyes wide open and shouted, "Phet!" In that instant my body, perception, and mind became unimpeded, all notions of solidity disappeared. "That is the absolute wisdom empowerment. *Supra tishta ye soha!*"[113] Saying this, he tossed barley grains skyward. From that time on, my mind remained relaxed and open. I felt no need to boast about spending

months and years in retreat; nor did I feel the need to focus forcefully in my meditation, nor cling to practice schedules. I knew the power of the lineage realization of absolute truth had been transferred to me. This karmically connected great teacher was none other than Guru Padmasambhava.

7. From the great yogi **Jampal Tsultrim Dragpa**, who had perfectly kept the three vows, he received in their entirety the empowerments, transmissions, and pith instructions of Jamgön Kongtrul's *Treasury of Kagyu Mantras*, a profound teaching of the Kagyu School; the great empowerments and transmissions of Chogyur Lingpa's *Heart Practice That Dispels All Obstacles*,[114] and the transmissions of many other nectarlike instructions, including Chogyur Lingpa's *Heart-Purifying Oral Advice*.

8. From **Rigdzin Pema Wangyal,** a greatly realized being hailing from the hidden valley of Pema Kö, he received the following teachings with empowerments, transmissions, and pith instructions: six volumes of terma teachings of the great tertön Jatsön Nyingpo; seven volumes of the great tertön Rigdzin Dorje Thogme;[115] the terma cycle of Dorje Dragngag; and the complete cycle of teachings of tertön Gampo Drodul Lingpa.

9. From **Garwang Sangye Dorje,**[116] a highly accomplished individual who had fulfilled the two aims through his compassion, wisdom, and joyful effort, he clearly and distinctly received empowerments, transmissions, and pith instructions of the entire terma cycle of Dudul Dorje, and in particular the lineage transmitted through Dudul Dorje's son.

10. From the renunciate yogi **Ngagwang Gedun Gyatso**, who had reached the higher realizations by practicing the two stages, he received all the empowerments, transmissions, and pith instructions of the cycle of teachings of the great tertön Pema Lingpa, as well as the transmissions of the *Hundreds of Thousands of Nyingma Tantras*. In addition he received many other profound and secret teachings from this teacher.

11. From **Ngagwang Jigme Lodrö,** who had accomplished the two aims

as a protector of all beings, he clearly, correctly, and melodiously received the entire *Kangyur*. His Holiness said that upon receiving these transmissions, he understood the great good fortune of a human rebirth.

12. From **Ngagwang Palden Zangpo**, a master of the glorious Taklung Kagyu School and an emanation of the lords of the three families, he received the bodhichitta vows of both Nagarjuna's and Asanga's lineages; the empowerments, transmissions, and pith instructions of the *Chakrasamvara*, *Hevajra*, and *Guhyasamaja*[117] tantras; and many other tantras of the new translation schools of Tibetan Buddhism.

13. From the renunciate sky-yogi **Jigme Trogyal Dorje**[118] he received transmissions for *Commentaries on Black Phurba* and many Nyingma tantras; and in particular the empowerments, transmissions, and pith instructions on the guru sadhanas, Dzogchen practices, and Chenrezig sadhanas revealed by the female tertön Dechen Dewe Dorje.[119]

14. From Vidyadhara **Orgyen Tsewang Palbar**,[120] who was such an exemplary bodhisattva that whoever met him made an enduringly meaningful connection, he received empowerments, transmissions, and pith instructions on Chogyur Lingpa's *Three Dzogchen Classes*, which is Chogyur Lingpa's extraordinary *semde*, *longde*, and *men-ngagde* terma.

15. From the Yamantaka yogi **Chökyi Jungne** he received the empowerments, transmissions, and pith instructions of many Yamantaka teachings, such as *Yamantaka, Lord of Life, Iron Locket, Iron Scorpion*, and *Ultimate Reverser*, and many additional teachings.

16. From the scholar and siddha **Ngedön Chökyi Gyatso** he received empowerments, transmissions, and pith instructions on many secret teachings of the great tertön Ratna Lingpa, as well as pith instruction on the five categories[121] and many other empowerments.

17. From **Ngagchang Orgyen Tenpa Rabgye**, who was born into the family of yogis and was replete with siddhis and realization, he received empowerments, transmissions, and pith instructions on Longchenpa's

Dzogchen *Four Heart Drop Cycles* and on nine volumes of Jigme Lingpa's teachings.

18. From Vidyadhara **Pema Könchog Rabten,** a master of the three wisdoms, he received teachings on Shantideva's *A Guide to the Bodhisattva's Way of Life,* Ngari Pandita Pema Wangyal's *Definitive Distinctions among the Three Vows,* Jigme Lingpa's *Treasury of Qualities,* and many other philosophical texts. In addition, a complete and detailed explanation of *Mirror of Poetry*[122] was given, along with thorough instructions on style and other topics of poetic composition.

19. From **Gyurme Tenpa Namgyal** of Kathok he received thorough instructions on *Secret Essence Tantra—The Net of Magical Illusions* based on two commentaries: *Starting with Könchog* by great omniscient Rongzompa and *Dispelling the Darkness of the Ten Directions* by omniscient Longchenpa.

20. From **Pema Thrinle Gyatso,** an outstanding lineage holder of the secret yanas, he received detailed and thorough instructions on *Secret Essence Tantra—The Net of Magical Illusions* according to the Mahayoga lineage of the great master Zurchen.

21. From **Ngagwang Chökyi Gyaltsen,** the unequaled bodhisattva and protector of all beings, he received the teachings of this master's own *Sadhana of the Extraordinary Three Deities of the Drugpa Lineage with Empowerments and Transmissions,* as well as other teachings of the Drugpa Kagyu and the Kagyu tantras in general.

22. From **Karma Legshe Phuntsok,** a holder of the practice lineage,[123] he received empowerments and transmissions of the *Chakrasamvara Tantra* and *Vajravarahi Tantra* according to the oral lineage teaching of the Karma Kagyu, as well as many other teachings of that lineage.

23. From **Ngagwang Jamyang Lodrö Gyatso,** a highly realized master and scholar, he received detailed commentary and instructions on *Hevajra Tantra* and many other tantras of the new schools.

24. From **Tsewang Tendzin Zangpo**, who was enriched with all the qualities of the noble ones, he received Jamgön Kongtrul's *Treasury of Vast Speech* and many other teachings.

25. From Lord **Rigdzin Pema Wangdrak**, who held the treasure of nectarlike pith instructions, he received in their entirety the empowerments, transmissions, and pith instructions of the great tertön Heruka Lhatsun Namkha Jigme's[124] visionary teachings called *Heart Practice of the Vidyadhara* and *Vajra Heart Hymns of the Clouds*.

26. From **Orgyen Sangngak Tendzin**, a great scholar of the mantrayana, he received many hidden secret instructions on *Dark Heart Nail Pith Instructions* and *Heart Drop of Jatsön Hung Nak* and many other secret tantra teachings.

27. From **Khenchen Ngagwang Khyentse Norbu**, who held the treasures of scholarship, morality, and goodness, he received detailed commentaries on *Mirror of Poetry*, *Source of the Jewel of Poetic Composition*, astrological texts of the black and white systems, and many miscellaneous texts on the arts and sciences.

28. From **Gyurme Gedun Rabgye**, a holder of the three vows and three baskets, he received comprehensive and detailed teachings on *Chart of Nerves and Muscles*,[125] *Four Medical Tantras*, and many other medicine teachings.

29. From bodhisattva **Jigme Kunzang Dorje**, a holder of the supreme treasures of scholarship, morality, and siddhi, he received teachings on *Definitive Distinctions among the Three Vows* and many other inner tantra teachings.

30. From the great spiritual friend **Pema Rinchen Norbu**, a noble bodhisattva and scholar, he received instructions on *Gradual Path of the Essence of Wisdom*, the transmissions for the biographies of Marpa,[126] Milarepa,[127] and Gampopa,[128] and the transmissions for many other teachings.

In summary, his studies began with reading and writing. From then on, he was instructed by many great siddhas and masters in both the ordinary and extraordinary branches of knowledge. The ordinary branches include the subjects of grammar, poetry, diction, astrology, and medicine. The extraordinary branch began with studies on foundational texts such as Ngari Pandita's *Definitive Distinctions among the Three Vows*, Dharmashri's commentary *Ripening the Wish-Fulfilling Tree*, and Jigme Lingpa's *Treasury of Qualities*. He continued with works on Madhyamaka and Prajnaparamita, the *Five Teachings of Maitreya*,[129] and similar texts. He then studied inner tantra texts such as Dudjom Lingpa's *Sharp Vajra of Awareness*, the *Secret Essence Tantra—The Net of Magical Illusions* and its commentaries by Rongzompa, Longchenpa, and Zurpa, and many other Nyingma tantra texts from both the kama and terma lineages. He absorbed these teachings and completely gained their realization. For a vast array of tantras and sadhanas he learned the ceremonial formalities associated with them: mandala creation, torma preparation and ornamentation, mudras,[130] melodies and rhythms, ritual musical instruments and their use, etc. Even such details as the correct method for wrapping a text or rolling a thangka had not been overlooked. In this way he preserved the lineage teaching of the great masters. Thus was he a consummate vajra master.

As is demonstrated again and again in the biographies that detail each of his previous incarnations, through study, contemplation, and meditation, he realized the meaning of interdependent coorigination and the two truths and reached the highest enlightened state. His supreme realization was not shed like the skin of a snake with each successive incarnation, but endured gloriously. Therefore, realizations and qualities and auspicious causes and conditions were inevitable. Holding the realization of previous lives, not mere titles, the moment he studied, everything was remembered. His treatises are praised by great academicians. Thus is he renowned as an excellent scholar.

As he himself said, just as he received the teachings, he put them into practice. From the ngöndro accumulations to the practices of the two stages, he was diligent and practiced as much as he could, and results came with very little effort. He dissolved all dualistic fabrications. The veil between meditation and postmeditation disappeared. Through the path of the four visions of the spontaneous clear light, both samsara and nirvana appeared pure from the beginning. The universe of all existing phenomena arose as the mandala of the kayas and wisdoms. He beheld inconceivable wrathful and peaceful deities of the three roots face to face, and the dharmapalas fulfilled his every request. Thus was he a great siddha.

Free from the limitations of the hopes and fears of the eight worldly concerns, he never acted with pretense or hypocrisy as worldly beings do. Thus was he a fearless sky yogi.

Through the action of skillful means, without partiality, he led both high- and low-ranking individuals, according to their capabilities, onto the path that leads directly to the state of the four kayas. Thus was he the great captain of enlightenment.

69

From snow mountains of the nine lineages flowed
Streams of blessings, powers, and pith words[131] of the nine yanas,
Coursing into your oceans of wisdom and devotion,
Adorning your heart with kama and terma's jewel.

70

From matchless captains, scholars, and siddhas,
Fonts of common and uncommon knowledge,
You, unsated, took huge gulps of wisdom.
Thus, you crossed the ocean of studying.

71

Again, again, mining the gold of study,
Refining it in fires of three inquiries,
Dispelling dark doubts with hundreds of lights,
You crossed the ocean of contemplation.

72

True, true, contemplation yields the wish-fulfilling jewel;
Unconstrained by the narrow path of analysis,
Meditation dawns beyond all thoughts and words.
Thus, you crossed the ocean of meditation.

73

Wisdom's magic gift: to realize the five visualizations and three aspects
    of suchness;
Wisdom's magic gift: to be seated on the vidyadhara throne of tenfold
    mastery;[132]
Wisdom's magic gift: to be sealed by the playful display of every kind of
    song and dance;
Wisdom's magic gift: your crown as the unique and unrivaled king of
    all vajra holders.

74

Brave, fearless Jigdral, strong with youthful confidence,
Always embracing Lady Yeshe's innate wisdom,
You constantly did deathless Dorje deeds with ease,
Fulfilling the four actions begun by Drodul Ling.

75

More, more, through three blazings, as one hundred suns, fulfilling
    one's own aims;
Still, still, through three gatherings, as thousands of lights, fulfilling
    others' aims;
Swiftly, swiftly, through four inspirations, with deeds beyond thought
    of two benefits,
Every place everywhere you filled with perfected heaps of the two aims.

76

Through three pure cities of vajra body,[133]
Through two stages of secret vajra skills,
Through naked awareness of vajra mind,
You, Jigdral, are "Fearless Vajra Wisdom."

77

Through the swift, effortless Dzogchen path,
All of samsara and nirvana
You realized in the buddhas' timeless way,
To become Garab Dorje's[134] equal.

78

By pith instructions, free of yay and nay,
The dharmakaya mother of great bliss
You met in the expanse of sheer elation,
As pure lands everywhere filled with your praises.

79

The vajra offering bowl of three immovables[135]
Fills with the melted butter of pure nonduality,
Kindling the six lamps burning bright from the beginning:
Samsara and nirvana, wisdom's rainbow body glows.

80

May I, henceforth, great protector,
At your lotus feet, hold the three delights,
And follow Dzogchen's swift path of clear light,
To fulfill, as you, the two aims.

This overview of his teachers and the teaching he received concludes the fifth heap of lightbeams.

His Holiness Dudjom Rinpoche in Tibet

THE SIXTH HEAP OF LIGHTBEAMS:
*Kyabje Dudjom's impartial, beneficial activities
for the teachings and beings*

Around age thirteen at Ma-ong Kota, a secret land of the hidden valley of Pema Kö, he gave the empowerments of *Treasury of Precious Treasures* to many ordained and lay practitioners, tulkus, and khenpos. It is said that this was the first time he gave these. He established two monasteries in Terkong Nang, his birthplace. One monastery was for ordained monks and the other for ngagpas. Dharma study, meditation, and other activities flourished at both. The monastery of fully ordained monks followed the three basic practices of the vinaya[136] passed down through the lineage inaugurated by the great Shantarakshita. The ngagpa monastery followed the perfect system of the ancient ngagpa lineages, performing *drubchens*, fire puja, and mantra recitation[137] based on the eight herukas, on *Embodiment of the Total Realization of the Lama*, and on Vajrakilaya. Both monasteries flew the victory banner of the kama and terma lineages uniting sutra and tantra, study and practice, and the stages of creation and completion. They performed vajra songs and vajra dances, mudras, and tunes in perfect accord with the traditional lineage of the vidyadharas that flowered at Mindröling Monastery in central Tibet.

However, local Sera Monastery officials, displeased with Kyabje's activities, claimed, "Without permission from the Tibetan government and Sera authorities, you cannot establish monasteries and gather monks." They continued making accusations and then took even stronger action. These circumstances became the cause for His Holiness to leave Pema Kö. He traveled to Lhasa to petition Tibetan authorities for the required permission. While waiting for their response, he did pilgrimage to Samye and other sacred sites in central Tibet, including Orgyen Mindröling Monastery. As no favorable response ever came, he was reluctant to go forward in Pema Kö. As predicted by Guru Padmasambhava, the world in general and the dharma and Tibet in particular would experience great misfortune during this current era. Around this time he sang the following song:

A Ho Ye
In Ogmin, in the midst of Copper-Glory Mountain's palace,
Vidyadharas, dakas, dakinis, are gathered together
In great bliss, on their charming and alluring peak. Thinking of that,
In my heart's core, I recall the one father, Lake-Born Dorje,

Whose body, with major and minor marks, outshines the world's glories,
Whose speech vibrates with tamboura songs of the secret channels,
Whose mind is the perfect, ceaseless nature of wisdom's clear light.
What feast could be better than seeing the Guru's joyful face?

Smiling, smiling, amidst joyful glances from bright, twinkling eyes,
Singing, singing, the secret sounds of dakini melodies,
Flashing, flashing, with swift dances, amazing and wonderful.
Again, again, the hope of seeing this is unbearable

Since the eye-bubbles of this miserable little child
Are thickly covered by the stained veils of duality thought,
And swell with regret at not having the fortune to see that sight.
With loud wails, I cried out, Lotus-Born, why have you not heard me?

If you hear, use your gold tool of wisdom and compassion, tear out
These thick cataracts, dark veils of ignorance, I beseech you,
Come, take my hand in yours, let me feel your fingers holding mine;
Lead me, only father, to your garden of great joy, please.

Right now, if I cannot be counted among the lucky ones,
Send vidyadharas, dakas, and dakinis to console me,
As I, to the endless bliss of Dewachen's glorious feast,
Joyfully run after you, father, on the gradual path.

Once this white-tailed eagle's body, youthful in three devotions,
Is fitted with a pair of soaring wings of View and Conduct
And fully endowed with the six strengths[138] of all pure samayas,
Then the citadel of Pema Öd will not seem so far off.

Gods and humans, male and female, all sharing good karma,
Say a prayer that we will rank with the vidyadharas, and—
Good! Good!—with laughter and enjoyment, all together,
Let us go, joined as one, never parting, to the pure land.

This is the longing melody sung by a youthful cuckoo,
Who heard its echoes in the speech chakra's playful dance of bliss.
Through this message calling out to the Guru's heart stream,
May a honey nectar of blessings rain down right now.

Around that time many fortunate devotees gathered to him, like swans
to a beautiful lake, to receive the empowerments, transmissions, and
pith instructions of the kama and terma lineages, as well as many other
Buddhist teachings. As they arrived, he gave teachings according to their
wishes. They were enthralled by his conduct and appearance: humble and
simple, yet replete with knowledge and wisdom. Devotion, pure perception, and bodhichitta naturally arose in whoever approached him, and
their realization increased. They talked about his goodness wherever
they went.

Soon he began to give the empowerments, transmissions, and pith
instructions for the *Treasury of Precious Treasures*, *Hundreds of Thousands
of Nyingma Tantras*, and *Four Heart Drop Cycles*; for the terma of Nyang-ral
Nyima Özer, Guru Chöwang, Terdak Lingpa, Dorje Lingpa, Ratna Lingpa,
Pema Lingpa, Dudul Dorje, Jatsön Nyingpo, Lhatsun Namkha Jigme, and

Dudjom Lingpa; and for many other Nyingma kama and terma teachings. He taught at Kongpo Dragsum Do, Kongpo Buchu Dechen Teng, Samye, and a great number of other locations in Tibet.

Then, later, in his early thirties he went first to Bhutan and did pilgrimage at Padro Taktsang,[139] where he decided to do retreat. There he revealed terma of Vajrakilaya and other teachings and had many beautiful visions and realizations. Then he went to Tashi Gang,[140] where he gave the empowerments, transmissions, and pith instructions of *Treasury of Precious Treasures* and Sangye Lingpa's *Embodiment of the Total Realization of the Lama*, as well as many other empowerments, transmissions, and teachings. He gave the blessings and personal instructions that devotees requested, thus fulfilling their wishes and bestowing what would bring benefit immediately and in the future. He sang the following song around this time:

A Ho
Primordially unchanging, innate nature of clear light,
Free of all artifice, enjoying the great bliss of union,
Self-born Vajra Queen, Noble Lady of the supreme secret:
So all is seen as dharmakaya display, come, console me!
In the sphere of the innately pure ground of phenomena,
Realization, wisdom's anointing from that single thigle,
View, vast and impartial, I give in ganachakra offering.
Empty-awareness dharmakaya Dakinis, enjoy this feast!
In the sphere of instantly perfect, endless clear light nature,
Wisdom's self outpouring far beyond fabrications of mind,
Meditation, sky-wide, I give in ganachakra offering.
Empty-brightness sambhogakaya Dakinis, enjoy this feast!
In the sphere of instantly diffuse wisdom and compassion,
Crazy wisdom deeds, beyond going, coming, keeping, giving,
Acts, free from yay and nay, I give in ganachakra offering.
Empty-appearance nirmanakaya Dakinis, enjoy this feast!
In the depths of clear radiant rainbow light of the six lamps,
Bright awareness, ceaseless configuring of wisdoms and kayas,
The four clear-light visions, I give in ganachakra offering.

Please enjoy this feast beyond mind, where all dharmas are ended!
The deeply luminous great thigle has no circumference,
The self-arising clarity of the four lamps shines undimmed,
Whatever appears is wisdom's turning, so why try so hard?
Relax, then, within the nature of primordial wisdom.
As false dualistic displays are freed in the unborn state,
Self-arising buddha nature fills samsara and nirvana.
Having found the protector's primordial kingdom within,
Spacious mind dawns, a blissful sun, shining from the heart's core.
Since we are all the heart sons and daughters of Kunzang Padma,
Following the true, secret, swift path of the supreme dharma,
Keeping to the vajra dance of the great rainbow-light body,
Let's start to stir the depths of samsara's three realms and help others!
Fortunate vajra brothers and sisters all gathered here,
Not hesitating, not doubting, firm in faith and devotion,
Not thinking "pure" or "impure," performing crazy wisdom deeds,
To the glorious ganachakra feast of deathless great bliss,
May all come as one, fulfilling the aims of that mandala.

In the marvelous area of Jong, in the province of Puwo, in the Drag Ge area, at the spot known as the "Glorious Neck" of Lion's Sky Fortress-Mountain, in the excellent and joyful gathering place of Vajra Yogini and her retinue, when I reached the age of twenty-seven, in the Male Iron Horse year (1930), on the tenth day of the waxing moon in the month of the Drozhin constellation, while I was making generous offerings to the dakas and dakinis of the three places,[141] spontaneously this song played in the trifling neck flute of the vidyadhara sprout Jigdral Yeshe Dorje.

At an unspecified date, somewhere in this time period, he sang this song:

A Ho
Wisdom's melody, clear light of utter simplicity,
Unceasing display, in union with nets of illusion:
Pervasive lord of all mandalas, Lake-Born Dorje,
Rain down blessings, so all is seen as dharmakaya.
Outwardly, self-born dakas and dakinis in charnel grounds;
Inwardly, the body's self-arising divine mandala:
Drunk with unending great bliss, youthful in vajra strength,
Dance to the deathless song of transformed inner channels.
All brothers and sisters gathered here by shared karma,
Enjoying this lavish ganachakra of great bliss,
May we have a place in Ogmin Padma Öd's palace,
All together, united as one, I wish and pray.

Thus this was spoken by Jnana at the request of Könchog Rabten.

Continuing on in Bhutan, he traveled to the valley of Bumthang[142] to do pilgrimage and to fulfill the requests of many devotees. There he met Pema Ösel Gyurme Dorje, who was the tenth incarnation of the great tertön Pema Lingpa. At the request of this incarnate lama, His Holiness gave the transmission of the entire cycle of Pema Lingpa and did the empowerments and transmission of the thirteen volumes of Sangye Lingpa's *Embodiment of the Total Realization of the Lama*. Afterward this tenth incarnation sent a messenger to His Holiness in Lhasa, asking, "Please edit and clarify the Vajrakilaya teaching of Pema Lingpa, so it will be easy to follow. I'm planning to do a drubchen of this annually with some other retreatants, so could you do this quickly?" As requested, His Holiness did the editing and sent it back. Pema Ösel Gyurme Dorje was very pleased, and they immediately made wood blocks to print it.

Around this time Kyabje went to the hidden land of Sikkim, as requested by the king, queen, princess, lamas, ministers, and subjects, and again gave the empowerments, transmissions, and pith instructions for

THE FOUR NOBLE TRUTHS

THE EXISTENCE OF SUFFERING

ITS ORIGIN

ITS CESSATION

THE WAY THAT LEADS TO ITS CESSATION

THE EIGHTFOLD PATH

1 RIGHT UNDERSTANDING

2 RIGHT THOUGHT

3 RIGHT SPEECH

4 RIGHT ACTION

5 RIGHT LIVELIHOOD

6 RIGHT EFFORT

7 RIGHT MINDFULNESS

8 RIGHT CONCENTRATION

Treasury of Precious Treasures, and in addition, of *Heart Practice of the Vidyadhara* and the termas of Lhatsun Namkha Jigme and many other teachings, empowerments, and pith instructions as requested by devotees. Thus he glorified the Buddha's teachings, particularly Nyingma teachings, in that area. Afterward in Sikkim he made pilgrimage to various holy sites, blessing and reconsecrating them. At Dragkar Tashi Ding, a geomantic energy point, he buried treasure vases and did ceremonies to recharge and balance the earth's energy. He gave many blessings and teachings, and those in attendance made life-long, meaningful connections.

Finally, he returned to Tibet thinking to do benefit by restoring balance at crucial energy points. In Kongpo Buchu he began building Zangdok Palri Monastery and founding two retreat centers, Rigdzin Ling and Sangchen Ösel Namdröling. [143]

Work Song to Commemorate Construction of the Glorious Copper-Color Mountain Temple in Kongpo Buchu

Lord of blessings, Padma Jungne,
Only precious refuge of your son,
Who, if devotion does not waver,
Will be led to lands of constant joy.
Your kindness, father, never deceives.
With yearning heart and mind, I pray,
May father and son be equal.

In lush, joyful valleys of east Kong,
In Buchu's secret pleasure gardens,
To help all beings, our past mothers,
May Copper-Glory Mountain Temple be raised,
And its aims succeed unhindered.
Keep dharma's victory banner firm,
Grant your blessings, kind Protector;
Friends, dakas and dakinis, please act,
Male and female dharmapalas, make this happen.

May the son's good wishes be fulfilled,
May your aims, noble lama, be achieved,
May the six kinds of beings be happy,
May this place prosper and be joyful.

Thus, again:

The upper reaches of glacial heights
Are the snow lion's roaming places;
If snow and lion are not parted,
His turquoise mane will surely brighten.
While the snow lion can roam anywhere,
Eh-O He knows just where to shake his turquoise mane!

Low-lying southern sandalwood forests
Are the striped tiger's roaming places;
If forests and tiger are not parted,
The tiger's stripes will surely brighten.
While the striped tiger can roam anywhere,
Eh-O He knows just where to show his bold stripes!

Turquoise lakes at low ends of valleys
Are the white-belly goldfish's roaming places;
If blue lakes and goldfish are not parted,
The gleam in gold eyes will surely brighten.
While the goldfish can roam anywhere,
Eh-O He knows just where to dart and shimmy!

Blue elevations stretching high above
Are the white-tailed eagle's roaming places;
If heights and eagle are not parted,
His three and six flight skills[144] will surely shine.
While the eagle can slice skies anywhere,
Eh-O He knows just where to spread wide his wings!

And once again:

In wide, expansive, high blue skies,
When the sun's royal parasol opens,
On the ground, lotus-flower gardens
Thrive, as cause and effect decree.

In the air, from depths of white clouds,
When shimmering honey showers rain down,
In valleys below, fruits and flowers
Bloom, as cause and effect decree.

In countries anywhere and everywhere,
When yogis and vidyadharas come,
In lucky practitioners, the two goods[145]
Dawn, as cause and effect decree.

Due to unfortunate, inevitable coming events, many bad omens appeared all over Tibet in the late 1940s. During that time Zangdok Palri Monastery was damaged by earthquakes. His Holiness, however, continued to bury treasure vases, build stupas, and do ceremonies to restore and balance the earth energy points where King Songtsen Gampo and many subsequent masters had built temples. In the 1940s, sectarian movements had started in central Tibet and many high government officials were influenced. Negative things were said about the other schools of Tibetan Buddhism, in particular about the Nyingma School, and about Guru Padmasambhava. They destroyed many statues of him, trampling them, tossing them onto trash heaps or into rivers. They loudly proclaimed what they'd done, saying, "How wonderful these activities are." Powerful Lhasa officials supported the perpetrators and issued directives ordering communities to organize welcoming parties for these individuals as they traveled around Tibet and to make arrangements to facilitate their activities. This was enforced by the central government military, such as it was. In brief, outwardly into human forms, the hearts and minds of asuras and lower-realm denizens were reflected again and again.

Around that time foreign armies entered Tibet. In the 1950s the Chinese Communist party, trying to restrengthen and stabilize their power, invited His Holiness the fourteenth Dalai Lama, the sixteenth Karmapa, the tenth Panchen Rinpoche, and many great teachers from all the schools of Tibetan Buddhism, as well as many powerful lay leaders, to China. Kyabje Dudjom Rinpoche was also invited and went as the representative of the Nyingma School. On the way he gave many blessings and teachings to Tibetan and Chinese devotees. The Communist Chinese entertained these distinguished guests with elaborate performances of dance, theater, music, gymnastics, and also wrestling contests. Kyabje had an attendant from the Kongpo area named Tashi, who had a naturally large and strong physique, and while they were attending a wrestling exhibition, without thinking it through and certainly without consulting His Holiness, he jumped out into the stadium. Kyabje thought, "This is a big mistake. He may be injured, even killed. Why couldn't he just sit here quietly?" He did prayers to Padmasambhava and the dharmapalas, and Tashi was able to rouse the spectators in a way that none of the Chinese wrestlers had been able to do. They began laughing and clapping. They presented him with flowers and scarves, which he brought back and offered to His Holiness. People began talking about the strength of Tibetan men.

After leaving China, His Holiness returned to central Tibet and began giving many teachings of the Nyingma kama, of the old and new termas, of *Treasury of Precious Treasures,* including their empowerments, transmissions, and pith instructions. Among those who attended were many renowned teachers such as the two great khenpo brothers, Minling Chen Gyurme Khyentse Norbu and Minling Chung Gyurme Ngagwang Chökyi Dragpa, Minling Trichen Kunzang Wangdu Rinpoche from Mindröling Monastery, Dordrag Rigdzin Chenpo and Chuzang Rinpoche from Dorje Drag Monastery, and the great Dzogchen lineage holder and yogi Chatral Sangye Dorje Rinpoche. Many other great khenpos, tulkus, renowned ngagpas, and thousands of lay practitioners, along with many Tibetan

*In Central Tibet, His Holiness surrounded by many lamas, khenpos, and tulkus
including the abbots of Mindroling and Dorje Drag monasteries*

government dignitaries and officials, were also present.

Sometime around 1955 he made a brief trip to his birthplace, Pema Kö, to perform additional beneficial activities for dharma and beings in that area. Then he returned to central Tibet.

In 1956, the Fire Monkey year TRE 2083, when Kyabje was fifty-three, the great state oracle, Nechung Chökyong, instructed the Tibetan government to make a request of Kyabje Dudjom Rinpoche. He was asked to subdue negative forces by doing special Dorje Drolö ceremonies. He was also asked to erect a dudul stupa[146] at the place in Tsela Gang mountain range resembling an elephant trunk where two rivers, Yarchab Tsangpo and Nyangkhe Tsangpo, meet.

In the midfifties the Tibetan situation deteriorated due to the expansion of the Communist state. Many Tibetans left the regions of their birth and traveled to Lhasa, thinking the situation would be more stable there. For numerous reasons, many great teachers, including Khyentse Chökyi Lodrö,[147] either made their way to central Tibet or departed for Bhutan, Sikkim, and Pema Kö. Around this time, His Holiness wrote the following poem:

Ready to Go from Kongpo to Central Tibet
or Other Undecided Destinations

I, a silken lion, do not need a palace.
The lion's glacial heights are my palace.
Anywhere I like, I shake my turquoise mane,
Roaming about, enjoying any snowy ravine.

I, the eagle, do not need a strong fortress.
The white-tailed eagle's high red cliffs are my fortress.
Anywhere I like, I spread my wings with six strengths,[148]
Slicing the high skies and vast blue expanses.

I, the tiger, do not need a rich mansion.
The tiger's forest thickets are my rich mansion.
Anywhere I like, I parade my bold stripes,
Heading toward good spots in sandalwood forests.

I, the golden bee, do not need fertile fields.
The humming bee's lotus beds are my fertile fields.
Anywhere I like, I burst out in song,
Gliding wherever sweet nectar can be gathered.

I, the yogi, do not need a family home.
All the yogi's good places are my family home.
Since the two aims are instantly realized,
Anywhere I go I like, heading out at ease.

Thus Dudjom spoke words of mad chatter.

Around 1957 His Holiness Dudjom Rinpoche with his family and wife, Sangyum Kuzhok Rigdzin Wangmo, went to Sikkim and then to Kalimpong, where they settled. Again His Holiness returned to central Tibet, this time, primarily, to get many Nyingma kama and terma texts and also many relics and precious ritual objects. In this time period in Kalimpong, having

*His Holiness Dudjom
Rinpoche with long-life vase*

performed land-blessing and ground-breaking ceremonies, he began to build Zangdok Palri Monastery with the assistance of Sharpa Tsenam.

In 1959, the Earth Pig Year TRE 2086, Tibetans lost their homeland, and His Holiness the Dalai Lama escaped to India. Many Tibetans were killed; many were separated from their relatives; and many lost their homes and belongings. Guru Padmasambhava had said in his predictions, "Even in the lower realms, there will not be such suffering as this." Thick black storming clouds of the five poisons covered and disrupted the blazing teachings and welfare of Tibetans.

Around 1960, the Iron Mouse year TRE 2087, Kyabje Dudjom Rinpoche was unanimously appointed head of the Nyingma School of Tibetan Buddhism by great Nyingma teachers, monks, and practitioners. This decision was supported by His Holiness the Dalai Lama and the Tibetan government-in-exile. He served in that capacity until his parinirvana in 1987.

Around 1961, through the sponsorship of Tsewang Gyaltsen from

Riwoche in Kham, he gave the empowerments, transmissions, and pith instructions of *Treasury of Precious Treasures* to thousands of disciples in Kalimpong, near the hidden valley of Sikkim. Again in Kalimpong at the beginning of 1962, through the sponsorship of the great teacher Kyabje Trulshik Rinpoche, he gave the empowerment and teaching of the Nyingma kama to many thousands of devotees: laymen and laywomen, ngagpas, tulkus and khenpos, yogis and yoginis. Thus, he restrengthened the Buddha's teachings, particularly Nyingma teachings, giving great hope at this crucial time to many Tibetans. Near the conclusion of the Nyingma kama teaching His Holiness Dudjom Rinpoche gave these following specific instructions and advice called *Rejuvenating Medicine of the Heart* to all the devotees who were present:

Dear Dharma Friends,

I will now briefly explain the essential history of the cycle of teachings I am presenting here known as the Nyingma kama. Some time ago I was asked whether the kama is a part of the Kagyupa teachings. The answer is no. Generally the "Nyingma" and "Sarma" designations refer to two distinct time periods in which the Buddhist teachings were translated into Tibetan. Therefore these names did not exist in India.

During the reign of Dharma King Trisong Deutsen and his sons, an august, noble assembly of over a hundred great panditas and translators gathered. Their common goal was to translate the Buddhist sutras and tantras and to establish the dharma by applying the methods of attentive study, meditation, and practice. The panditas were some of the most revered names in the history of Tibetan Buddhism: Shantarakshita, Guru Padmasambhava, and Vimalamitra. Also participating were the Tibetan translators: Vairochana, Kawa Paltsek, Chok Ro Lui Gyaltsen, Ma Rinchen Chok, and Nyak Jnana Kumara. The resultant corpus of teachings is known as the Nyingma, the ancient, translations.

Years later King Langdarma destroyed the teachings and the dynasty of Tibetan kings was broken. The descendants of the

His Holiness surrounded by many masters in the 1960s
after giving the Nyimgma kama teachings

dharma kings settled in Ngari, the upper region of Tibet. Later
still, during the reign of King Lha Lama Yeshe Öd and his brother
Zhiwa Öd, the translator Rinchen Zangpo and others once again
began the process of translating the Buddhadharma into Tibetan.
From that time on those translations came to be known as Sarma,
new translations.

There are those today who think that the Nyingma School lacks
the sutra teachings and the Sarma School lacks the tantra
teachings. These are the errors of insufficient familiarity with and

incomplete study of the teachings. Both the Sarma and Nyingma schools have complete teachings of both sutra and tantra. There have been scholars who arrogantly asserted the wrong view that since Langdarma destroyed the ancient translation tradition, all subsequent Nyingma teachings must be inauthentic and the fabrication of many individuals. Only uneducated dummies have entertained doubts upon hearing such false accusations. This view is absolutely incorrect. When it is said that he destroyed the Buddhist teachings, this refers in general to the destruction of monastic institutions. He could not destroy the mantra system nor the practice of ngagpas for several reasons. For one, he was afraid of the power of the great ngagpa Nubchen Sangye Yeshe. Furthermore, ngagpas didn't wear monk's robes, and since the persecutors could not read their minds, they were left alone. Therefore, these lay, white-robed ngagpas[149] protected the volumes of sutra and tantra and kept the heart of the teaching through their study, contemplation, meditation, and practice. By their kindness the secret teachings exist as a wish-fulfilling jewel even down to this present time, and, as a result, we can all enjoy them.

After the king's death and in the wake of his destruction of the dharma in central Tibet, three disciples of Shantarakshita, named Mar, Yo, and Tsang, escaped to Kham, in eastern Tibet. Lachen Gongpa Rabsal and ten others from the U and Tsang regions took vinaya ordination from these three masters. After the assassination of King Langdarma, the monastic tradition was restarted in central Tibet, and that is known as the beginning of the later or Sarma schools of Tibet. Soon thereafter the great translator Rinchen Zangpo arrived and gradually many other translators came as well. The Kadam, Sakya, and Kagyu schools developed and so did others. Jamgön Tsongkhapa came from the lineage of the Kadam School, and from him the tradition of the Gaden or Gelugpa began.

Late in the life of King Lha Lama Yeshe Öd, the Nyingma

tertöns began to appear. Our Nyingma teaching can be divided into two lineages: the long lineage of kama and the close lineage of terma. The teachings that were passed on from mouth to ear in unbroken succession from Buddha Samantabhadra up to your own root lama are known as the long lineage of kama. The kama teaching is vast and profound, containing pith instructions for both sutra and tantra but primarily for the three divisions of the Nyingma inner tantras, *Do, Gyü,* and *Sem*:[150] *The Sutra Which Gathers All Intentions (Do Gongpa Dupa),*[151] or Anuyoga; *Secret Essence Tantra—The Net of Magical Illusions (Gyü Gyutrül Drawa),* or Mahayoga;[152] and *Sem, Long,* and *Men-ngag de,* or Atiyoga. In woodblock form alone the number of tantras in the kama teachings is over 440, and that number is far exceeded by the kama teachings recorded in handwritten form.

Foreseeing the degeneration of the teachings and beings in times to come, Guru Rinpoche kindly hid an inconceivable number of treasure troves containing dharma, wealth, blessing substances, and so forth in glaciers, rocky mountains, lakes, and many other places. When the time was right, tertöns emanated, opened the treasure doors, and spread the teachings they contained. These teachings then are known as the close lineage of the termas. This lineage comprises inconceivable pith instructions, yogic activities, and ritual practices of the creation and completion stages connected primarily with *ka gong phur sum.*[153] From early on and up to the present, more than one hundred major and over one thousand lesser tertöns have appeared.[154]

Let's return to the kama lineage. From the sutra point of view, they contain vinaya and bodhisattva teachings. From the tantra point of view, they contain kriya, upa, and yoga teachings. And from the extraordinary Nyingma point of view, they contain three inner tantra teachings: Mahayoga, Anuyoga, and Atiyoga. The Mahayoga teachings are based on the root tantra *Vajrasattva's Net of Magical Illusions*[155] and on many branch tantras specifically related to the mandalas of body, speech, mind, quality, and activity. The Anuyoga teachings on the nine yanas are related to the mandala of *Condensed Sutra Mandala of the Great Assembly*.[156] The Atiyoga teachings are pith instructions that can be divided into three classes: the outer, inner, and secret classes. The outer is based on the *Mind Class of Eighteen Mother and Son Tantras*.[157] The inner is based on the *Space Class of the Vajra Bridge*.[158] The secret class is based on the Seventeen Tantras.[159] Therefore this kama teaching is the foundation and heart of the Nyingma School, and from ancient times it spread beautifully in Tibet. Study the religious history of the Nyingma School and the biographies of its masters, and you will see why the Nyingma kama tradition is so important.

The Nyingma teachings were preserved and spread through group practice and retreat, mandalas, sadhanas, pith instruction and oral explanation of *Secret Essence Tantra—The Net of Magical Illusions*, etc. In brief, the activities of study and practice continued without decrease in central Tibet at Dor-Min, in Kham at Ka-Pal, and the territory in between at Zhe-Dzog,[160] and at most other Nyingma monasteries.

Now the negative intentions and unthinkable power of savages have destroyed and uprooted all the monasteries, lineage holders, and practitioners in Kham and central Tibet. Not even one copy of the teachings remained, and so this unlucky era began. Even after this immense tragedy in Tibet, I was able, though with much hardship, to move the books I already had in Pema Kö to India.

Out of his sense of responsibility for the continuation of the lineage, Zha De-u Trulshik Tulku Rinpoche urged me again and again over a long period of time to give empowerments and transmission of the kama teachings. Recently, without regard for hardship, he came from the Shar Khumbu region to Kalimpong and sponsored these teachings. Because of this we are able to pervasively spread the complete Nyingma kama lineage by empowerment and transmission. Sunk as we are in this difficult time, at this very moment we can connect with the life force of the lineage, and so be assured that it has not died. For this we can rejoice.

When I was about twenty years old and receiving these teachings at Mindröling Monastery, I, along with many great teachers, including Khenpos Chen and Chung[161] and numerous other lamas and tulkus, received this kama teaching in its entirety, as well as *ka gong*[162] and many other empowerments, transmissions, and pith instructions from Khenchen Dorje Chang.[163] Among all of us he told me specifically, "You have completed the principal teachings of the kama and terma; the pith instructions, empowerments, and transmissions. Now you must hold the Nyingma lineage, which means you must keep and preserve all the volumes of the kama and terma and never neglect an opportunity to spread these teachings." He said this to me several times. Now when I reflect on his words I see them as prophetic.

Moreover when I received the teaching of *Treasury of Precious Treasures*, Phugtrul Rinpoche said, "Among all the students of the two Jamgöns there is none other than myself who has given the teachings of *Treasury of Precious Treasures* five times; you, however, will give them ten times." With much laughter he said this many times to me. I thought to myself, How can that be possible? But now I have given these teachings nine times, and I realize his words were also prophetic.

I, an old householder father, don't have a single good quality except that of perceiving all my root teachers as accomplished masters and scholars and as Guru Padmasambhava come again in human form. Never did I perform even a single small action against these teachers, not even one that might appear inappropriate. That is my principal quality, and sometimes I get a little proud that there isn't anyone else who has kept the lineage as purely as I.

At this time there are over two thousand in attendance here: about thirty-seven tulkus; around sixty khenpos and lobpöns;

monks and ngagpas form the majority; and the rest, about one quarter, are laymen and laywomen. In ancient times when tantric empowerments were given, the teacher had confirmed in advance that each participant could keep the teaching and samayas, which meant that only a limited number of individuals were involved, and as a result at any particular time the dissemination of the teaching was never widespread. However, there is a saying, "Vinaya teaching follows the traditions of the country in which it finds itself." In these days everyone is very happy to receive empowerment, even small children. And nobody is happy if anyone is excluded. When I ask whether you will do the practice, everyone together says, "I will, and I will keep the samayas." Even though you say this, it is very difficult to maintain. Promising to do it but then not doing it is the cause of obscuration and annoyance to me, to you, and others around you.

If someone isn't interested, even if you invite them to come, they won't. Therefore, whoever comes, must be devoted disciples. So I am giving the transmission and empowerment without hesitation. *Moon Lamp Sutra* says there isn't a single sentient being without buddha nature. Therefore no one is incapable of receiving the teaching. For the uneducated ones who are not really ready to receive the vajrayana, these teachings will become naturally self-secret. Therefore, I feel I am not in error to make the teachings available to everyone.

To really receive the empowerment, you must know the precise meaning of the words used and then take that meaning into meditation. Without knowing the meaning, the feel of the bumpa as it touches your head or tasting the water from it will not necessarily mature the mind. However, the root of mantrayana is pure perception, and therefore to see the lama as the principal deity of the mandala and the empowerment substances as blessing nectar, and with devotion free of doubt to view the mandala and hear the names of the deities purely, will have great benefit. In that manner receive the empowerment.

After receiving the empowerment you have to protect the samaya. Your relation to the vajrayana samayas can be compared to a snake's options for movement when placed into a hole in bamboo: keep samaya and go straight up to the pure lands, destroy samaya and go straight down to the lower realms. There are only two ways to go. There is no third way. You need to understand that keeping samaya and practicing dharma, rather than merely an obligation, brings great benefit to oneself. There are many samayas to protect and many dharmas to practice, but you must always remember to bring them all into a single essential practice. In general, all of us who claim to be practitioners soon discover that our actions are not in accord with dharma, and that is our biggest mistake. Therefore don't confuse your high purpose with your actual behavior. Your actions should be the same in private as they are in public. If your mouth proclaims, "I take refuge, I take refuge," and "I act for the benefit of all beings," but you act like the ringleader in your own circus of self-important, ego-clinging tricks, then in reality you ignore karma and samaya and this is no good.

Buddhadharma does not exist outside, but only in one's own mind. For that reason our teacher[164] said, "Do not do any negative activities. Perform the perfect virtues. Discipline your own mind. This is the teaching of the Buddha."

In summary:

All activities, big and small, performed with a mind tainted by the three poisons are negative and must be abandoned. When you abandon those, you abandon any harmful action to others. That completes the teachings of the vinaya.

Any activity free from thoughts tainted by the three poisons, whether big or small, is virtuous and must be performed. When activities are not mixed with the three poisons, beneficial thoughts toward others will arise naturally, and whatever activities you perform will fulfill the three vows of the bodhisattva.

Positive or negative thought produces virtuous or unvirtuous action. Therefore mind alone is the source of good and evil. Protect and discipline your own mind. All the 84,000 teachings that Buddha gave, were given in order to discipline the mind. When you have disciplined this rough, wild mind, naturally all ordinary habitual patterns and perceptions will decrease. Gradually all will be seen in its purity, thereby completing the samayas, the vajrayana vows.

When you discipline the wild mind, good thoughts will come naturally. The beautiful term "bodhichitta" that we hear so much about is nothing other than a good heart. With regard to the vajrayana samayas in particular, they are not like the vinaya vows, which are based on the actions of body and speech, but are based instead on the mind and so can be easily damaged. For example, if from deep in your heart anger arises toward a vajra friend, at that very moment you have committed the third root downfall of the vajrayana. If in your heart you harbor contempt for the beliefs of another religion, let alone for another school of Buddhism, you have committed the sixth root downfall. After damaging the samaya, if you don't immediately purify that breach, then for as long as you delay the process of purification, for that long will obscurations become heavier and heavier. Therefore not even the smallest breach of samaya should be neglected, but rather immediate action must be taken to purify it.

From the moment you receive the empowerment of any deity of the three roots, you must practice and meditate on the body, speech, and mind of that deity as your samaya. And if it happens that you can't perform the many recitations of the numerous deities, then meditate and practice on Vajrasattva, who is the lord of all mandalas, and it will be the same as meditating on each of all the mandalas separately. Vajrasattva practice is also particularly effective for purifying all broken samayas, obscurations, and downfalls. Therefore using a sadhana such as *The Single Seal That Will Shake the Depths of Samsara* as a daily practice and reciting the hundred-syllable mantra at least twenty-one times is very important.

In conclusion, all of you have now received this profound empowerment and teaching. To make it ever more meaningful, apply all your capabilities to it as often as you're able, perform meritorious activities and practice, and carry it into your daily activities. You'll be doing yourself a great kindness. So many people came together here without messengers or advertisement, which demonstrates that we're truly connected through dharma and past aspiration. Through renewed aspirations, we can increase that connection to such an extent that in our next lives I think we will certainly come together again.

Therefore let all of us, teachers and disciples, wish together for the increase of the precious teachings of the Buddha, the source of benefit now and in the future. As for the crown jewel of all lineage masters, the protector of the Land of Snow,[165] and all the great lineage holders, we wish that their lotus feet firmly remain for a long time to come and that all their beneficial activities will increase. We wish that the entire world in general, the holy land of India in particular, and the Land of Snow especially, be immediately free from the torment of the suffering of degeneration, and may all enjoy the prosperity of a new golden age of joy and peace. Please pray for this from the bottom of your heart.

I have one request directed to all the lamas and tulkus concerning a big hope of mine. Because of my age, my health, and so forth, it will be difficult for me to give and spread the teaching on a large scale. I was able to give the transmissions and empowerments this time to all of you, and this makes my heart very happy. Now I ask you to keep this father's precious jewel as his rightful heirs, to take on the responsibility to prevent the profound pith instructions of the wish-fulfilling jewel from ever decreasing. It is so important that you do this. This copy of the cycle of Nyingma kama teaching which I have here is now the only one in existence.

All the rest have been destroyed. If we lose one page from this cycle, then it is gone forever. Therefore you lamas and tulkus please make as many copies of this as you are able. Practice it yourselves. Teach and spread it to other people. Act in as many different ways as you possibly can to ensure its continuation for a very long time to come. Do your best to keep it in the very core of your heart.

Because of activities such as this one, we can understand why he is called the regent of Khenpo Shantarakshita, Lobpön Padmasambhava, and Dharma King Trisong Deutsen, who came at the right time.

Later in 1962 in Tso Pema, in northwest India, the holy place where Mandarava and Guru Padmasambhava practiced, and where that Guru transformed a conflagration into a lake, many students gathered from regions throughout the Himalayas, such as Ladakh, Gazha, Khunu, Parti, and Nyungti. He rained down the teachings and empowerments of the Nyingma kama and the *Hundreds of Thousands of Nyingma Tantras* on all those devoted followers. Around this time the following song was sung:

Playful Display of the Original Nature:
A Song and Dance of Ultimate Fulfillment

A Ho Ye
In the pure land of Dewachen,
Dharmakaya Lama, Amitabha, dwells.
I pray, please look upon your child kindly,
Bless me with the supreme empowerment.
Clear light empty awareness, without center or borders:
Is this not your realization, Lord?
Original nature beyond movement and change:
Is this not Amitabha, limitless light?
Not for a moment have I been separate,
Never separate, still I was unaware.

At the instant of awareness,
Buddha Amitabha is gone,
Dewachen's pure land vanishes—
Within mind's unborn nature, sha ra ra,
In the play of awareness and empty bliss, ya la la,
Whatever arises is the sparkling dharmakaya.
Holding to the pure land is a delusion,
The label "buddha" is a hurdle of attachment.
Amitabha is not outside, look within.
This finding the dharmakaya through oneself, a la la!
This being happy, always and ceaselessly, e ma ho!
This again is the sublime lama's kindness,
This again, the profound blessing of pith advice.
Let's sing the noble song of supreme happiness,
Let's step to the dance of ultimate fulfillment.

A Ho Ye
In the pure land of Tala Mountain,
Sambhogakaya Lama, Chenrezig, dwells.
I pray, please look upon your child kindly,
Bless me with the supreme empowerment.
Self-luminous awareness, not veiled, not obscured:
Is this not your realization, Lord?
Wisdom's energy, compassion's instant arising:
Is this not Chenrezig, Lord of Compassion?
Not for a moment have I been separate,
Never separate, still I was unaware.
At the instant of awareness,
Buddha Chenrezig is gone,
Tala Mountain vanishes—
Within mind's unborn nature, sha ra ra,
In the play of awareness and empty bliss, ya la la,
Whatever shines forth is sambhogakaya's rich nature.
Holding to the pure land is a delusion,

The label "dharma" is a hurdle of attachment.
Chenrezig is not outside, look within.
This finding the sambhogakaya through oneself, a la la!
This being happy, always and ceaselessly, e ma ho!
This again is the sublime lama's kindness;
This again, the profound blessing of pith advice.
Let's sing the noble song of supreme happiness.
Let's step to the dance of ultimate fulfillment.

A Ho Ye
In the palace of Copper-Glory Mountain,
Nirmanakaya Lama, Orgyen Pad Jung, dwells.
I pray, please look upon your child kindly,
Bless me with the supreme empowerment.
Self-liberating awareness, timeless and lasting:
Is this not your realization, Lord?
Wisdom and kayas, mind's self-born nature:
Is this not Padma, self-born from a lotus?
Not for a moment have I been separate,
Never separate, still I was unaware.
At the instant of awareness,
Buddha Padma Jungne is gone,
Copper-Glory Mountain vanishes—
Within mind's unborn nature, sha ra ra,
In the play of awareness and empty bliss, ya la la,
Whatever appears is nirmanakaya play-energy.
Holding to the pure land is a delusion,
The label "bodhichitta" is a hurdle of attachment.
Pad Jung is not outside, look within.
This finding the nirmanakaya through oneself, a la la!
This being happy, always and ceaselessly, e ma ho!
This again is the sublime lama's kindness;
This again, the profound blessing of pith advice.
Let's sing the noble song of supreme happiness.

Let's step to the dance of ultimate fulfillment.

A Ho Ye
In the place of great bliss, on the crown chakra,
The root lama, peerless protector, dwells.
I pray, please look kindly upon your child,
Bless me with the supreme empowerment.
Instant wisdom, in the fourth time, beyond the three times:
Is this not your realization, Lord?
Awareness, the root of all phenomena:
Is this not the root lama?
Not for a moment have I been separate,
Never separate, still I was unaware.
At the instant of awareness,
The root lama is gone,
So-called pure lands vanish
Within mind's unborn nature, sha ra ra,
In the play of awareness and empty bliss, ya la la,
Whatever arises is the lama's true nature.
Holding to the pure land is a delusion,
The label "buddha's human form" is a hurdle of attachment.
The lama is not outside, look within.
This finding the Buddha through oneself, a la la!
This being happy, always and ceaselessly, e ma ho!
This again is the sublime lama's kindness;
This again, the profound blessing of pith advice.
Let's sing the noble song of supreme happiness.
Let's step to the dance of ultimate fulfillment.

A Ho Ye
In the pure land of Blazing Fire Mountain,
The supreme yidam, Lord of Herukas, dwells.
I pray, please look upon your child kindly,
Bless me with the supreme siddhis.

Awareness itself, glory of samsara and nirvana:
Is this not your nature, divine one?
Wisdom hero's egoless realization:
Is this not Dorje Zhönu, ever youthful?
Not for a moment have I been separate,
Never separate, still I was unaware.
At the instant of awareness,
The assembly of yidams is gone,
Blazing Fire Mountain vanishes—
Within mind's unborn nature, sha ra ra,
In the play of awareness and empty bliss, ya la la,
The pure world and its beings are the yidam's true nature.
Holding to pure lands as places is a delusion,
The label "real buddha body" is a hurdle of attachment.
The yidam is not outside, look within.
This finding the divine assembly through oneself, a la la!
This being happy, always and ceaselessly, e ma ho!
This again is the sublime lama's kindness;
This again, the profound blessing of pith advice.
Let's sing the noble song of supreme happiness.
Let's step to the dance of ultimate fulfillment.

A Ho Ye
In the pure land of Pristine Celestial Sky,
The supreme dakini, Dorje Phagmo, dwells.
I pray, please look upon your child kindly,
Bless me by removing obstacles.
Innate and uncontrived nature, vast as space,
Is this not your spacious nature, dear friend?
Wisdom and empty bliss, beyond meeting and parting:
Is this not the Wisdom Dakini?
Not for a moment have I been separate,
Never separate, still I was unaware.
At the instant of awareness,

Dorje Phagmo is gone,
Celestial Sky pure land vanishes—
Within mind's unborn nature, sha ra ra,
In the play of awareness and empty bliss, ya la la,
The world and its sounds are the wisdom mother's true nature.
Holding to pure lands is a delusion,
The label "Great Mother" is a hurdle of attachment.
The dakini is not outside, look within.
This finding the Supreme Mother through oneself, a la la!
This being happy, always and ceaselessly, e ma ho!
This again is the sublime lama's kindness;
This again, the profound blessing of pith advice.
Let's sing the noble song of supreme happiness.
Let's step to the dance of ultimate fulfillment.

A Ho Ye
In charnel grounds of so many pure lands,
Oceans of oath keepers and dharmapalas dwell.
I pray, please look upon your child kindly,
Bless me by fulfilling my actions.
Perfect pristine awareness, without effort,
Is this not the heart essence of oceans of oath keepers?
Guarding against dividing samsara and nirvana:
Is this not the ultimate protector?
Not for a moment have I been separate,
Never separate, still I was unaware.
At the instant of awareness,
Dharmapalas and protectors are gone,
Sacred charnel-ground places vanish—
Within mind's unborn nature, sha ra ra,
In the play of awareness and empty bliss, ya la la,
All thoughts are the self-liberating play of dharmapalas.
Holding to so-called sacred places is a delusion,
To label "protectors" as such is a hurdle of attachment.

The protector is not outside, look within.
This finding the oath keepers through oneself, a la la!
This being happy, always and ceaselessly, e ma ho!
This again is the sublime lama's kindness;
This again, the profound blessing of pith advice.
Let's sing the noble song of supreme happiness.
Let's step to the dance of ultimate fulfillment.

Dharma friend Lama Sönam Chöphel asked me, "Please sing a song in accord with your realization of whatever comes into your mind." I thought to myself, "Heh, why can't I do this? I had a good teacher who was like Padmasambhava returned in the flesh. I touched my head to his feet and received profound instruction. I met with Dzogchen, the essence heart-blood of the dakinis. Though I have no big stories to tell, nor anything to brag about, for example, like staying for a long period of time in a sealed cave, still I was never separated from the original flow of natural wisdom. Therefore I have no expectations or suspicions about anyone. I'm not a great practitioner, but my practice is Dzogchen. I'm happy. Thus I'm worthy to sing the song of ultimate fulfillment." As a dummy donkey is happy with his penis, so this gypsy, Jigdral Yeshe Dorje, at the shore of Tso Pema at Zahor in India, without shyness sang this as it came to mind.

In the early 1960s Tibetan exiles—ordinary men and women, political leaders, and great teachers alike—under the leadership of His Holiness the Dalai Lama had one unanimous thought: to restrengthen their culture and their educational system in India. Therefore, many great scholars were invited to Dharamsala,[166] and H.H. Dudjom Rinpoche was among them. They gathered there to set up the curriculum and write the texts for primary and secondary schools already established.

While the curriculum was being formulated, Nono Tsering Paljor invited His Holiness to Ladakh. Around that time Chögyam Trungpa Rinpoche came to visit, and His Holiness asked him to do a mirror divina-

*Masters and heads of the four schools of Tibetan Buddhism with
His Holiness the Dalai Lama in the 1960s in Dharamsala, India*

tion regarding this trip. In the mirror Trungpa Rinpoche saw a statue of
Guru Rinpoche moving forward, but a tether was attached to the form.
H.H. Dudjom Rinpoche requested that the Ladakhis do prayers to remove
any obstacles related to his visit. They did so, and he traveled to Ladakh
where he stayed for two weeks giving empowerments and teachings, performing a fire puja, and giving his blessings.

    Though Tibetan culture and religion were nicely taking root in their
new environment, a few high Tibetan officials had a different idea about
how to maintain and strengthen Tibetan culture and political autonomy.
They said, "Due to a lack of unity, we lost our country. Now is the perfect
opportunity for change. Let us call ourselves Tibetans rather than identify
with our local region. Let's have a single school of Tibetan Buddhism rather
than the excess of traditions that exist currently." That message made many
people nervous, particularly devotees of the Nyingma, Kagyu, and Sakya
schools. On the street they began saying, "If we make one school, which
will it be?" "This is only a plan to destroy the schools of Nyingma, Kagyu,

and Sakya." "Look how the Tibetan settlement schools are running these days. Morning and evening prayers are Gelugpa prayers, and the religious teacher in each school is Gelugpa." Rumors spread among the refugees, and people began saying, "In Tibet the Communist party gathered all the children, giving them a Communist education and way of life. In exile, the children are gathered and given Gelugpa teachings." The official statements and actions, therefore, didn't promote unity; rather, the strategy created deep dissension in the hearts of many Tibetans.

Meanwhile H.H. Dudjom Rinpoche's Kongpo disciples, residing primarily in one settlement in Orissa, India, requested that he give his support to their wish that this settlement be declared a place where his disciples could remain without being scattered to other camps. To comply he went to Tso Pema and Dharamsala and asked Tibetan officials to fulfill this wish.

Around that time Kathok Öntrul Rinpoche, the head lama of Kathok Monastery, was traveling with Kyabje. He had the ability to do mirror divinations. Kyabje asked him, "Read our situation in the mirror." He did and said he saw a Padmasambhava statue wrapped in barbed wire.

On the train ride back to Kalimpong, Kyabje had a stopover in Old Delhi. Dzongsar Gona Rinpoche had come to meet with him in a first-class waiting room that had been made available. The author of this biography and his family were part of Dzongsar Gona Rinpoche's entourage. During the meeting, the party had the good fortune to receive blessings from His Holiness.

His next stopover was in Siliguri. It was said that there were those jealous of Rinpoche's flourishing activities, and with sectarian sentiments and political motivation, told the Indian intelligence organization that he was collaborating with the Chinese Communist party and was receiving a salary from them. When he and his party arrived, the police put him under house arrest. As news of this spread, his disciples were shocked and saddened. They'd also heard that authorities were going to transport His Holiness by train from Siliguri to Panchimari, the site of a prison for Tibetans detained for political reasons. Many students from Sikkim, Darjeeling, Bhutan, and Kalimpong planned to prevent the train from

His Holiness Dudjom Rinpoche in the early 1980s

leaving by lying on the railroad tracks. But by then His Holiness the Dalai Lama and his officials, the king of Sikkim, and the king, queen, and ministers of Bhutan, and important figures from India and Nepal, as well as thousands of students, had already written letters to Jawaharlal Nehru, the Prime Minister of India. After a few days His Holiness was released from house arrest in Siliguri and returned to his home in Kalimpong.

Sometime around 1964 he made another trip to Tso Pema and gave a variety of teachings to fulfill the wishes of many devotees. Around 1965, the Tibetan government-in-exile was planning the establishment of a university that would support all four schools of Tibetan Buddhism, and to further the plan, government officials requested support for this endeavor by asking the heads of the four schools to nominate scholars from each of their lineages to act as representatives. To fulfill their wishes His Holiness invited Khenchen Palden Sherab, Khenchen Thubten Tsondrü, Mewa Khenchen Thubten, and Yardrok Taklung Tsetrul Rinpoche. Among these four, the first two went to the gathering. These were the first steps toward the establishment of an institution of higher education for Tibetans in India.

Toward the end of 1965, sponsored by the great Drikung Kagyu lineage holder, Ladakh Togden Rinpoche, he gave the *Treasury of Precious Treasures* cycle of empowerments and transmissions in Tso Pema.

In the autumn of 1967 the first modern university for Tibetans was in fact established in India by the Tibetan government-in-exile, at first as a department of the prestigious Sanskrit University in Varanasi and later as an independent institution in Sarnath called the Central Institute of Higher Tibetan Studies. H.H. Dudjom Rinpoche called upon Khenchen Palden Sherab and Khenchen Thubten Tsondrü to move to Varanasi with the twin objectives of founding a department of Nyingma studies and teaching. Khenchen Palden Sherab Rinpoche went first, and there in Varanasi he met the ten students His Holiness had contacted to be the first students. He became a founding member of the Institute for Tibetan Higher Studies and the chairman of Nyingma Studies. The first ten students were Taksham Tulku, Taklung Tsetrul Pema Wangyal, Tulku Rangdröl, Khenpo Pema Sherab, Khenpo Chökyi Gocha, Lama Rinchen Phuntsok, Shedrub Namgyal, Lozang Tenphel, Pema Tsering, and the author of this biography. With courage, commitment, and determined effort, Khenchen assumed the responsibilities of department head and instructor in the philosophy of the Nyingma School. Beginning with ten students in that first class, seventeen years later in 1984 when he resigned from his position, the total enrollment in the Nyingma department had reached over eighty. His Holiness was very pleased with the work he'd done.

In 1969, the Earth Bird year TRE 2096, sponsored and organized by the Tsechu Association led by Golok Tulku, he gave empowerments and transmissions on *The Eight Herukas— Embodiment of All the Sugatas* at old Ghoom Monastery in Ghoom, Darjeeling. Attending were Minling Trichen Rinpoche, Dzongsar Khyentse Thubten Chökyi Gyatso,[167] Dungse Thinley Norbu Rinpoche, as well as dakini Sangyum Kuzhok, Dungse Shenphen Dawa Rinpoche,[168] Nyoshul Khen Jamyang Dorje, Sakya Khenchen Sangye Tendzin Rinpoche, Sera Gomde Rinpoche, Khachöd Rinpoche of Pema Yangtse Monastery in Sikkim, Lobpön Longdröl, Lama Karpo and Lama Nagpo Pema Wangchen, Jetsün Kuzhok Pema, and yogi Sönam Kazi,

Ladakh Nono Rinpoche, Tsetrul Pema Wanggyal Rinpoche, and many other great scholars, teachers, ngagpas, and men and women practitioners—thousands came, including the author of this biography.

Around 1973, the Water Mouse Year TRE 2099, a Chinese disciple, Lama Sönam Chökyi Gyaltsen, invited His Holiness and all his family to Dudjom Ashram in Hong Kong. There he gave many great teachings, empowerments, and transmissions to all the Chinese devotees.

From there Tarthang Tulku Kunga Deleg, yogi Sönam Kazi (the former minister of Sikkim) and his daughter, Jetsün Kuzhok Pema, and many other devotees invited him to come to the United States. First, he went to California and visited the centers established by Tarthang Tulku, the Nyingma Meditation Center and the Nyingma Institute, where he gave many empowerments, transmissions, and blessings to Tarthang Tulku, Gyatrul Rinpoche, and a large number of American students. He also blessed and consecrated Odiyana, Tarthang Tulku's retreat land in northern California.

As Sönam Kazi requested, His Holiness and entourage came to New York and gave many empowerments relating to the three roots as well as Dzogchen instructions. The wishes of Sönam Kazi, Jetsün Pema, and many other devotees were thus fulfilled.

From New York they went to England, France, and then Zurich, Switzerland. In all these places he gave general Buddhist teachings on the four renunciations,[169] devotion, refuge, and bodhichitta, and empowerments, transmissions, and pith instructions of the nine yanas, fulfilling all the wishes of his devotees. During Kyabje's visit to Switzerland, the author of this biography was in a sanitarium there and wished to see him and receive blessings but couldn't arrange that. The biographer made a phone call, and His Holiness gave him the great opportunity of hearing his sacred voice.

After fulfilling the wishes and needs of his devotees, he returned to his beautiful home, Namdröl Khangzang, in Darjeeling. Darjeeling is to the south of Sikkim, a land blessed by many great masters who in the past had come there and done retreat. The great tertön Dorje Lingpa resided there, and the name "Darjeeling" is derived from his name. Namdröl Khangzang was the primary residence of His Holiness at that time, and there, every day, he received a continual flow of students and visitors, giving them advice, empowerments, transmissions, and pith instructions. He also edited volumes of the ancient masters' teachings, which had been spoiled and mixed with the deluded conceptions of many individuals over many generations. He refined, corrected, and edited those teachings, fulfilling the wishes and requests of many teachers and devotees.

Around this same time, the outer and inner aspects[170] of the Nyingma monastery, Dudul Rabten Ling, in Orissa were completed. They invited His Holiness to do the consecration, but he was unable to attend. He told them that if they would do ceremonies and offerings on the dates he gave them, he would do consecration prayers at the same time. The sangha and congregation did as he suggested, and on that day grains of consecration rice fell from the sky. Seeing miraculous blessings such as these, many in attendance established an unshakable devotion.

In Samtse, Bhutan, around 1974 the great dharma patron, the Royal Queen Grandmother of Bhutan,[171] Azhe Phuntsok Chödrön, sponsored and arranged for His Holiness to give the empowerments and transmissions of Pema Lingpa's entire terma. Great teachers attended, such as Kyabje Dilgo Khyentse Rinpoche, Kyabje Dodrubchen Rinpoche, and many other great khenpos, lamas, tulkus, and ngagpas from all over India, Bhutan, Sikkim, and Nepal, as well as many thousands of devoted male and female lay practitioners.

Around 1975, the Wood Hare year TRE 2102, His Holiness moved to Kathmandu, Nepal, and this became his main residence. Around that time he composed the following autobiographical letter at the request of Dobum Rinpoche, director of Tibet House in New Delhi, India:

> I am the wanderer called Dudjom Jigdral Yeshe Dorje. I was born in the hidden land of Pema Kö in the Wood Dragon year of the fifteenth rabjung (1904). My father, Khengla Jampal Norbu Wangyal, was descended from the royal family of Kanam. At about the age of three, I was recognized as the incarnation of the great treasure revealer Dudjom. His disciples took me in, and so I entered the gate of dharma. My tutors, knowing that the

foundation of knowledge is reading and writing, set me on a course of constant study and ensured that I memorized the daily prayers and rituals. They educated me in physical, verbal, and mental conduct so as always to avoid wrongdoing and behave correctly. They employed history, stories, elementary principles, and the like, so that with these various methods of teaching, my eye of wisdom opened a little.

As I grew in years and wisdom, accordingly a succession of learned and realized masters looked after me with their love and compassion. Grammar, poetry, astrology, medicine, and the other ordinary sciences I picked up in bits and pieces. As for the extraordinary sciences I studied just a few scriptures on the middle way, the teachings of Maitreya, *A Guide to the Bodhisattva's Way of Life*, and teachings on the three vows. In particular, it was the ripening empowerments, liberating instructions, tantric commentaries, profound pith instructions, and so on from the ocean of kama and terma of the Nyingma tradition of mantrayana with which I was chiefly concerned. Beginning with the thirteen great activities of a vajracharya,[172] which include the performance of rituals, torma making, decorative arts, dance, drawing, chanting, and music related to various classes of practice, I applied myself assiduously to learning the tradition of the lineage of the vidyadharas without neglecting anything. At times, I devoted myself to practice, first the accumulation and purification of the ngöndro practice, and then the main practice of the creation and completion stages, with the phases of approach and accomplishment,[173] and I did my best, diligently accumulating ounces into pounds. But, unfortunately, thanks to my having the title of "lama," all I really did was to serve as the slave of distraction posing as "benefiting the teachings" and "helping beings." The result was that in the end the realization and qualities I gained from practice were as copious as the hair on a tortoise.

Whatever nectar of dharma I received, and whatever I learned,

I taught and spread as much as I could to people everywhere, according to what they required. Even though I'm not a member of the illustrious club of scholars, in order not to refuse people's demands, and in the hope that it might be of some small service to the teachings, I wrote *History of the Nyingma School of Tibetan Buddhism, Fundamentals of the Nyingma School of Tibetan Buddhism, History of Tibet,* commentaries on *Definitive Distinctions among the Three Vows,* practice instruction manuals[174] for the many cycles of sadhanas, pith retreat instructions,[175] and other works. They are being compiled and edited—more than twenty volumes have already been published—and these I leave as the achievement of my learning, set down in writing without any expectation or fear.

Thanks to the kindness of my sublime masters, my eyes of pure perception are not blind. I've never accumulated the bad karma of forsaking the dharma by bearing ill will toward or criticizing other teachings or individuals. I have always managed to keep a good heart without any crookedness or hypocrisy. So I do not have the slightest doubt that I can count myself a disciple of the compassionate Lord Buddha, our teacher, among the lower levels of his fourfold retinue. About this I sometimes feel a little sense of pride, and yet I wonder whether these thoughts are virtuous or unvirtuous. Still, here is a brief summary of my story, the story of an old yogin.

Dudjom[176]

Kyabje Chatral Sangye Dorje, the great light of Dzogchen teaching, founded a retreat center at Yangleshö, the secret land where Guru Padmasambhava transformed into Vajrakilaya, subduing all negative forces, balancing the elements, and bringing forth all auspiciousness. This pith instruction was written in the 1970s to Yölmo Lama Dawa who was one of the retreatants there:

Dedicated practitioner at Yangleshö, fortunate one named Dawa, who practices from his heart, I give you these instructions with love from my heart.

To take full advantage of the life that is so difficult to obtain, resolve to free oneself from the ocean of samsaric suffering, trust that the three jewels are the infallible source of refuge, and do not be mistaken about the results of virtuous and unvirtuous actions. In particular, devotion to the root teacher, love and affection for samaya brothers and sisters, the bodhichitta of compassion toward all mother sentient beings, and the reduction of grasping due to the knowledge that all compounded things are impermanent are known as the four everlasting wealths of a practitioner and should be regarded as indispensable. The lama and yidam are inseparable from one's own mind. In the development stage, meditate all appearances to be as empty as the moon's reflection on water; all repetitions and utterances as the sound-emptiness of mantra. All this is the display of one's own single awareness of dharmata, the true nature. Within the space of dharmata, benefit and harm are nonexistent. So-called nirvana and samsara are labels corresponding primarily to hope and fear.

When you recognize the original inherent wisdom as it is, activity will only add delusion; therefore, hold the fortress of awareness with nonaction. Let naked, ordinary mind go free. Then "abiding" and "nonabiding" will be nothing more than names. If thoughts arise, let them come, and let them self-liberate. If they don't arise, then let that be, and relax in that self-occurring state. If the faults of meditation—torpor and scattering—should arise, dispel them on the spot. When the clear light pervades both night and day without interruption, then, *a la la*! How wonderful! There'll be no need to hope for results in a future life. Please, practice diligently in this way.

Thus written and sent by Jigdral Yeshe Dorje.

His Holiness
in the mid-1970s

In 1976-1977, the Fire Dragon year TRE 2103, he traveled with his family to France, England, the United States, and some other countries, where he gave many teachings and empowerments and secret teachings on Dzogchen as requested by the students.

In 1976 through the beautiful motivation, devotion, and effort of Yeshe Rangjung (John Giorno) and others, a beautiful house was bought for Yeshe Nyingpo[177] as a residence for His Holiness in New York City. Also at that time he was invited by the great teacher Chögyam Trungpa Rinpoche to Colorado, where he gave the following teaching:

In this world are many dear things, and among them, the precious dharma is most dear. This dharma was taught by Buddha Shakyamuni, who countless aeons ago attained dharmakaya for his own benefit, and then through his compassion emanated many rupakayas to benefit others. In order to benefit beings, you have to take on forms and conventions similar to theirs. Therefore, he performed the twelve deeds, for example, transferring from Tushita heaven to take birth in this world. Turning the wheel of dharma helps other beings only if it is done according to the readiness and capabilities of those beings. For Shravakas and Pratyekabuddhas, those with average understanding, he taught the elimination of nonvirtuous activities. To those with bigger minds and greater wisdom, he gave the bodhisattva teachings, and along with the vows for body and speech, he taught the principal discipline, training the mind. And to those of the highest intelligence, he gave secret, mahayana tantra, which surpasses the causal yanas.[178]

When you first enter the dharma, the key distinction between a Buddhist and a non-Buddhist is the taking of refuge; recognizing the infallibility of the three jewels with total confidence, take refuge from your heart, and that is your dharma foundation. Following refuge, bodhichitta is the central pillar of dharma. Sentient beings are as pervasive as space. Therefore, our parents of past lives are pervasive as space, and we need to practice for their benefit.

He taught shamatha and vipashana, as well as Dzogchen, and bestowed empowerments and blessings on the Vajradhatu students.

Complying with the wishes of the great teacher Khyentse Pema Ösel Dongak Lingpa, Pema Garwang Lodrö Thaye collected and compiled all the principal teachings of the great tertöns, starting with the first tertön, Sangye Lama, and titled it *Treasury of Precious Treasures*. Thanks to the kindness of these two great masters, even at this worst moment in Tibetan history, these teachings survive. Similarly, H.H. Dudjom Rinpoche undertook to make collections of all the kama teachings of the greatest siddhas and scholars who in their realization were comparable to the buddhas. His collection included the works of such masters as Garab Dorje, Manjushrimitra (Jampal Shenyen), Shrisingha, Jnanasutra, Vimalamitra,

Guru Padmasambhava, Sangye Sangwa (Buddhaguhya), Lalitavajra, and all the great Indian masters. Also included were all the native Tibetan masters such as the great translator Vairochana, Wisdom Lady Yeshe Tsogyal, Nyak Jnana Kumara, Nub Namkhai Nyingpo, Nub Sangye Yeshe Rinpoche, Zhang Yeshe De, Chok Ro Lui Gyaltsen, Kawa Paltsek, Dharma King Trisong Deutsen, So Yeshe Wangchuk, and Zurchen Shakya Jungne, Zurchen Sherab Drak, Rongzompa, Yungtön Dorje Pal, omniscient Longchenpa, the two Mindröling brothers (Minling Terchen Gyurme Dorje and Lochen Dharmashri), and many other great teachers. These teachings, which focus on the nine yanas in general and the three inner tantras in particular, were compiled and edited into a single series called *Collection of Nyingma Kama*. Completing this collection was one of his dearest aspirations. Whenever he returned from his travels, he continued his work on this. The total collection came to fifty-eight volumes.[179]

Now, as it turned out, late 1977 through early 1978 would be the time period in which His Holiness gave his last major teachings. Therefore, this period was the **perfect time**.[180] The **perfect place** was Orgyen Dongak Chökhorling, the monastery of H.H. Dudjom Rinpoche in Boudnath, Nepal. Boudnath is the site of the stupa built by previous incarnations of Guru Padmasambhava, great master Shantarakshita, and King Trisong Deutsen during the time when the teachings of Buddha Kasyapa, the third of the one thousand buddhas of this Fortunate Aeon, were still extant. The **perfect teacher** was H.H. Dudjom Rinpoche, the regent of Guru Padmasambhava. He possessed all the qualities of the great masters and was teacher to an array of great teachers. The **perfect retinue** included such students as Kyabje Trulshik Rinpoche, Dzongsar Khyentse Thubten Chökyi Gyatso, Palyul Choktrul, Palri Kyabgön, Gangteng Tulku Kunzang Pema Namgyal, Lhalung Sungtrul, Dungse Thinley Norbu, Dungse Shenphen Dawa, Khenchen Thubten Tsondrü, Khenchen Palden Sherab, Shar Khumbu Tengpoche Tulku, De-u Rinpoche, Tsang Gampa Gomchen, Dzatrul, Dragtrul, Nagtrul, Doshul Lama Gyalchog, Ladakh Nono, Ladakh Chöje Tulku, Gyatrul Rinpoche, Yogi Lama Tsewang Lhagyal, Yogi Khetsun Zangpo, Mön Ngagchang Lama Karpo, Yogi Lama Nagpo Pema Wang-

*His Holiness
Dudjom Rinpoche
in the early 1980s
at Yeshe Nyingpo,
New York City*

chen, Lobpon Longdröl and Lobpon Nyingkhula, and so forth, the great
masters from the Nyingma School of Tibetan Buddhism. It included
Khenchen Thrangu Rinpoche and Vajracharya Tenga Rinpoche, Drigung
Yudra Tulku, Kuzhok Tsechu, and Dazang Tulku, Bhutan's Je Khenpo
Kunleg, and Khenpo Khedrub and so forth, and a great many other masters
from the practice lineage of the Kagyu School of Tibetan Buddhism. It
included Kyabje Chögye Trichen Rinpoche, Traruk Rinpoche, Dongthog
Tulku Tenpai Gyaltsen, Khenchen Rinchen, and many other great masters
from the Sakya School of Tibetan Buddhism. The retinue also included
many others possessing the great wealth of the three trainings and of the
realization of the two stages from among the two assemblies, a total of over
ten thousand devotees. The **perfect teachings** were the *Dudjom Tersar* cycle

that included both his own and his previous incarnation Dudjom Lingpa's teachings, along with the corresponding empowerments, transmissions, and pith instructions. These are the heart treasures of Guru Padmasambhava and Yeshe Tsogyal; profound teachings, precisely customized for this era; powerful teachings able to remove obstacles and negativities immediately and simultaneously bring prosperity and longevity; wondrous teachings ultimately leading to the supreme enlightenment of the transcendental rainbow wisdom body.

In 1978, the Earth Horse year, TRE 2105, in May or early June, at the request of the Tibetan government-in-exile, he led the ganachakra ceremony of Guru Padmasambhava one hundred thousand times. Many monks, nuns, and teachers of the four schools of Tibetan Buddhism attended at Ka Nying Shedrub Ling Monastery[181] in Boudnath, Nepal.

Around that same time Kyabje had asked Ngagchang Khetsun Zangpo to undertake the construction and administration of a Nyingma institute which would come to be known as Wish-Fulfilling Nyingma Institute (Shedrub Döjo Ling). The author of this biography received a letter from His Holiness requesting that he serve as its abbot. Without hesitation he accepted, and, complying with Kyabje's instructions, over the course of the next two years he taught the monks *Six Categories of Taking Refuge*,[182] a Tibetan grammar text[183] with a commentary by Situ Panchen Dharma Kara,[184] the second chapter of *Mirror of Poetry*, and Chandrakirti's *Entering the Middle Way*.

Then early in 1979, the Earth Sheep year, TRE 2106, His Holiness again traveled with his entourage to France, England, and America. His first stop was France where he went to his center, Dorje Nyingpo, in Paris and then to Dordogne where he gave many teachings and blessings, fulfilling the wishes of many devotees. That autumn he came to his center, Yeshe Nyingpo, in New York. In October and November he gave teachings on the tathagatagarbha to the public, explaining how the buddha nature is inherent in every sentient being. A few days after that, he performed the refuge ceremony for a large audience and then a public Padmasambhava empowerment. This was followed by a weeklong teaching on *Sharp Vajra of Awareness*.

In February 1980, the Iron Monkey year, TRE 2107, at the Chinese Mahayana Temple in Cairo, New York, he led a ten-day retreat with many members of Yeshe Nyingpo and other Nyingma practitioners. He gave teachings on the Six Bardos, *Purifying the Limbs and Body through Meditation on the Five Dhyani Buddhas,* and the large and small vase wind practices.[185]

In May of 1980 the whole entourage flew to California on the West Coast of America. Khenchen Palden Sherab, Gyatrul Rinpoche, Chagdud Tulku Rinpoche, Lama Ngagchang Gönpo Tseten Rinpoche, and the author of this biography together with many Tibetans and Westerners were at the airport to receive him. He stayed at a beautiful home in Berkeley that had been arranged by the Bay Area Yeshe Nyingpo Center.

That evening he gave the empowerment and teaching on the Twenty-one Taras to hundreds of students. His manner of introducing the empowerment was amazing in its level of detail and in how he had tailored it to his audience of Western students. Customarily a lama will read from the text and proceed to the ceremony, but on this occasion His Holiness talked about Tara. He explained why she is regarded as the mother of all buddhas. He pointed out that she emanates an appropriate form that is an expression of one of the three kayas, depending on whether beings are completely lost in obscurations, partially obscured, or free of all obscurities.

He described how through the great aspirations of Shantarakshita, King Trisong Deutsen, and Guru Padmasambhava the Buddhadharma came to Tibet and how a great many Indian and Tibetan teachers and scholars translated the teaching into Tibetan. He told the participants that there were two methods of presenting the teachings, one scholarly, the other more practice oriented, and that the teaching this evening would be from the practice tradition. He clarified that the practice-oriented teachings had come down to us through two unbroken and flourishing transmissions known as the kama and the terma and that these tonight were terma teachings. He said that the combination of qualified teacher and qualified student is the most auspicious circumstance for receiving empowerment. At the very least we should try to increase our bodhichitta, devotion, and pure perception. After that, he began to talk about the four empowerments and their significance:

> In general there are two aspects to the presentation of the vajrayana teachings: the ripening empowerments and the liberating instructions. Then by practicing the two stages you will actualize the state of Buddha Vajradhara. Tonight I will give the ripening empowerments: the outer empowerment of the vase, the inner empowerment of the secret nectar, the secret empowerment of wisdom, and the ultimate empowerment of the absolute word. The first is the vase empowerment of the body. The second is the sacred empowerment of speech. The third is the wisdom empowerment of the heart. The fourth is the ultimate empowerment of clear light of Dzogchen, which is beyond the effort of giver, giving, and receiving.
>
> The vase empowerment bestows the vajra body blessing that removes body and channel obscurations, which thereby opens the way to the swift actualization of nirmanakaya buddhahood. The secret empowerment bestows the vajra speech blessing that removes the obscurations of speech and wind, which opens the way to the swift actualization of sambhogakaya buddhahood. The wisdom empowerment bestows the vajra mind blessing that removes the obscurations of the mind and thigle, which opens the way to the swift actualization of dharmakaya buddhahood. The absolute word empowerment bestows the body/speech/mind blessing that removes the obscurations of inseparable body/speech/mind and very subtle propensities, which opens the way to swiftly actualize svabhavikakaya buddhahood.

At that time the author of this biography thought how fortunate these Westerners were to receive such thorough explanations and how lucky he was to be a part of this group. After completing the empowerment, Kyabje explained the mandala offering and talked about samaya, saying:

Samaya is the life force of the empowerment. If you have the realization that you, the deity, and the lama are inseparable within the three vajra states, there is no need to observe any additional samaya. All the hundreds of specific samayas come together in that state. If you don't have that realization, then at the very least you must restrengthen your bodhichitta, your love, compassion, devotion, and faith; do mantra recitation as often as you can, and even if for only a short period of time, relax your mind in the natural state; and reduce your clinging to worldly concerns.

The next day he received many visitors and met with board members of the center. A few days after, he gave the empowerment of the *One Thousand Buddhas of This Fortunate Aeon*.[186] He began the teaching with a verse to explain the visualization:

One thousand arms are the thousand universal monarchs.
One thousand eyes are the thousand buddhas of this
    Fortunate Aeon.
Emanating as needed for beings, Lord Chenrezig,
To you I pay homage.[187]

He gave a thorough explanation on how to prepare oneself to receive the empowerment and how to visualize the one thousand buddhas.

The sangha members of the West Coast Yeshe Nyingpo Center had arranged a grand long-life ceremony for him according to the *Heart Drop of the Dakini* tradition and scheduled it for the first weekend of his visit. The weekend came, and after the ceremony was completed, His Holiness began giving teachings on the six bardos:

First is the bardo of birth and life; second, the bardo of meditation; third, the bardo of dreaming; fourth, the bardo of death and dying; fifth, the bardo of the true nature; and sixth, the bardo of becoming. These six can be abridged to four: the bardo of birth and life, the bardo of death and dying, the bardo of true nature, and the bardo of becoming. Of these four the bardo of birth and life is most important because right now we all have a precious human birth with the eighteen endowments.[188] We have available to us teachers who are to a certain degree well qualified, and the teaching we receive is a wish-fulfilling jewel, the very precious teaching of the sutras and tantras. It is rare to have such a precious opportunity. Don't waste your time when you have everything going for you.

First, you should contemplate the significance of the four thoughts that can turn the mind from the futility of samsara. Train your mind again and again by returning to that contemplation. Combine this with a deep, heart-felt devotion to the three jewels and the three roots, which are brought into one state in your root teacher who is the embodiment of three kinds of kindness and inseparable from Guru Padmasambhava. What is devotion? It is having joy and appreciation for your opportunities, for the lama and the dharma.

What are these four thoughts? First, think how difficult it is to obtain the freedoms and endowments of the precious human body. Second, consider how life and compounded things are impermanent. Third, recognize the inexorability of karma, of results invariably following from causes. Fourth, observe that none of the three realms of cyclic existence is beyond trouble and suffering. The main point of this contemplation is to reduce attachment and grasping to the activities of samsara.

Then begin the practices of the extraordinary ngöndro. Knowing the supreme qualities of the three jewels and thoroughly understanding the difficulties of samsara, **take refuge** with clarity and a profound aspiration to achieve the state of buddhahood beyond samsara. It is imperative to **develop unshakable bodhichitta** to benefit all the limitless numbers of sentient beings who have experienced uninterrupted difficulties throughout all their lifetimes. Develop unconditional love and compassion to liberate all beings from suffering. Again and again practice wishing bodhichitta and performing bodhichitta according to your capability, combining it with emptiness meditation.

To achieve the dharmakaya and the rupakaya enlightenment, we must remove the two obscurations, and this can be accomplished by accumulating both merit and wisdom. There are many methods of accumulation, but one that is simple and brings big results is the **mandala offering** practice. The means to instantly destroy all faults, downfalls, and obscurations is to **meditate on Vajrasattva**, who is lord of all the families of deities, and to recite the hundred-syllable mantra, the king of the secret mantras. To remove obscurations and increase merit quickly, the ultimate essence of the vajrayana path is **guru yoga** combined with meditation on shamatha and vipashana. Whoever follows these practices is making their life more meaningful, and therefore, the bardo of birth and life is more meaningful.

As I said, this bardo of birth and life is so very important. If you can recognize this bardo as nothing more than a dream and a magical display and combine that recognition with uncontrived bodhichitta born from your heart, then you will master this bardo of birth and life. When you master the bardo of birth and life, you will master all the other bardos. And if you achieve that, you will have become a great hero or heroine, not frightened by birth, sickness, old age, and death. Then there will be no need for special instructions concerning the bardo of death and dying.

However, to make sure the bardo of death and dying will be a journey under your control, make sure right now you really understand that the time of death is uncertain, the cause of death is uncertain, and life is impermanent. Because compounded things are not free from the four endings, they are impermanent. Therefore, the end of gathering is dissipation, the end of building up is falling down, the end of birth is death, and the end of coming together is separating. Therefore regard everything you see in samsara as dreamlike. Your current circle of closest friends is as fleeting as acquaintances bumping into each other at a fair. It's all one big magic show. It was like that in the past, it's like that now, and in the future it will be the same. Why be troubled by fear and attachment? It won't help. Therefore, think, "I will never be afraid or attached," and keep on thinking it as often as you can in this, your current life. Then make offerings of all your belongings, including your body, to the buddhas and bodhisattvas of the ten directions, particularly to Amitabha. Just as you would plan for a trip, plan for your death, considering how and where you'll go. Your destination is Dewachen; your conveyance is togal, trekchö, and phowa practice; your attitude, without any fear or sadness, is joyful and confident. Now, when you possess vitality and all your faculties, is the time to practice generosity, giving as much as you can to others, thereby accumulating merit. If you can't do this now, how will you do it when death is near?[189] You'll be sick and your mind scattered. Your feelings of attachment to and worry about your life, loved ones, and possessions will be even more intense when you have no alternative but to leave everything as it currently stands. To avoid that eventuality, prepare now, perform virtuous activities, ensure that you have no fears and regrets. Now we all have the great fortune to receive these clear light, Dzogchen teachings, and if you practice them with joyful effort and commitment, you can in this very lifetime achieve the level of a vidyadhara. If that level is not attained, then at the very least your mind will be clear, stable, and relaxed at the time of death. Rehearse your lama's instructions once more like an actress glancing at herself in the mirror just before going on stage, then die with a smile of joy and confidence. With courage born of an unshakable view allow the dissolving stages to gradually occur, and you will have the fortunate opportunity to be liberated in the dharmakaya or the sambhogakaya.

Thus, he thoroughly presented the teachings.

*His Holiness Dudjom
Rinpoche in 1980*

After this visit to the Bay Area, His Holiness with the Sangyum and family accepted the invitation from Kyabje Phuntsok Phodrang of the Sakya lineage to visit his monastery, Sakya Thegchen Chöling, in Seattle. There he gave the Guru Padmasambhava empowerment and teachings as requested. From Seattle he returned to his Yeshe Nyingpo center in New York City and stayed for a few days completing some legal documents for the center.

Again he traveled to California and then up to Oregon, where he visited Tashi Chöling, the Pacific coast Yeshe Nyingpo retreat center, which was established near Ashland through the effort of Gyatrul Rinpoche and sangha. His Holiness blessed the land and made offerings to the three roots and dharmapalas. He gave blessings, empowerments, and teachings, and then returned to New York.

Through the wishes of His Holiness and the contributions of the sangha members and dharma patrons of Yeshe Nyingpo, and particularly the effort of John Giorno, a large parcel of land with a motel was purchased near Greenville, New York. This facility was fully furnished, complete with a large kitchen and dining area (that could, according to local regulations, accommodate one hundred people) and also included a playground and a swimming pool. He named it Orgyen Chö Dzong. He obtained this beautiful place with the vision that all Buddhist teachings, particularly the Nyingma teachings of Tibetan Buddhism, could be established, maintained, and spread. Because of this, he decided to open this center on the tenth day of the sixth month,[190] followed by a one-week group retreat.

In order to do preparations for the opening of the retreat center, Dungse Shenphen Dawa Rinpoche, Khenchen Palden Sherab Rinpoche, Lama Rinchen Phuntsok, the author of this biography, and some other members of Yeshe Nyingpo, all went to Orgyen Chö Dzong. For many days we worked on the building that would become the temple, cleaning it, painting its walls, windows, and doors, placing the carpet and raising prayer flags in five colors, making sure all the arrangements were complete. Then His Holiness Dudjom Rinpoche and his wife, the great dakini Rigdzin Wangmo, with entourage arrived, and the sangha greeted them with a reception.

In the morning of the tenth day disciples from all over the United States and Europe were gathered in anticipation of the arrival of the great Vajracharya Dudjom Rinpoche and the vajra consort, Sangyum Kuzhok. On the pathway to the temple Khenpo Thubten Rinpoche and Khenchen Palden Sherab Rinpoche had drawn all the eight auspicious symbols[191] and the seven royal treasures.[192] As His Holiness and the Sangyum approached, Khenchen Palden Sherab Rinpoche walked ahead with a white scarf and fragrantly burning incense as a traditional offering of respect. Lining each side of the walkway were Dungse Shenphen Dawa Rinpoche, Khenpo Thubten Rinpoche, Sogyal Rinpoche, Tulku Thondup, Tsetrul Pema Wangyal Rinpoche, Gyatrul Rinpoche, Lama Rinchen Phuntsok, and the author of this biography. The sangha members were there as well: many

H.H. Dudjom Rinpoche on the throne during the tenth day opening cerermonies of Orgyen Chö Dzong, with Khenchen Palden Sherab Rinpoche giving explanation of mandala offering translated by Sogyal Rinpoche. Left to right are Khenpo Tsewang Dongyal Rinpoche, Gyaltrul Rinpoche, Khenpo Thubten Rinpoche, Khenchen Palden Sherab Rinpoche, Sogyal Rinpoche, Shenphen Dawa Rinpoche, and His Holiness.

ages, many skin colors, colorfully dressed, white scarves draped delicately over folded hands at their heart centers, holding bright flowers and wafting incense. Out of the blue sky the blazing sun formed a brilliant canopy above the unshakable throne, mother earth, adorned with endlessly beautiful ornaments. Surely, Guru Padmasambhava and Yeshe Tsogyal, the three roots, and an ocean of dharmapalas must have been there in the rays of the sun on this auspicious occasion. When they arrived at the door, His Holiness began chanting the *Prayer of the Eight Noble Auspicious Ones That Swiftly Accomplishes All Wishes* followed by the special invocation prayer of Guru Padmasambhava and his retinue of dakas and dakinis that comes from the *Seven-Chapter Prayer of Guru Padmasambhava*. After completing these prayers, His Holiness and all the sangha members entered the temple, and he took his seat on the lion throne of devotion. He taught the importance of this tenth day which marked the birth of Padmasambhava and the significance of Padmasambhava for all sentient beings, especially in this degenerate time. Then he gave the empowerment of *Heart Drop of the*

Lake-Born Vajra, one of his great termas. Afterward, the sangha arranged for the performance of a long-life ceremony for His Holiness in which they could present their offerings and lay out a large mandala representing the body, speech, and mind of the buddhas. To begin this elaborate mandala offering, Khenchen Palden Sherab gave a talk with extensive explanations of the mandala offering, starting with the five perfections. After the mandala offering, the nine-day retreat began. Every morning His Holiness taught from *Meditation Instructions of the Nine Yanas*.[193]

After concluding the retreat, he returned to the Yeshe Nyingpo Center in New York City and stayed a few days giving teachings and audiences to many sangha members. There, open to the public, he gave the empowerment of the *One Thousand Buddhas of This Fortunate Aeon*. Soon after, he went to Paris and Dordogne in France, fulfilling the requests and wishes of many dharma practitioners.

Toward the end of September he and his entourage returned to New York City, where he taught Longchenpa's *Precious Garland of Four Dharma Points*. Following this he went to Orgyen Chö Dzong where once again students from all over the United States and Europe, along with many tulkus and khenpos, had assembled. On this nine-day retreat he taught every morning from his own book, *Fundamentals of the Nyingma School of Tibetan Buddhism*. Every afternoon at the request of His Holiness, Khenchen Palden Sherab Rinpoche provided clarification and detailed explanation of what had been presented that morning. Many students felt incredibly fortunate to be gaining a good understanding of the basic Buddhist philosophy and tenets presented through careful reasoning and logic.

Each morning commenced with ngöndro practice beginning with a devotional *calling the lama from afar* known as *Spontaneous Song of the Original Nature*, followed by the four thoughts that turn the mind, refuge, bodhichitta, etc. During the day shamatha, vipashana, creation stage, and completion stage were practiced, and in the evening those who had received the empowerment of Vajrakilaya, practiced that and did dharmapala prayers. He gave everyone in attendance instructions for inserting all one's conceptions about phenomena into the vase of clear luminosity.[194]

After completing this retreat, His Holiness and the entire entourage took a trip to Howe Caverns, which are deep, large, and filled with many limestone formations that could be interpreted as symbols. Amazing! There was even a lake, the underground Lake of Venus, upon which they took a boat ride.

After this excursion, he returned to New York City, where he stayed two weeks before traveling to France in November of 1980. In Paris he gave the numerous teachings and blessings that his students had requested, and then he went to Dordogne, the location of several Nyingma retreat centers. One of these was established with the blessing and inspiration of Lord Tertön Longchen Yeshe Dorje, commonly known as Kyabje Kangyur Rinpoche, and his dharma heir and son, Taklung Tsetrul Pema Wangyal Rinpoche. At that retreat center His Holiness gave teachings and instructions to the three-year retreatants. Having fulfilled their wishes, His Holiness went back to Nepal in January 1981.

At the airport many lamas, khenpos, tulkus, and ngagpas had gathered from all over Nepal, Tibet, India, and Sikkim to receive him. Since His Holiness had stayed a long time in the West, every day hundreds of devotees, from renowned teachers to unknown yogis, took this opportunity to see him. Due to the large number of visitors, he eventually began giving group audiences from the balcony of his house in Kathmandu to devotees gathered in the courtyard below, who stood with folded hands, some doing prostrations with falling tears. He chanted the prayers of Guru Rinpoche. When he threw the rice, many tried to catch it in their shawls or skirts, or simply picked it up from the ground. He held many of these audiences.

Around this time his Chinese disciple, Guru Lau (Sönam Chökyi Gyaltsen), came with about twenty students to see him, and as they requested, His Holiness gave many teachings, transmissions, and empowerments. The author of this biography served as translator. Again, as requested by Guru Lau and his disciples, His Holiness gave an audience in which he showed them his entire collection of relics, amazing objects that he had either discovered himself or inherited from other great tertöns and masters. The biographer also had the great fortune to see them and receive their blessings. In this way he fulfilled the wishes of all the disciples and students. He also continued working on and collecting the Nyingma kama teachings.

In late 1981 he went to Hong Kong, once again fulfilling everyone's wishes by giving empowerments, teachings, and pith instructions. Then he returned to Nepal to celebrate losar.[195]

In the spring of 1982 he and his entourage went to France, first Paris and then Dordogne, where that summer he led a retreat at his center called Orgyen Samye Chöling. He gave Dzogchen teachings and empowerments to students gathered from Europe, the United States, and Asia.

When His Holiness and Sangyum Kuzhok arrived in New York that November on the day before Thanksgiving, many lamas, khenpos, tulkus, and students were there to greet him with great joy and respect, and to all of them he gave his blessings. In December he gave teachings on shamatha from the Dzogchen perspective.

Around this time the Kyabje Penor Rinpoche had invited His Holiness to attend the graduation ceremonies marking the fifth anniversary of the Nyingma shedra[196] that Penor Rinpoche had established. Unable to attend, he sent this letter to be read during the commencement proceedings:

> To the Head of the Namling Do-ngag Rigpa Jungne Nyingma Shedra and all officers and students.
>
> Supreme Tulku Pema Norbu of Palyul Namgyal Jang Chub Ling Monastery, where Buddhadharma is maintained and made available to others, I praise your courage and vast intention to preserve the heart teachings of the Nyingma School, both sutra and tantra, and generally all Buddha's teachings, but particularly the Nyingma which is distinguished from the other schools by six distinctive features.[197] I praise your intention to maintain and spread every detail and subtle point of sutra and tantra teachings connected with the nine yanas, as well as the other traditional fields of study. With this intention you established the Nyingma College in southern India five years ago. On this special anniversary the joy in my heart is a lotus fully bloomed, and I toss the petals of appreciation and praise with a heart of goodness.

Today is the day that the great omniscient Longchenpa attained the level of no-more-study and transformed his body into the original, natural form of immortality. A great many of you have completed your study of philosophy and supreme Madhyamaka, and on this significant day and in accord with the system and tradition of modern times, you are receiving the auspicious diploma, a symbol of honor and praise for your achievement.

From this beginning, in the future many perfect beings will come whose activities will benefit the Nyingma teachings. May this aspiration spread throughout the dharmadhatu like a white cloud canopy.

And also may you department heads, administrators, and sangha members unite your intention and effort into this college, which will support the study and contemplation of all its students.

As for you student intellectuals, you must work in harmony, and keep your moral conduct as stainless as a white lotus, and your study impartial, embracing the knowledge of all the ordinary and extraordinary sciences— brought through great effort and aspiration by Khenpo Shantarakshita, Lobpon Padmasambhava, King Trisong Deutsen, and many emanated translators and panditas—and the commentaries on those sciences by the great teachers of the kama and terma. These teachings are pure gold. Generate the resolute courage, as indestructible as diamond, to make these teachings shine as the sun all over the world and make it available to all who are connected. And at the same time don't waste this wonderful opportunity to joyfully apply yourselves to further study. This is a friendly reminder, composed with good-hearted affection.

I send this letter with an abundance of white lotus petals and prayers and aspirations from the big city of America, New York. Dudjom Jigdral Yeshe Dorje, who is in the line of the secret mantrayana of the ancient school, sends this on the eighth day of January 1983; Tibetan royal era 2109, eleventh month, twenty-fifth day.

At this time he also composed the following letter to Kalön Wangdu Dorje, the home minister of the Tibetan government-in-exile:

To the lotus feet of the Minister Kalön Wangdu Dorje, possessor of beautiful wisdom and loving-kindness welling up from the depth of your devotion.

I tell you, receiving your letter was like seeing your face. I'm glad you are well. Here, this old one's health is in balance. I have a few dharma centers in America and France. Because they requested me to come, I could not refuse. So earlier this year I arrived in France. Here and there are a few dharma students; here and there, a few retreatants. To fulfill their wishes I gave teachings which lasted for a few months. Now I've arrived in America, nominally to teach dharma, but in fact wandering in scattered activity.

As you mentioned, Shinje Tramdö[198] and Chujin Tongdog[199] are both in the *Treasury of Precious Treasures*. Along with these two practices, you should add the long-life sadhana and the long-life sutra and do them repeatedly even though at this time you are not approaching the end of your life. But if you do them now, it will strengthen your health and increase your longevity. I thought this was important, and so I am telling you. It is very good that you are doing the White Tara long-life practice these days.

You also asked about the meaning of "supreme nonfocus"[200] during the principal practice. Whether practicing either the creation or completion stage, if there is any focused grasping, that is incorrect. Relax your mind in an uncontrived manner, without grasping, which is known as the "supreme nonfocus." When you relax in the natural state, immediately thoughts will arise. Catch them as soon as they do and recognize them with mindfulness. Don't judge the movement as bad. Just look at this movement. The moment you look, the object and the watcher disappear without a trace, and there is great vastness. That is the nonfocus state. A great teacher[201] said if you abide with the movement in its own place, it will be liberated in the dharmakaya. As he said, if you are at ease within that movement, not pursuing it, there is the openness of emptiness regarding what is to be relaxed and who is relaxing. That again is the dharmakaya. The essence is empty, the nature is clarity, and the expression is compassionate concern arising in every direction without obstruction. Thus the three kayas are already complete within one's own self, and each individual must discover it. This teaching is the extraordinary method of Dzogchen.

Regarding daily practice on Hayagriva, that is very good. Obstacles cannot disturb your life. Practicing this daily is not only beneficial for you but will benefit the affairs of the Tibetan government as well. I'm not being partial regarding religion, but during this time the teachings of the ancient school are of profound benefit to all beings and the teaching.

As you requested, I carefully did a divination, and it indicated that your health and activities will be good, and that though your proposed resignation will not easily be accepted, it will happen if you insist. Not merely accommodating you with lip service, I will certainly pray for your health always.

This old man, sooner or later this summer, is returning to Nepal. In the meantime I will continue to send letters. Hopefully soon I will have the great pleasure of seeing you again. Please keep this in the depth of the ocean of your mind, O Honored One.

Old Dudjom sends showers of flowers of auspiciousness and prosperity from Yeshe Nyingpo Dharma Center of America, New York, February 9, 1983.

His Holiness was going to be celebrating the Water Pig year losar at the New York City Yeshe Nyingpo, and everyone was busy preparing for the New Year celebration. Early in the morning family members and retinue individually offered him khatas and wished him long life. The festivities lasted three days, and on the third day his American students arrived, and he received them. They offered scarves, flowers, candles, burning incense, and gifts.

In New York at that time his routine included morning and evening meditation sessions, and following lunch he answered letters and received visitors. During that stay in New York he received a number of visitors, including the great teacher His Eminence Shamar Rinpoche, the Honorable Prince of the Kingdom of Sikkim, and Mr. Om Pradam, the permanent Bhutanese delegate to the United Nations. Many other Bhutanese dignitaries visited, as well as many renowned Tibetan scholars and officials, and in addition many Western students. He received them all, giving blessings and answering questions, and thus he fulfilled their wishes.

In the Water Pig year, TRE 2110, on March 23, 1983, he, the Sangyum, and family went to Los Angeles as arranged by the Los Angeles Yeshe Nyingpo Center. Gyatrul Rinpoche and Chagdud Tulku Rinpoche, and many Chinese, Tibetans, and Americans received him with great respect at the airport. After arriving, he called the author of this biography to come as translator and attendant, which he did immediately. On April 8, His Holiness presided at the dakini tsok, and Yeshe Nyingpo sangha members as well as students from other areas participated. On April 9, he taught that the source of samsara and nirvana is the mind, which is primordially empty and tranquil. Thus he let fall the rain of Dzogchen teachings to many students. The following day he gave the three roots empowerment, which is one of his own termas.

On April 13, students came from all over the West Coast, to receive transmissions they had requested for *Mountain of Burnt Offerings* and for his mind-terma dharmapala prayers. The next day he presided at the *Mountain of Burnt Offerings* ceremony. Sangha members of all the Yeshe Nyingpo Centers on the West Coast wanted to offer His Holiness a long-life and obstacle-reversing ceremony. So the following day, led by the great dakini Sangyum Kuzhok, and joined by Dungse Shenphen Dawa Rinpoche, Chagdud Tulku Rinpoche, Gyatrul Rinpoche, and the author of this biography, that ceremony was performed with students from all over the United States.

H. H. the Dalai Lama visits with H. H. Dudjom Rinpoche at Yeshe Nyingpo in 1979.

The following Sunday he gave the *One Thousand Buddhas of This Fortunate Aeon* empowerment to hundreds of students. On the tenth day of the Tibetan calendar, which fell on April 22, he presided at the Guru Rinpoche tsok and gave the empowerment for his terma *The Gathered Essence of the Cycles of Seven Great Tertöns.*[202] On April 27, full moon day, he gave empowerments of *Long-Life Sadhana of the Vital Force of Immortality* and *Condensed Essence of the Heart of Vajrakilaya*, both of which had been revealed by Tertön Zilnön Namkhai Dorje. During that empowerment he said, "Guru Padmasambhava intended these two teachings to be practiced in these degenerate times, and so at this juncture they are replete with power and blessings. When I received this teaching from the great tertön himself, my life and activities flourished and were fulfilled, and likewise it will be of great benefit for you to practice this." On May 1, he gave the empowerment of Green Tara to hundreds of Chinese and Western students. During this stay in Santa Monica, he received many students, and the media came to interview him. He fulfilled all their wishes and gave blessings, prayers, and transmissions.

On May 7, His Holiness and the entourage returned to New York. Toward the end of May he gave bodhisattva vows to many lamas and sangha members in the New York area. Then on June 4, at the request of Yeshe Nyingpo students, he gave Dzogchen teachings. On June 10, he celebrated his birthday. Many American and Chinese students came and made offerings with gifts, candles, incense, and white scarves, wishing His Holiness long life and to remain for hundreds of years. And afterward, according to the Western tradition, everyone had birthday cake and delicious sweets, as well as other foods and drinks. Around this time, Tibetan government-in-exile officials asked His Holiness to write a letter which would speak to all the people of Tibet:

To the Tibetan people.

I request the ear of all brothers and sisters of Tibet who have great zeal for the Tibetan cause and at the same time are deeply devoted to virtue. As you all know, today we face a situation worse than any other in our recorded history or in our spoken legends. At this time all Tibetans should arouse courage as unshakable as a vajra and commitment as powerful as a blazing fire by bringing to mind the ancient dharma kings, and in particular *Me Ön Sum*[203] and the three, *Khen-Lob-Chö*,[204] plus all the lineage masters of every school of Buddhism as well as the many kings and subjects of history. All of them spent their wealth, bodies, and lives many times to bring rich dharma and culture to Tibet. For this we can be proud. Even non-Tibetans now are praising these accomplishments. This rich heritage we all should protect and maintain and spread without in-fighting and power struggles. Remember, the beauty of the peacock feather is in its distinct colors.

This is the responsibility not of just a few of our brothers and sisters, but of all Tibetans. It is repayment of the kindness of all those great beings and teachers. It is service to the whole of Tibet, a source of benefit and happiness for future generations of

H.H Dudjom Rinpoche making a mandala offering to H.H. the Dalai Lama during his first visit to the USA, with great aspirations that His Holiness's peace mission to the United States goes smoothly and that his compassionate activities be fulfilled

Tibetans. You all must recognize this and keep it in your hearts. Reject all slanderous thoughts stemming from the self-importance that proclaims my region, my religion, my customs are superior to yours, or I'm a big shot and you're a small fry, and so forth. All Tibetans must join together to fulfill the wishes of the fourteenth Dalai Lama. Day and night unite your intention as you would to lift the four corners of a great carpet. Please do this.

Old Dudjom sends this simple reminder, a good and unpretentious wish, in the Water Pig year, sixth month, on an auspicious day.

At the end of June, he and the entourage went to Orgyen Chö Dzong to lead a three-week summer retreat. At the retreat center many students came from all over the United States and Europe, as well as Asia. On July 2, the three-week retreat began, and he gave his own teaching, *Mountain Hermitage Retreat Instructions*, and other empowerments and transmissions to the retreatants. At this time many students, including Dungse Shenphen Dawa Rinpoche, Tulku Rangdröl Rinpoche, Jigme Khyentse Rinpoche, Chöje Tulku, and Lama Rinchen Phuntsok, and the author of this biography were there. Everyone was happy and delighted to be with him, and the retreat went beautifully.

During his stay at Orgyen Chö Dzong, His Holiness wrote the following letter to be read at the Kalimpong shedra inauguration ceremony. The letter calls to mind the main purpose of the Zangdok Palri Monastery in Kalimpong and encourages the effort to continuously uphold that original goal of the founders. It is addressed to all its lamas, sangha members, and dharma patrons:

> To the lamas who hold the full richness of realization and the power to inspire others along the path to liberation and who are deeply rooted in the two stages.
> To the dharma patrons who are determined to support the precious dharma teachings of the Buddha and who have opened the doors of generosity.
> To the congregants who radiate the moonbeams of a good heart and who are always thinking how to assist the monastery.
> To all of you this is addressed.
>
> Because of the courageous, joyful, extraordinary activities of the chief artist Phuntsok Zangpo and the continued assistance of the dharma patrons and the support of the members of the Tsechu Association, today we are able to establish at Zangdok Palri Monastery of Kalimpong a shedra, the root of both scholarship and practice. On this occasion I am delighted, a joyful lotus is blooming from the depth of my heart. I play the sitar of praise and appreciation to all of you who lift the carpet with your united intention.
>
> In general, Buddha Shakyamuni gave many profound and vast

*His Holiness Dudjom Rinpoche at the groundbreaking ceremony
of the Glorious Copper-Color Mountain Monastery*

teachings suited to the readiness of the individuals. These
teachings spread to many parts of the world according to need and
capability. In Tibet, Land of Snow, three great beings—the second
buddha, Guru Padmasambhava, the great abbot of Nalanda
University, Shantarakshita, and the one who ruled this vast land
with awesome power and maintained it according to dharma,
King Trisong Deutsen, the emanation of Manjushri—displayed
their kindness by building Samye Monastery, an object of refuge,
complete in both its outer and inner aspects.

When the monastery was completed, all the Buddha's
teachings from the hinayana to the essence teachings of Atiyoga—
including the commentaries on these teachings composed by the
six ornaments and two supreme ones[205] predicted by Lord Buddha
in his vajra words—and the teachings of many other great ones
were brought by hundreds of panditas and lotsawas. These
teachings encompassed not only the inner science, but also the
science of language that dispels the errors of imprecision, the

science of logic that cleanly cuts contradictions of meaning, the science of healing that restores equilibrium among elements that have disproportionately increased or decreased, and the science of art that reveals the principles behind the beauty and humor in artistic productions. These panditas and lotsawas translated, corrected, and established these five sciences, the extraordinary and general knowledge, and all their branches.

Practice on the meaning of these profound pith instructions, combined with study, leads to the highest realization, as it did for the twenty-five disciples and the many male and female siddhas who filled the valleys of Tibet. The glorious master Atisha praised this growth of Buddhadharma, saying, "Even in India it never increased like this."

The thousand-spoked brilliant sun of the ancient translation school radiated over the whole of Tibet, and from that time the practice lineages known as the Eight Great Chariots and the academic lineages known as the Ten Great Pillars[206] gradually developed. Thus the Nyingma is the mother, the source, of all the Buddhist teachings of Tibet. And why has this essence of the great lineage continued even into the present for the use of many fortunate beings? The answer is the twenty-five mahasiddha disciples as well as the many masters of kama and terma who reached the state of Vajradhara. Only by their kindness is the teaching still here. To repay their kindness and to benefit sentient beings, we all have the responsibility to courageously preserve and joyfully maintain the teachings that are the source of benefit now and in the future until samsara is emptied.

Don't waste the good efforts of the dharma patrons and those who have taken the responsibility to establish this shedra. Instead you must follow the example of those ancient scholars and siddhas. We are all following the One Teacher, Shakyamuni. We are all entering the glowing light of a single mandala. It is said in the teachings that vajra brothers, sisters, and friends go together

Glorious Copper-Color Mountain Monastery in Kalimpong

like a flame and its wick until they reach the union state of Vajradhara. Therefore, never lose your bond of harmony. Keep your moral conduct as stainless as a fresh white lotus. Don't pretend to study, merely tallying the number of texts you've read. Deeply study sutra, tantra, commentary, and other traditional sciences. Especially study the subtle philosophical points of the ancient school, understand the distinctive points of the different doctrines, and become familiar through observation and participation with each lineage's distinct style of doing things. These are the specific responsibilities of all you students.

In general, I and the late honorable dharma patron Sharpa Tsenam, members of the Kalimpong Tsechu Association, and many devotees from all directions, who took the Buddha's teachings to heart and through a continuous expenditure of wealth without regard for hardship, working directly and indirectly, and for a very long time, endured in the effort that resulted in the Zangdok Palri Monastery of Kalimpong that is now to some degree complete. From the standpoint of architectural design it represents the extraordinary architectural living mandala to be found in no other school than the Nyingma. This is not to emphasize the physical structure alone, but rather the design, which is capable of kindling the realization of the lineage. Therefore this dharma mansion is radiating blessings, and whoever connects with it will experience the truly meaningful.

Since the beginning of this project, we, the living and those now gone, all had the same thought and hope that this would become one of the monasteries that would maintain the shedra and drubdra of the Nyingma tradition, as well as Buddhist teachings in general. As we had these wishes, so also did the Wish-Fulfilling Jewel, the fourteenth Dalai Lama, whose wishes were communicated in several letters from the Council of Religion of the Tibetan government-in-exile that expressed that this monastery should become the mother monastery of the Nyingmapa. I know this is old news, but I wanted once more to bring into focus the goals related to this monastery. By the power of establishing this shedra in this new place today, in the future the ancient great secret translation school will spread in every direction and become available to all those who are fortunate, and they will reach enlightenment within a single lifetime. By that same power the people of the world will not even hear the names of bad things, but will always enjoy the amazing prosperity of joy and peace. May this aspiration spread as a white canopy of clouds in all directions. Simultaneously I throw the white lotus petals, wishing goodness at the beginning, in the middle, and at the end from this day forward.

Practitioner of the Nyingma secret mantrayana, vidyadhara of the divine clan, Dudjom Jigdral Yeshe Dorje, sends this on the second day of the goodness of wisdom.[207] May it bring prosperity.

Still at Orgyen Chö Dzong in August of 1983, and unable to accept the invitation to speak at the opening of an art exhibition in Japan focusing on Tibetan culture in general and the Nyingma School in particular, he addressed the following letter to its organizers:

A memorandum to Honorable Toshika Zukiriyama, whose wisdom eye is wide open and whose motivation is beautiful, and the entire group that made this exhibition possible.

The primary function of your team has been to organize educational exhibitions of cultures from around the world, and in this case you are featuring the Buddhist tradition, specifically the culture and religion of the Nyingma School of Tibet. Your joyful enthusiasm and considerable effort have culminated in this beautiful day of fulfillment. I shower the petals of auspiciousness and goodness. The delight I feel is as if a lotus had bloomed in my heart. On melodious instruments I play songs of praise and appreciation to the deeds that issued from your good hearts.

Perfect teacher, Buddha, gave many varieties of profound and vast teaching corresponding to the capabilities of individual sentient beings. These teachings spread throughout the world according to the capability of the people. Only through the kindness of the second buddha, Padmasambhava of Orgyen, and the great abbot Shantarakshita of Nalanda did the teachings come to the Land of Snow. About Guru Padmasambhava, Buddha Shakyamuni said in the *Mahaparinirvana Mahayana Sutra*, "Two times four years after my mahaparinirvana, on the island of Dhanakosha an individual will be born who is greater than I myself." Moreover, in the *Manjushri Mayajala Tantra* one stanza reads, "Glorious Buddha born from a lotus, / Possessor of the all-knowing wisdom treasure, / Regal source of various displays, / Buddha distinguished as the holder of mantra and awareness." Thus was his coming predicted in praises, and not just in these two examples, but many times in sutra and tantra. Through his immeasurable compassion this second buddha pacified and dispelled all negative forces, clearing the way for construction that proceeded so smoothly and quickly the outer and inner aspects seemed to arise like a magical emanation. No sooner was Samye completed than the complete range of Buddhadharma, from Shravakayana to Atiyoga, the essence teaching of the Buddha, as well as the commentaries of the qualified masters and siddhas, and also the treatises on the sciences of language, logic, healing, and art were brought by hundreds of panditas and lotsawas, who then completely translated, corrected, and established all these major and minor teachings.

The twenty-five disciples of Padmasambhava and male and female siddhas who filled the valleys of Tibet practiced these profound instructions and reached the highest stage of realization within a single lifetime. The remarkable growth of Buddhadharma in Tibet was unparalleled even in India and was praised by unequaled teacher Jowo Je Dipamkara. Thus the incomparable, sacred, ancient translation school of the Nyingma rose like a brilliant sun; a sun that for the Tibetan people will never set. Atop this massive foundation some new translations (*sarma*) were subsequently added. The old and new translations together eventually resulted in the Eight Chariot practice lineages and the Ten Great Pillar academic lineages. Therefore, the ancient translation school is the source and mother of all the schools of Tibetan Buddhism. The Nyingma is the essential dharma of the fourth buddha.[208]

Furthermore, from this beginning arose the unmistakable elements of a traditional style. Your exhibition includes a three-dimensional model of an early temple exquisitely rendered by skilled craftsmen. The actual temples represented the perfect outer mandala. The exhibition also includes cast statues, sculpture, reliefs, and paintings symbolizing the Buddha's body, speech, and mind. These objects represent the inner aspect of the mandala. Also exhibited are a variety of musical instruments that accompany the vajra dances and the vajra songs which carry all the desirable qualities of the path and are able to crush habitual patterns.

Due to your courage and joyful effort, without concern for difficulty or expense, you brought this dawn of the Nyingma teaching and art into your home country of Japan. By this auspicious circumstance, it is my hope that in the future the sun of the entire ancient school will shine in your country and that all fortunate beings will reach enlightenment within a single lifetime. By that power may not even the names of evil and destruction be heard and may you always enjoy glorious and amazing peace and happiness. May my aspiration spread as a cloud canopy. I throw the white lotus petals that bring goodness to the beginning, middle, and end of this inauguratory event.

This secret vajrayana, Nyingma practitioner, mantra holder Dudjom Jigdral Yeshe Dorje of the divine clan of vidyadharas sends this in the Water Pig year on an excellent waxing moon day in midsummer, 1983, the year of the unequaled teacher, king of the Sakyas, who revealed his array of major and minor marks at Lumbini garden 2,607[209] years ago, and of the second buddha, Pemakara of Odiyana, who appeared on the lotus at Sindhu Lake 2,523 years ago. May it bring auspiciousness.

At that time at Orgyen Chö Dzong, there was a very old Coca-Cola machine that required only a single quarter for a pop. His Holiness and Sangyum Kuzhok were walking near it, and he wanted to use that machine, and she said, "I don't have any change." He reached into his chuba, fumbled around and came out with a quarter, which he placed in the slot, and after pressing the button, out came a can of soda. He took it, shook it up, and threw it on the floor where it burst amidst peals of laugher. After the retreat he stayed on one month more at Orgyen Chö Dzong.

His Holiness had long before decided to return to Nepal to complete his work of collecting and editing the Nyingma kama and had already made

His Holiness Dudjom Rinpoche with His Holiness Dilgo
Khyentse Rinpoche in Dordogne, France

travel arrangements for leaving the U.S. in September. The day of his departure arrived, the entourage had packed the car, everything was loaded and ready for the trip down to New York City, the airport, the flight to France, and then on to Nepal.

Then several Western students approached Shenphen Dawa Rinpoche. They parleyed, and then included Sangyum Kuzhok in a discussion that lasted for an hour. They then announced that His Holiness would not go to Nepal after all, and that instead, the scribes would be flown to the United States. They said the United States was better for his health. After the luggage was pulled out of the car, the author of this biography went to the room that His Holiness and the Sangyum were in. He was smiling and said, "So many people talking about so many things, and now I can't leave." Not long after that the four Bhutanese scribes including Lobpon Nyingkhula arrived at Orgyen Chö Dzong.

He remained in New York another four months, after which in 1984 he and the scribes went to France where he continued editing the Nyingma kama, as well as giving teachings and audiences. That summer at Orgyen Samye Chöling they held a large retreat with over seven hundred participants. He gave retreat teachings, empowerments, transmissions, and instructions, showering blessings on all the students in accordance with their wishes. He received an invitation from the Guru Lau to consecrate his newly built monastery. His Holiness had told him long before, "If you complete the monastery in Taiwan, I'll come to dedicate it." They decided to go through the United States on their way to Taiwan.

From France they arrived in New York and stayed for a week at the Yeshe Nyingpo center, giving audiences and blessings. After completing arrangements for passports and documents at the Taiwanese Consulate, they were scheduled to leave for California on September 29, 1984. That morning, however, His Holiness wasn't making any preparations for his imminent departure. In fact, he was relaxed and talking with Khenchen Palden Sherab Rinpoche even though his attendants kept coming in to remind him that if they were going to make their flight, they'd have to leave soon. They became increasingly concerned, but he said, "It's okay to miss the plane." When they did finally leave, there was no traffic on the road, and they made it to JFK Airport in less than twenty minutes.

At the airport in California, Gyatrul Rinpoche, Chagdud Tulku Rinpoche, and many students met him. He stayed in a beautiful private home for about one week. Many came to see His Holiness, such as Lama Tharchin Rinpoche, Ngagpa Yeshe Dorje Rinpoche, and Lama Lodrö Rinpoche, who is the representative of Kyabje Kalu Rinpoche on the West Coast, as well as hundreds of others to whom he gave audiences. He gave the empowerment of Guru Padmasambhava and blessings to everyone.

At the beginning of October the entourage flew to Taiwan through Japan. At the Taipei airport a great teacher of the Nyingma School Very Venerable[210] Palyul Dzongnor Rinpoche, the Chinese master Guru Lau, the head of the Tibetan-Mongolian Department of Taiwan, some Tibetans, and hundreds of Chinese came with white scarves and a huge welcome

His Holiness Dudjom Rinpoche in Taiwan in 1984,
attended by the author

banner in Chinese, English, and Tibetan. From the airport they went straight to Tai Chung Monastery. On October 10, which is also Taiwan National Day, he consecrated and opened the temple, giving the empower-ment of Guru Padmasambhava to hundreds of Chinese students. That night His Holiness and the entourage were invited to a large banquet. The following day he gave the empowerment of Vajrasattva to the members of the Vajrayana Buddhist Association. During his stay he continued giving personal instructions and guidance to Guru Lau, as well as other students.

After His Holiness had completed all the dharma activities that had been requested of him in that area, Guru Lau invited him and his entourage to the other cities where he'd established a Vajrayana Buddhist Association center. His Holiness blessed the Taiwan center, and visited and consecrated a large tract of land that would be the future site for a monastery and retreat facilities. Next they traveled to Kaohsiung, blessed the center there, lodged that night at the Grand Hotel, and the next day returned to Tai Chung Monastery. Shortly after that they continued to Taipei and did a blessing for the center there. He gave the empowerment of Guru Padmasambhava and a refuge ceremony to hundreds of Chinese.

Having fulfilled the wishes of the students of Taiwan, His Holiness accepted Guru Lau's request to visit Hong Kong at the end of October. At the Hong Kong airport a large crowd of Chinese students received him. He and his party stayed at the New World Hotel where he gave the empowerments and teachings for *Long-Life Sadhana of the Vital Force of Immortality*, Vajrakilaya, and Medicine Buddha, as well as bestowing personal instructions, transmissions, and blessings on many students. After completing activities in Hong Kong, they went through Bangkok to Paris and then to Dordogne, where he gave many teachings to the three-year retreatants, as well as blessings and teachings to all the other disciples.

His Holiness Dudjom Rinpoche

81

Within the vast dharmadhatu, innately pure,
Inner and outer vajra skandhas[211] ebb and flow,
Forms of emptiness—peaceful-wrathful, mother-father[212]
Are all perfected in your buddha mandala.

82

Every animate and inanimate sound
Flows as the effortless speech of emptiness;
Silent self-reciting vajra tones arise
To grace your speech chakra with unending bliss.

83

Dispelling duality where nothing needs dispelling,
Joining meditation and after where nothing needs joining,
Ending samsara and nirvana where nothing needs ending,
Finding all good in the rich space where nothing needs finding.

84

Not opened by duality's key of effort,
But by the spontaneous method, clear and bright,
The rich treasury of dharmakaya space
Yields to scholars through inexpressible means.

85

In realizing all sights, sounds, and thoughts
As pure and deathless vajra nature,
Your good deeds, natural and pervasive,
Brought countless beings to lasting joy.

86

Clearly arising from primordial emptiness,
Unceasing compassion yields the wealth of three kayas.
Through your wisdom of yore, free of mental strife,
Attainments came without hardship or effort.

87

> Buddha's heart teachings, nectar of kama and terma,
> From good vases of powers, transmissions, and pith advice,
> You poured into three treasure bowls[213] of lucky disciples,
> Raising the Nyingma victory banner to the world's peak.

88

> East to west, across the world's length and breadth,
> Upon all mankind's beautiful colors
> You showered the nine yanas, as needed,
> Bringing countless lucky beings to lasting joy.

89

> Across the dharmakaya sky of twofold purity,
> Moves the sun's chariot of your past bodhichitta wishes,
> Bright with the power of thousands of rays of loving-kindness,
> Stirring beings and teachings, lotus gardens, everywhere.

90

> Men of great power, glory, wealth, and lineage,
> In joyful devotion, with their crown chakras,
> Again and again, bowed down to your lotus feet,
> While you were crowned with sweet humility!

91

> You, perfect moon of the buddhas' three secrets,
> Pride of a hundred thousand stars of beings,
> Though all praised you with constant garlands of smiles,
> Yet pride and self-conceit swelled not in you.

92

> From all directions all practitioners
> Thronged to the dancing stage of your blessings.
> Not tailoring words nor assuming guises,
> You rested in your natural state. Marvel!

93

> More and more, five impurities come near, near.
> Again, again, all joy and wealth flee far, far.
> Zig zag, the four elements waver, waver.
> Side to side the darkness of beings grows and grows.

94

> Rumbling with evil karma's five impurities,
> Out of dark, frightful clouds of greed and anger,
> A fierce hailstorm of harsh, cruel actions fell and
> Blighted Tibet's harvest of beings and teachings.

95

> On your strong shoulders, armed with a courageous heart,
> Buddha's doctrine, especially the Nyingma School,
> You raised high on the white banner of pure study and insight:
> Hero of two benefits, in samsara and nirvana.

96

> Four elements go awry, wealth's element ebbs,
> Human minds waver, human consciousness falters,
> Youth's vigor is stunted, youth's fresh bloom fades:
> Mind's unrelenting time, this darkened time.

97

> In these dark degenerate times,
> When the sun of joy and ease dimmed,
> When the din of war and disease grew loud,
> Then you came, Guru Rinpoche's regent.

This is a brief account of his dharma activities, how he worked to benefit the teachings and beings. All over the world he touched and opened the hearts of beings, from beginning practitioners to renowned teachers. This completes the sixth heap of lightbeams wherein has been described his activities to secure the Buddhadharma in general and Nyingma teachings in particular.

His Holiness Dudjom Rinpoche receiving
yellow-scroll terma papers at the age of thirteen

The Seventh Heap of Lightbeams:

*a brief explanation of Kyabje's enthronement as a great tertön and
regent of Guru Padmasambhava and of how Guru Rinpoche and
wisdom dakini Yeshe Tsogyal entrusted him with terma*

In His Holiness Dudjom Rinpoche's own words:

> The Lake-Born Lama gave me the name of Garwang Drodul
> Lingpa,[214] a lion's name, even though I'm just an old dog. In previous
> lives I was blessed by the kindness of the father and mother gurus,[215]
> and by following them, have developed some good karmic
> connections. I was born with unshakable devotion to them, and
> therefore I received signs of their blessings again and again. When
> just a young boy, I began finding treasure caskets, which were my
> portion to discover. I kept them and had countless visions.
> Specifically, when I was thirteen years old, I saw Guru
> Padmasambhava directly. Right after that, a few girls, who were
> playing with me, placed in my hand a code[216] and some actual
> rolled, yellow papers[217] covered with symbolic syllables. Around that
> time amazing magical appearances and events occurred. But
> because place, time, friends, and retinues made conditions fall
> under the control of others, and many inner and outer
> circumstances were discouraging, I offered all those yellow, rolled
> papers to the great mother Nabza Karmo.[218] From that time on I
> decided to maintain and spread the termas of all the past tertöns, to
> the extent that I was able, and to rid myself of the hopes and fears

associated with the revelation and transmission of new termas, preferring a relaxed and simple way of life.

Again, when still a boy, near the shore of the river of Ma-ong Kota in Pema Kö, he was playing with other children. At that time he found a small, beautiful, black stone similar in shape to a *nyida*.[219] The inside was hollow, and when he shook it, it made a sound. The author of this biography had the opportunity to see this object in His Holiness's own hand. Many other disciples said that it was the key[220] to his termas. His stepfather, Lama Kunrab, said that His Holiness started revealing terma at age five.

As for how he revealed the teaching of *Vajra Subduer of Demons, Crazy Wrathful Blood-Drinker Pema*, Guru Padmasambhava declares in the root terma text:

> Since this heart-drop of the condensed secret meaning of all root texts was too precious to hide in the external world, I buried it instead in the vast spacious mind of the magical being who is my emanation filled with the power of awareness wisdom. Samaya.

The great teacher tertön said:

> When I was thirteen years old, I began a short retreat in which I practiced Dudul Dorje's Dorje Drolö terma. Suddenly the text of the *Vajra Subduer of Demons, Crazy Wrathful Blood-Drinker Pema* with its unique system of recitation and visualization arose in my mind. This happened again when I was twenty-four and practicing the Dorje Drolö of Dudjom Lingpa.
>
> Concerned that sharing this teaching with others would shorten my life[221] as indicated in the samaya, I practiced this teaching secretly, even though outwardly it appeared as if I was practicing the Dorje Drolö terma teachings of those other two tertöns. I had great confidence in the power of this new terma.

Then when I had passed through the turbulence of the degeneration-causing obstacles that occur at around the age of fifty, the time was right, and being urged repeatedly by the supreme tantric practitioner Gyurme Yönten Gyatso to reveal the very secret practice of *Vajra Subduer of Demons, Crazy Wrathful Blood-Drinker Pema,* I released the secret seal and revealed this teaching.

As for how he revealed the teaching of *Heart Drop of the Dakini,* Kyabje's own words are given:

I was twenty-five. It was the tenth day of the waning half of the tenth month in the Earth Dragon year. Yogi Trulshik Dorje, urged by the dakinis, arrived unexpectedly and said, "You have to write a very concise and precise dakini sadhana right now." I had been thinking to write just such a sadhana and had considered taking some time as usual to compose it, but when he said this, the complete sadhana and its meaning arose instantly and clearly in my mind. Without moving from my cushion or changing the words as they came, I wrote them down. Although it could be regarded as mind terma, I never called it that. I handed it to him on the spot. Trulshik Dorje went to Crystal Cave at Yarlung and practiced on this *Heart Drop of the Dakini,* getting many signs of achievement and gaining great confidence in the sadhana. He repeatedly asked me to set down in writing the outer, inner, and secret instruction sections of the practice that would round out the cycle. I couldn't bear the constant disturbance to my ear, so I added many branch practices related to the original.

Later, a connection to this profound teaching arose for a highly placed Lhasa government official, Honorable Tsewang Rigdzin Namgyal. He asked for elaboration, so I added additional stanzas to the visualization portion of the practice to make it easier to follow. During that time period, I completed the whole body of these dakini teachings.

His Holiness Dudjom Rinpoche in Tibet

Connected to this *Heart Drop of the Dakini* mother practice is the father practice on the lord of the family, Guru Padmasambhava, called *Heart Drop of the Lake-Born Vajra*. His Holiness said:

> For the fortunately connected students, I released the secret seal of the casket[222] spontaneously arisen from the space of awareness.

Thus, he completed the cycle of teachings called *Heart Drop of the Lake-Born Vajra*.

When he was thirty-three years old and practicing at Buddha Tsephug Cave in Kongpo with a retinue of disciples, His Holiness got sick. One of his chief disciples, Dzogchen yogi Trulshik Dorje, led the others in hundreds of repetitions of the *Heart Drop of the Dakini* ganachakra for his quick recovery. About this His Holiness said:

> During that time early one morning I had a dream. A lady loudly sang this prayer:
>
> > Ram Yam Kam Om Ah Hung
> > The ganachakra torma offerings of pure awareness are displayed
> >   in the skull cup of dharmadhatu.
> > The variegated desirable qualities of the rainbow rays and points
> >   of the six lamps shine.
> > These are the wondrous, inconceivable samaya.
> > To the assembly of the deities of the three roots, our self-
> >   awareness,
> > This offering is made in the state of nondual equanimity.
> > We purify conceptions in the great bindu.
> > Liberate the enemy and obstructer, duality, in the unborn
> >   expanse.
> > Please act! Awaken deluded appearance into the primordial state.
> > Having fully realized the wisdom of the spontaneous four visions,
> > May we be enlightened in the originally pure youthful vase body.

When I woke up, I didn't forget a single word and wrote down the illusory appearances of the dream. That very day auspiciousness came, and I completely recovered from my sickness the next day.[223]

As for the manner in which the sadhana of the activity heruka, Vajrakilaya, was discovered, it is described in these words of Yeshe Tsogyal, which are part of the terma:

> The secret teachings and pith instructions of all the tantras in a single state, the heart drop essence of the hundred thousand Vajrakilaya teachings is called *Vajrakilaya, the Razor That Destroys on Contact*. It condenses the personal Vajrakilaya practices of the three great masters.[224] Just as Guru Padmasambhava bestowed these teachings so dear to his heart on the assembly of king and subjects, so they practiced them. To secure the Vajrakilaya teachings for future generations, the majority have been transmitted orally, many have been hidden as earth treasures, and some have been hidden in the wisdom mind-stream of various individuals. Of all these this is the ultimate essence, free of wordiness and fabrications, yet all the core meanings are here. Its extraordinarily sharp power and blessing are greater than any other.
>
> When Guru Padmasambhava was leaving for the southwestern subcontinent to subdue the cannibals, he inconspicuously handed me, Yeshe Tsogyal, the woman from the Karchen clan, the profound secret teaching as a parting gift. So precious is this teaching, I chose not to hide it in any common way and instead sealed it in the heart of the one with pure wisdom mind and good fortune who is no different from me. Samaya Gya Gya Gya. Guhya.

In the words of His Holiness:

> In the Fire Ox year, 1937, on the full moon day in the Trumtö month, I, Jigdral Yeshe Dorje, was thirty-four years old and doing

His Holiness Dudjom Rinpoche being handed a phurba
and teaching by Yeshe Tsogyal in a dream

practice to make the dharma nectar medicine according to the Vajrakilaya sadhana, *Sword of Meteorite*, at Padro Taktsang in Bhutan. In a dream a woman with a beautiful dress and ornaments whom I knew to be Yeshe Tsogyal handed me a six-inch clearly detailed meteorite phurba and said, "This is the actual ritual implement that Guru Rinpoche held here in this place, when he transformed into Dorje Drolö and put under oath all the eight classes of mighty invisible beings, and in particular the *gyalpo* and *senmo*.[225] Later, at Gungtang Mountain Pass, Guru Padmasambhava gave me this phurba as a farewell gift.[226] Now I'm

His Holiness
Dudjom Rinpoche

giving this to you. You must keep it as your heart treasure." She began to put it in the fold of my chuba, and at that moment I was so happy, I grabbed it quickly, and thought, I'm going to receive an empowerment. I touched it to my forehead and throat. When I touched the heart center, instantly that phurba and I became inseparable. The upper part of my body was as it is now, but my lower body had become an iron phurba with sparking flames. I was chanting the Vajrakilaya mantra and felt the whole earth tremble and shake. At that moment that girl said to me, "That is the real empowerment and blessings. This is the treasure of all tantra teaching and pith instructions in one single state. Don't neglect this, it has great purpose. Do you remember completely receiving these teachings, empowerment, and pith instructions from Guru Padmasambhava in ancient times?" Then she pulled my hand, extending my arm, and I woke up. At that very moment I remembered many things past, and, particularly, all the Vajrakilaya teachings I'd received came clearly into mind. If transcribed directly as it was arising within the expanse of rigpa, this Vajrakilaya teaching would be much larger than those of the two tertöns.[227] There were even many instructions and action practices that those did not include.

Revealing terma involves you in a lot of work with little to show for it, so I set it aside. However, at the age of forty-five, in the Earth-Mouse year in the first month of the lunar calendar on the tenth day, urged by many internal and external circumstances not to neglect my own share of the teaching, I transcribed a small portion of these teachings as the heart drop of the root teachings. Dakinis and ocean of dharmapalas, you are the owner of these teachings. Please secure them *I-Thi*.[228]

Right after transcribing the root teachings, *Vajrakilaya, the Razor That Destroys on Contact*, in an illusory vision a beautiful turquoise female dog appeared in front of me and with a joyful expression said:

> In the place where all samaya keepers gather,
> Whether in a garden far from samaya corrupters
> Or in the assembly hall of the samaya keepers,
> These will be the symbolic words of the noble ones:
> By maturing the aspirations and good karma of the past
> In order to benefit all beings in the future,
> This secret treasure, which is the supreme essence,
> The heart realization of the three masters,
> Is the creation, completion, and great completion stage.
> Bound by the strap of the essence of the nine yanas,
> The lines of letters appearing as rainbows in the sky,
> Carry a vast meaning in a few words.
> This is the heart essence of the three lineages of
>   Samantabhadra.
> Know this to be the teaching for this time and
> Instruct individuals, who have these names:
> Jnana, Vajra, Karma, Mani,
> And Punye, Padma, and Odiyan.

They will spread this teaching to the four large tropical areas
    and the four big valleys.
It will rekindle the fire of the lineage teachings just a little—
Particularly, for the one keenly interested in the essential
    meaning,
Who possesses the self-appearing good marks,
The child born in the Monkey year,
Who will dissolve in the space of the dharmakaya of
    Samantabhadra,
The marvelous self-born, who emerged from space.
I, the female dog, who looks like a ferocious tiger pouncing
    on the enemy,
In ancient times in the cave of Yangleshö
I kept the vajra command of the Great Guru.
I make this announcement for those who are karmically
    connected,
Who have not deceived, are not deceiving, and will not
    deceive samaya.

She said that and then disappeared.

During this retreat at Padro Taktsang, he discovered an eighteen-inch
meteoric phurba. This sacred relic is in the possession of the family and
held in high regard.

His last revealed teaching preserves the essence teaching of the gracious,
compassionate teacher, Lord Buddha. It is a reminder to his students of the
supreme object of refuge. It enjoins them to combine mindful alertness
with compassion and emptiness to uproot the demon of ego. When this is
accomplished, it will lead to the originally enlightened mind in the vast
expanse of Samantabhadra's great bliss. This teaching is known as *The
Prayer That Brings the Recognition of Our Own Faults, That Reminds Us of
the Object of Refuge, That Purifies Our Misdeeds, That Makes Perfectly Clear
What to Take Up and What to Abandon*. His Holiness said:

*Companion dakini reminding the Sangyum
to request His Holiness to write the teachings*

Regarding this combination of purification practice and prayer of
aspiration, one night during the waxing moon of the tenth month
of the Water Pig year my wisdom consort, Rigdzin Wangmo, had
a dream in which a girl whom she was used to seeing in her
dreams appeared. The girl said, "Please ask Rinpoche to write a
prayer," and then she disappeared. In that same month on the
tenth day she came again in a dream and said, "You haven't asked
him yet." Next day we talked about it casually, and I said, "There's
a shortage of pray-ers, not prayers." She said, "Please, just write a
prayer without regard to length."

Guru Rinpoche appearing as a dancer singing a song that would be
His Holiness Dudjom Rinpoche's final teaching

I thought I should write a prayer evoking supreme wisdom-compassion, one that would alleviate the fear of disease, war, and famine. Due to the business of traveling, it was delayed.

On the tenth night of the twelfth month, *Gyal Dawa*, the girl came again. She said, "Don't neglect my request for a prayer. It is very important." That's the dream she had. I thought, "I'll write it

on the full moon day." So on the night of the fourteenth I prayed
with single-pointed devotion to Guru Rinpoche to grant blessing
that the prayer would be beneficial and then fell asleep. Early in
the morning of the fifteenth I dreamed I was sitting in front of the
shrine in a very large building that looked like a temple. Suddenly
a young white man dressed in white with his hair falling loosely
over his shoulder appeared at the entrance. He was playing the
cymbals melodiously and dancing the swirling, joyous dance of
the Ging. He came closer and closer, singing:

> If you want to establish the dharma,
> Establish it in your mind.
> In the depth of mind, you will find Buddha.
> If you wish to visit the buddha fields,
> Purify ordinary deluded attachment.
> The perfectly comfortable buddha field is close by.
> Develop the joyful effort to practice,
> That is the essence of the teaching.
> Without practice, who can gain the siddhis?
> It is hard to see one's faults,
> But to see them nakedly is powerful advice.
> In the end when faults have been cleared away,
> The enlightened qualities increase and shine forth.

At the end of this he rolled the cymbals. Then he crashed them
together, and I awoke. After I woke up, I did not forget what he
had said. I understood it to have been advice on practicing what
to accept and what to reject. I was sad that although I had actually
seen the face of my only father, Guru Padmasambhava, I had not
recognized him.

*I, Jigdral Yeshe Dorje, old father of the Nyingma, wrote this from my
own experience. Sarva Mangalam.*[229]

A few notable events related to Kyabje's activity as a tertön are briefly listed to round out this presentation:

- At the age of thirteen he saw Lake-Born Vajra Lord Orgyen and Yeshe Tsogyal. From them he received empowerments, instructive notification regarding his terma and how he was to reveal it, and the name Garwang Drodul Lingpa Tsal. Thus was he enthroned as the regent of Guru Padmasambhava.

- Wisdom dakinis offered yellow paper scrolls, and he began discovering profound terma. From that time on, the immeasurable pure visions expanded, enabling him to see clearly all terma that belonged to him.

- In the Buddha Tsephug Cave, by practicing on the Buddha Amitayus, all the long-life nectars began overflowing from the skull cup, and he saw Buddha Amitayus.

- At Mön Padro Taktsang, while practicing on Vajrakilaya, he saw Yeshe Tsogyal and discovered the entire Vajrakilaya Sadhanas.

- Breaking the secret seal on the amulet of self-arisen awareness of clear light luminosity, he revealed *Heart Drop of the Dakini* and *Heart Drop of the Lake-Born Vajra*, which are powerful and blessed practices for this era, the heart essence of Guru Padmasambhava.

These are some of his main termas. Otherwise he focused more on maintaining, protecting, and spreading the kama and old terma teachings than on revealing new terma teachings himself.

98

As bodhichitta heart-wishes from past lives ripened in virtue's lake of the
world's beings,

You bloomed—thousand-petaled white lotus, smiling with beauty of the
two merits,[230] and instantly

The sun of Lake-Born yab yum, with the inconceivable three roots,
dharmapalas, and others,

Rushed to touch you with garlands of prophecies, advice, blessings—in
visions, dreams, and face to face.

99

Jewels, rubies, sapphires, diamonds, gold, and so on,
Things of beauty, thousands of perfumed petals,
All marvelous worldly objects, loved and desired,
No one needs any urging to gather them up.

100

Similarly, around you, holy tulku,
Wisdom's assembly of three roots and protectors,
As bees in a beautiful lotus garden,
Again, again, full of smiles, hastened to gather.

101

From Orgyen yab yum's joyous skies,
Summer's drums' unceasing song
Rolled out the name "Drodul Ling,"
Sounding it in ten directions.

102

Guru yab yum imprinted, mind to mind,
Profound secrets of the three inner tantras,
Sealing them deep within vast wisdom's clear light
As foretold, within your mind's terma stream.

His Holiness Dudjom Rinpoche
in Tibet

103

"When the darkness of evil grows strong,
And the wisdom of beings grows weak,
You will come and show freedom's path." Thus,
Padma gave you throne and dominion.

104

Wisdom dakinis swaying in waves of smiles,
Sweetly uttering melodious words,
With their tender hands your own terma code[231]
Held out, but your heart turned to ancient termas.

This completes the seventh heap of lightbeams concerning his appointment as regent of Guru Padmasambhava, entrustment with terma by wisdom dakini Yeshe Tsogyal, and enthronement as a great tertön.

His Holiness Dudjom Rinpoche in full ceremonial robes

THE EIGHTH HEAP OF LIGHTBEAMS:

an enumeration of how he preserved and spread
the teachings of the ancient great tertöns through empowerment,
transmission, and pith instruction, and by emending texts
that had been annotated incorrectly

1. When Kyabje was thirty years old, he resided at the hermitage of Ösel Thegchog Ling at Chöding Rinchen Pung. While there, he compiled two sadhanas at the request of Garwang Sangye Dorje. They were based on the *Quintessence of All Dharma Realizations* that had been revealed by Tertön Dudul Dorje. The two sadhanas are called *Heart Essence of the Vidyadharas* and *Heart Drop and Secret Practice of the Lama.* He supplemented these sadhanas with various practice instruction manuals.

2. At the age of thirty-five on the twenty-ninth day of the miracle month, an excellent day for the gathering of dakinis, he emended the *Profound Secret Essence* sadhana revealed by Taksham Nuden Dorje and named it *Profound Secret Essence of the Nirmanakaya Dakini.* This emendation had been requested by the high official Tsering Paljor, the reincarnation of Lhacham Pema Sal.

3. Then he compiled the *Convenient and Easy to Follow Practice of Ngöndro* using the root text *Heart Practice of the Vidyadhara* revealed by Mahasiddha Lhatsun Namkha Jigme. Döndrub Namgyal, the king of Sikkim, and the practitioners from the Pema Yangtse Monastery had made the request. The practitioners wanted it for use in their own daily practice and for use by other followers of the lineage as well.

4. At the age of forty-seven in the Iron Tiger year at Rigdzin Gatsal in
Kongpo Buchu, he compiled *Joyful Feast of Practicing on the Ocean of
Dharma*. The text is based on *All-Gathered Dharma Ocean* revealed by
Yarje Orgyen Lingpa,[232] the incarnation of Prince Lhaje. *All-Gathered
Dharma Ocean* is a terma that is the heart essence of the oceanlike secret
teachings dear to Guru Padmasambhava. In Kyabje's own words:

> I compiled this according to the pith instructions of the true
> lineage teachers in honor of my crown jewel, Gyurme Ngedön
> Wangpo, from whom I received the complete empowerment of
> this *All-Gathered Dharma Ocean*, and who was the supreme inner
> heart disciple of the great chariot of the secret teaching, Pema Ösel
> Dongak Lingpa.

In addition he composed several practice instruction manuals to
accompany this sadhana.

5. While Kyabje was residing at Rigdzin Gatsal, his monastery Ogmin
Palri had recently been completed. The monastery is located at a geograph-
ical power point and modeled both inside and out on the pure-realm
palace of Padmasambhava. To commemorate the event and to simplify
guru yoga for himself and the monastic practitioners, and also at the behest
of Trulshik Dorje, His Holiness merged seven great guru yoga treasures
into one. He combined and condensed them into the composition known
as *Granting All Wishes, Joyful Feast of Accomplishment, the Practice on the
Heart Essence of the Lama*. About this Kyabje said:

> I, Jigdral Yeshe Dorje, whose wisdom lotus blossomed a little by
> the sunlight of the great kindness and teachings of the great
> teacher of Odiyana, Padmasambhava, wrote this when I was age
> forty-eight in that time of year when everyone enjoys the feasts
> and luxuries of summer.

In addition His Holiness wrote condensed sadhanas and various practice
instruction manuals related to this larger sadhana.

Line drawing of His Holiness Dudjom Rinpoche that was approved by him

The seven original guru yoga instructions were given out of kindness and compassion by the great teacher of Odiyana, embodiment of all the buddhas of the three times. He gave these profound teachings to the king and other disciples. Specifically thinking of the tormented beings in the future times of degeneration, he hid these teachings in many different locations throughout Tibet. Subsequently they were revealed one after another at the appropriate time. The seven termas include the following texts:

- *Essence of the Lama* cycle revealed by that famous king of tertöns and siddhas, Guru Chökyi Wangchuk from Lhodrag Kharchu Namkechen in southern Tibet
- *Gathering of the Eight Herukas* revealed by the body emanation of the great translator Vairochana, Orgyen Dorje Lingpa, from the secret cave of Ngomshö Namchag Drag
- *Embodiment of the Heart Essence* revealed by the emanation of the Mahasiddha Langdro Lotsawa, Chögyal Ratna Lingpa, from Nyalme Geridrag

- *Lama, Ocean of Jewels* revealed from Lhodrag Mendö Drag Singhe Dongpa Chen (the Rocky Mountain Which Has the Face of a Lion) in southern Tibet by Vidyadhara Pema Lingpa, who was the emanation of the princess Lhacham Pema Sal
- *Gathering of Victorious Ones* revealed by Zhigpo Lingpa Gargyi Wangchug Tsal, who is an emanation of Prince Murub Tsenpo, from Chung Tsang Drag (Rocky Mountain of the Garuda Nest)
- *Quintessence of All Dharma Realizations* revealed at Puwo Dongchu Dechen Sangphug by Tragtung Dudul Dorje, who was the emanation of Drogben Khyeuchung Lotsawa
- *Ultimate Gathering of Sugatas*, which is the terma teaching of His Holiness, himself.

6. In the beautiful park near the main temple of Lhasa[233] in the Water Dragon year at age forty-nine, Kyabje was approached by Sinphug Lama Jamyang Yeshe Singhe, the spiritual and worldly heir of the tertön Dorje Lingpa. He offered His Holiness many precious objects with a white scarf and requested, "Would you write a condensed and essential version of *Union of the Lama and Buddha Amitayus*, which is a terma teaching of Tertön Dorje Lingpa?" As requested, His Holiness kept the essence teaching of Dorje Lingpa as the basis and adopted many great teachings similar to Dorje Lingpa's and put together a clear and easy-to-practice sadhana, known as *Feast of Immortal Practice of the Inseparable Guru and Buddha Amitayus*. The scribe was Norbu Wangyal.

7. The tenth speech emanation of Terchen Pema Lingpa, Sungtrul Pema Ngagwang Chökyi Gyaltsen, established new ceremonies to be performed at regular intervals at Lhalung Rabgye Ling Monastery as well as other practices. He asked His Holiness, "Would you edit Terchen Pema Lingpa's sadhana of Vajrakilaya so that it's easy for everyone to follow?" To oblige, His Holiness used Kunkhyen Tsultrim Dorje's sadhana and a few other teachings by Pema Lingpa together with Guru Padmasambhava's own tantric instructions as the foundation, and without changing the root terma words, he composed a sadhana known as *Ornament of Enjoyment*

and Fulfillment of the Action of the Heart-Secret Razor of Vajrakilaya from the Terma Cycle of Pema Lingpa. He was age forty-nine in the Water Dragon year and was residing near the Jokhang. The scribe Norbu Wangyal assisted him. In addition he wrote many other action and accomplishment practices connected with this sadhana.

8. In the autumn of the same year with the fruit ripe on the trees in front of the Jowo cathedral,[234] His Holiness had a wish to benefit the many vajrayana practitioners he'd met who lacked both understanding and realization of tantra due to their habitual patterns and broken samayas. Urged by the highly accomplished yogi of the two stages Sangye Dorje Tsal, the true king of renunciates, to compose a sadhana to accomplish that objective, Kyabje compiled a simple-to-follow sadhana called *Ornament of the Heart of Buddha Samantabhadra That Will Purify and Renew the Samayas of the Secret Yana of the Tantra Which is Connected to the Self-Liberating Peaceful and Wrathful Deities from the Terma Cycle of Siddha Karma Lingpa.* He used the kama lineage sadhana of the great Nyingma charioteer Maha Lotsawa Dharmashri and the Zhitro terma of Karma Lingpa as his primary sources. He incorporated many technical teachings and pith instructions by Guru Padmasambhava as well. Sangye Dorje Tsal served as the scribe. In addition to this he wrote many shorter versions of this practice, which purifies broken samaya by means of the peaceful and wrathful buddhas, and practices to help the deceased.

9. All the members of the precious sangha of Chökhor Rabten Tse, the monastery praised by His Holiness as "the principal source of Buddha's teaching in the southern direction," made offerings to Kyabje and repeatedly requested, "Please make a condensed and easy-to-follow sadhana suitable for occasional and daily practice; one which will stand as a beacon of goodness for generations to come." To fulfill their wish, at the age of fifty-one in the Wood Horse year in front of the cathedral of Jowo Rinpoche in Lhasa, he composed *Excellent Path of the Vidyadharas, an Easy-to-Follow Heart Practice of the Lama.* He used the *Embodiment of the Total Realization of the Lama,* the most important earth terma of Tibet, revealed by the great

tertön Sangye Lingpa, as his root source. In accordance with the qualified masters of this lineage, he pared away extraneous words[235] to make it concise and added what was necessary to make it clear.

10. Regarding kabgye terma, there are nine lineage-blessing rivers. The first five are exalted as the five kabgye heart treasures of Guru Padmasambhava:

- *The Eight Herukas—Embodiment of All the Sugatas* revealed by Terchen Ngadak Nyang-ral Nyima Özer is esteemed as the *heart practice* of the eight herukas
- *Totally Complete Secret of the Eight Herukas* revealed by Terchen Guru Chökyi Wangchuk is commended as the *heart-blood practice*
- *Self-Born, Self-Arising Eight Herukas* revealed by Terchen Rigdzin Godem Chen[236] is honored as the *heart-essence practice*
- *Heart Mirror of the Eight Herukas* revealed by Terchen Pema Lingpa is valued as the *life-force practice*
- *Essential Secret of the Eight Herukas That Subdues Negative Arrogance* revealed by Terchen Samten Dechen Lingpa is praised as the *body practice*.

In addition, kabgye sadhanas from four other great tertöns are as follows:
- *Completely Condensed Totality of the Wrathful Mantras of the Eight Herukas* revealed by Terchen Dorje Lingpa
- *Heart of Accomplishment of the Eight Herukas* revealed by Terchen Jatsön Hungnak Mebar
- *All the Eight Heruka Practices Condensed* revealed by Terchen Rigdzin Longsal Nyingpo
- *Embodiment of the Eight Wrathful Herukas* revealed by Terchen Pema Ösel Dongak Lingpa.

These nine converged when at the age of fifty-two, His Holiness composed a threefold sadhana, the stages of which are named *Heart Activities of the Eight Glorious Herukas*, *All the Pith Instructions of the Eight Herukas Coming as One Form*, and *Heart Essence of the Eight-Heruka Practice That Will Subdue the Garrison of Obstacles and Enemies*. These were written at glorious, spontaneously accomplished, indestructible Samye Monastery along with many supplementary sadhanas, all of which are included in his collected works.

11. At the age of fifty-nine in the Water Tiger year in Kunzang Forest midway down the slope of Richen Pünpa Mountain, he emended the entire empowerment section of the *Three Sections of Dzogchen Teachings.* He named it *Ornament of the Heart of Vidyadhara Guru Samantabhadra.* The ngagpa teacher Chödrag Gyatso was the scribe. In Kyabje's words:

> When Lama Orgyen Tsewang bestowed the complete teachings and empowerments of Chogyur Dechen Lingpa's terma *Three Dzogchen Sections,* he asked me to edit it so that it would be clear and easy to follow. I kept his request in my heart, though its fulfillment was delayed. Then, the sixteenth Karmapa, Gyalwang Kunzang Rigpai Dorje, urged Lama Orgyen Tsewang to finish editing that particular text. Finally the lord of the mandala, Khyentse Chökyi Lodrö, encouraged me to do this emendation.

12. *Tree of Lotus Flowers, from Heart Practice of the Lama, Ocean of Jewels* revealed by Terchen Pema Lingpa had accumulated layer upon layer of additions from many generations of lineage practitioners and schooled and unschooled village ngagpas. The sadhana had fallen into extremes: unnecessarily elaborate in some sections and so condensed in others that the true meaning had been lost. Seeing this, His Holiness thought that he should emend this sadhana to make it suitable for contemporary practitioners. When Ngagpa Tendzin Kunleg and several other practitioners of the Pema Lingpa tradition asked him to edit the text to bring out its true meaning and to make it easier to follow, he compiled *Ornament of the Heart of the Vidyadhara.* About this emendation he said:

> To make this fruitful, when I was sixty-eight years of age on the full moon day of the fourth month, *Saga Dawa*, of the Iron Pig year, I edited and completed this. I also wrote supplemental sadhanas connected to this cycle.

13. At the age of sixty-nine on the tenth day of the *Drozhin* month in the Water Horse year at his Darjeeling residence, Namdröl Khangzang, His Holiness composed *All-Pervading Activity*. The text is an emendation of the *Secret Practice of the Peaceful and Wrathful Embodiment of Samantabhadra's Mind* revealed by Pema Lingpa, with additions from the authentic lineage teachings of other great masters. Kyabje said:

> Ngagpa Tendzin Kunleg, who came from the medicine valleys of the south[237] and was devoted to the lineage of Pema Lingpa, requested me to edit an easy-to-follow and correct version, saying that it will be very beneficial for all the Pema Lingpa lineage. He urged me again and again to do this.
>
> Recently the yogi Orgyen Tsering from Trin-gon Sangngag Chöling Monastery in Parti in Himachel Pradesh, India, also urged me to finish this work and offered to sponsor its publication as soon as it was completed. As requested, I wrote it.

This is a brief presentation, and those interested in more details can consult the collection of Kyabje's own works.

105

> Heart drop of India and Tibet's past vidyadharas,
> Profound kama and terma's wish-fulfilling jewel,
> You raised high on the victory banner of the three wheels,
> Fulfilling the two benefits for all who wished.

106

> Orgyen Rinpoche, only refuge of dark times, how great!
> Great is your wisdom and compassion, unfailing protector.
> Protector, by your three secrets, as earth and sky upheld,
> Upheld are these times by you, Jigdral, fearless hero.

107

> Ganges' pure water, streaming from past tertöns,
> Its course muddied by unskilled imitators,
> You set right through three unerring modes of thought,
> Preserving the ter-nying teachings as foretold.

108

Time after time, from glacial heights of kama and terma, scholars and
  siddhas—like Nyang, Gur, Rong, Long [238]—flowed,
Deepest of deep dharma, water of eight qualities, vehicle to the rainbow
  body in one life.
Again and again, streams of your heart-wishes, brimming with empowerments, pith advice, commentaries,
In place after place, watered fields of lucky beings, where the two siddhis
  bloomed and swayed in soft rippling waves.

109

> In life after life, you, Protector,
> As buddhas and buddhas' heirs counseled,
> That, exactly that, you fully did.
> "Good! Good!"—the song breaks out everywhere.

This completes the eighth heap of lightbeams of how he preserved and
spread the teachings of the ancient great tertöns by empowerment, transmission, and pith instruction, and, in addition, by emending those that had
been misinterpreted.

*His Holiness Dudjom Rinpoche underneath an orange tree
in Santa Monica, California, in 1983*

THE NINTH HEAP OF LIGHTBEAMS:

*the final activities of the precious nirmanakaya that terminate
where all phenomena are exhausted in the true nature*

In January of 1985 during an extended stay at his center in Dordogne, His Holiness asked his wife, Sangyum Kuzhok, "When is the moon coming full?" The Sangyum answered, "In a few more days." That evening he thoroughly and repeatedly performed the dharmapala and aspiration prayers. Later that evening in conversation with her he said, "I have well completed what was mine to do regarding the Buddha's teachings in general and the Nyingma teachings in particular. Henceforward, there is no need for me to do prayers and offerings to the dharmapalas, so please don't put any more offerings into the bowls." She said, "Why are you acting with such a small mind?" On another occasion he said, "Now I've completed all the aspiration and dedication prayers for the well-being of those connected to me. For the living I've prayed that their lives be long, that they have prosperity and good health. For those who have passed on, I prayed that their negative deeds be purified. Therefore, I have no regrets about leaving anything unfinished." And he continued, "Generally, if gifts offered with devotion are accepted and then not used to do the prayers and good deeds that have been requested, this is wrong livelihood and will impede development and progress on the path in this and future lives. Recognize that all samsaric activities are a dream, a display of magic, and with this understanding reduce grasping and clinging. Always keep this in your heart and never forget the four renunciations, devotion, pure perception, and bodhichitta. Give your heart to Guru Rinpoche, seeing him as the embodiment of all the objects of refuge. Realize that all of phenomenal existence is the three-kaya mandala of the glorious guru." All these instructions he gave in casual conversations.

110

 All-pervading lineage lord, lama supreme!
 Supreme teachings, all beings you helped, to the end,
 Ending in Copper-Glory Mountain, when done with life.
 Life-long dakini[239] heard you speak thus at parting time:

111

 "Bringing fruitful harvests of benefits to beings,
 Swift as lightning, dharmapalas, you act. Yet, no more
 Need I make daily and special prayers and offerings.
 Now, let the ritual bowl and plate rest a while.

112

 "For Buddha's teachings and the Nyingma lineage,
 Whatever was decreed, now I have completed that.
 Likewise, for the living and dead who relied on me,
 I left no dedication or blessing prayers unsaid.

113

 "Ill-using dharma gifts from the living and dead,
 Not keeping in mind their good and proper use,
 Makes irresistible wealth a heavy yoke.
 When life is done, how dry the desert. Alas, woe!

114

 "All wealth given out of devotion,
 Don't forget to seal with prayers for the living and dead,
 When giving, think of the three jewels,
 And you and others will always benefit, no doubt.

His Holiness Dudjom Rinpoche

115

> "All inner, outer displays of samsara,
> Not lasting, not forever—illusion's play—
> Though arising within vast, open freedom,
> Lure the mind with fond grasping, time after time.

116

> "All samsara and nirvana, one together,
> In primordial emptiness, is the sphere of peace;
> Yet constancy's queen, the law of interdependence,
> Karma's illusory rule, never should be breached.

117

> "Impossible to measure all of samsara.
> Impossible to know how long life will last.
> Impossible to tell where joy or sorrow starts.
> Impossible to undo the laws of karma.

118

"Now your life in the body, now what you do,
This double mirror of your past and future,
Shows why you should benefit self and others
And keep turning your mind to deeds of virtue.

119

"Fortune and misfortune, gain and loss,
Rise and fall, all meeting and parting:
Samsara's dancers dancing. This play,
Duality's child, take not for truth.

120

"In three realms, dark clouds are lit by falsity's lightning.
Birth, old age, sickness, death, thunder loud, always in bloom.
Unwelcome hail of sufferings rains down. Even so,
Birth, death, these are dream's children: from the beginning, naught.

121

"All joys and sorrows are mind's false illusions.
Mind itself is like a barren woman's child.
Thus, what happens, all forms and colors, are jokes.
Relax in vast great bliss, free of contrivance.

122

"Keep devotion and selfless bodhichitta in your heart,
Guard your three doors with mindfulness, alertness, modesty,
Strive to offer and share the magical display of wealth,
Do what you intended, and you will never have regrets.

123

"Bodhichitta: without it, the heart of dharma is lost.
Pure perception: without it, the root of tantra rots.
Deep devotion: without it, visions and siddhis shrivel.
Strong confidence: without it, the two aims are trampled down.

124

> "On the lama, sole refuge and wish-fulfilling jewel, set
> On your crown, meditate with heart's unfailing devotion.
> Whatever arises, see as the lama's mandala,
> And the creation stage will perfectly awaken.

125

> "The lama, supreme refuge, source of all good qualities,
> Beyond is and is not, inside and outside, yay and nay,
> Within the nondual clarity of wisdom's innate light,
> When seen as self nature, the completion stage is upon you.

126

> "From true nature, unmarred by thought or effort, what arises
> Arises innately from its origins as emptiness.
> Emptiness and what arises are not two, truth is thus.
> Thus, creation and completion are one in the lama.

127

> "All the words of the buddhas and lineage lamas
> Hold in the pistil core of your heart without fail.
> Then, in the pure land of Copper-Glory Mountain
> We will meet in the mandala of no more parting."

Guru Dewa Chenpo, the Buddha of Great Blissfulness

One evening in that same time period while still in Dordogne his eyes gazed widely into space, and he stopped speaking. His behavior seemed to indicate that he was making preparations to depart for the Pure Land. At that moment great dakini Sangyum Kuzhok and the family members and disciples who were present were overwhelmed with sadness and speaking through tears requested in one voice, "Please don't enter nirvana. What ceremonies should we do to keep you here with us?" He replied, "I'm a wayfarer already on the road. There's no need for ceremonies now." Again all his students, particularly Sangyum Kuzhok, said, "Kathmandu is your main residence; most of your disciples are in Asia; therefore, it's there you must return. Recognize this, and don't go just yet." She repeated this insistently. He said, "Once a traveler is on the road, it is difficult to turn back. However, if you wish, you can all do the brief reversing ceremony from *Heart Drop of the Dakini*." When he said that, everyone was trying to find the text. Their minds were agitated, and they were unsuccessful. His Holiness raised himself up in his bed, extended his hand, and said, "Give me the book." Immediately he pulled out the text and gave it to them. At this juncture the Western doctors, who had been called when the episode began, now arrived and began their examination. He was rushed to the hospital nearby.

As this news spread to all parts of the world, Nyingma centers, East and West, began doing the long-life ceremonies indicated by Sangyum Kuzhok. Khenchen Palden Sherab Rinpoche and I, Khenpo Tsewang Dongyal, and his American disciples, from the East Coast to the West Coast, began doing prayers: *Spontaneously Fulfilling All Wishes*, *Prayer That Removes All Obstacles*, Tara prayers, and in particular lots of Vajrasattva practice, *Long-Life Practice of the Tantra*, and *Long-Life Practice of the Sutra*. Back into the ocean we released many thousands of fish ransomed from the fish markets. After a few days His Holiness came back home from the hospital.

He had been ready to completely release his life force and to direct his intention to the pure Glorious Copper-Color Mountain of Guru Rinpoche, but for the benefit of his students, especially Sangyum Kuzhok, he reinvigorated his compounded elements and remained, but in that state where all phenomenal conceptions are exhausted in the dharmakaya.[240] To the disciples who had the opportunity to visit him during that time, he smiled and said simply, "Are you okay?" Otherwise he didn't engage in conversation. Whenever he saw an image of Guru Rinpoche, he immediately placed it on his head and said, "This traveler is taking a long time to return." In this way he fulfilled the wishes of those who requested that he remain, and at the same time awakened in those who were grasping to substantiality, a vivid understanding of renunciation.

128

> When fields of disciples in all directions
> Were ripe with nectar of the two benefits,
> Then the mandala of your form body
> Began turning toward dharmakaya space.

129

> From your face with millions of major and minor marks,
> Joyful eyes of sun and moon looked skyward,
> While red and white channel breath-winds gathered
> To unite in the invisible central channel.[241]

130

> Then, vajra consort, children, disciples, all
> Distressed, and weighed down by heavy sadness, said:
> "Che ma! Buddha Padma's regent that you are,
> How could you do this without thinking of us?

131

> "Arya, through birth and death's illusory dance
> You came to certainty of vast unborn space.
> For us, unprotected ones, holding to dreams,
> Stay a while longer. Protector, please remain."

132

> Everyone, a chorus of distress,
> Hands raised to the crown chakra,
> Let streams of tears rain down while
> Whispering in the Protector's ear.

133

> Noble, compassionate protector of beings,
> Your face, a sublimely beautiful mandala,
> Your eyes, gazing all the while with loving-kindness,
> Your voice, the sound that liberates. Thus, you spoke:

134

    "Through the body's impermanent aggregates,
    All beings in every place, without exception,
    I helped toward lasting good, without hope of reward.
    Now is the time to let go of everything.

135

    "Youthful in naked awareness, beyond birth and death,
    A meditation master, beyond now and after,
    On samsara and nirvana's stage, beyond good and evil,
    I will leap to the dance, past dark veils, beyond all hope and fear.

136

    "I, the envoy who fulfilled great aims,
    Cannot be kept by anything
    From joining Padma yab yum's feast
    And enjoying the heroes' welcome!

137

    "Since I cannot withhold from you what you ask,
    The dakinis' profound heart-drop terma,
    Ritually asking them to withhold welcome,
    Prepare, each of you to do it right now!"

This is a brief explanation of His Holiness's last activities in his precious nirmanakaya body in this world, including his dwelling in the state where all phenomena are exhausted. Thus the ninth heap of lightbeams is concluded.

Golden stupa containing the relics of the
dharmakaya body of His Holiness Dudjom Rinpoche

THE TENTH HEAP OF LIGHTBEAMS:

H.H. Dudjom Rinpoche's dharmakaya mind enters the dharmadhatu, the beneficial effects of his kudung, and its installation in the golden stupa for the benefit of generations to come

Early in the morning of the eighteenth day of the eleventh month of the Fire Tiger year, TRE 2113, January 17, 1987, his dharmakaya mind merged with the dharmakaya mind of Samantabhadra Guru Padmasambhava. At that moment outside and inside the house many shimmering rainbow lights appeared, celestial music sounded, and the delicious fragrance of incense pervaded.

138

Alas, alas, glorious lama, sun,
Sunk in dharmakaya sleep, in the west.
All beings in the dream world of samsara
Are once more enveloped by dark ignorance.

139

Lord Lama, treasure of compassion,
Beyond eye's reach of duality's child
For now your body is folded away,
How hard is this for the small child's mind.

140

Alack, alas! Lord of wisdom and compassion,
Buddha and the second buddha's regent, you were both.
In troubled times, troubled beings are unaided.
Putting us out of mind, out of sight you went. How sad.

141

In dharmakaya sky, beyond thought, dawns the good,
Spontaneous, boundless, nirmanakaya rainbow:
Ever-expanding arc of good deeds helping beings.
Now, once again, dharmakaya space enfolds it.

142

In vast sky, dancers' stage of beginningless space,
Self-reciting vajra songs never cease humming.
Every possible sweet and delicious fragrance,
Within, without, wafts, rippling, rippling, everywhere.

143

As you entered the dharmakaya womb,
All at once, without anyone's urging,
The continents and mountains, the whole earth
Seemed, for a moment, in peace, to stand still.

144

> In the sky of ordinary mind,
> Thick storm clouds of misery gather.
> Tears of sadness, strong torrents,
> Pour down faces, as earth, drenched.

145

> Then, the children, students, and others, all
> Their wet faces trembling with tearful mist,
> In hoarse, choked tones, together in one voice
> Prayed, meditating on the two stages.

Complying with French law, the authorities were immediately informed of his passing, and when they arrived, were astonished to witness his glowing complexion and the flexibility of his body free of rigor mortis. Dakini Sangyum Kuzhok notified the author of this biography by phone. He then called Kyabje's students in the New York area, and together they did Vajrasattva practice.

His Holiness stayed in the meditation state for about fifteen days, and his body became the size of an eight-year-old boy. It was agreed that the ancient Tibetan technique of packing the body in salt for its preservation should be used.

During the forty-nine days following Kyabje's mahaparinirvana, Dungse Shenphen Dawa, Nyoshul Khen Rinpoche Jamyang Dorje, Taklung Tsetrul Pema Wangyal, Rahor Khenpo Thubten, Chogtrul Rangdröl, Parti Tulku, and the author of this biography, together with many Western students, all did the offering ceremony of Vajrasattva to the dharmakaya kudung. These ceremonies were beautifully conducted by Lama Karpo and Namdröl Zangpo of Bhutan who took responsibility to be *umdze* (chant master) and *chopön* (shrine master) respectively. His Holiness Dilgo Khyentse Rinpoche and Sogyal Rinpoche attended to pay their respects to Kyabje. Sakyong Mipham Rinpoche led a delegation representing Vidyadhara Chögyam Trungpa and the Dharmadhatu organization. Gyatrul Rinpoche, Venerable Guru Lau, Lama Rinchen Phuntsok, and many of their students also attended. His Holiness the Dalai Lama sent representatives, as did other schools and subschools of Tibetan Buddhism. From all over the world many of his disciples came to southern France and participated in these extensive ganachakra offering ceremonies.

On the last days of the forty-nine-day period everyone circumambulated his residence, the location of his dharmakaya kudung, and chanted the mantra of Guru Padmasambhava as a beautiful light rain fell. In the salt many different sizes and colors of relic pills appeared.

The disciples from many different countries, such as Nepal, Sikkim, Ladakh, France, and Bhutan, wanted to keep his dharmakaya kudung in their own countries. They wrote many letters requesting this honor, all of them appealing to the fact that he was their principal teacher. Keeping the body of such a highly realized being, according to the tantra teachings, will benefit the earth and its inhabitants in general and in particular will balance the energy of the country in which it resides. All the letters came, and finally Sangyum Kuzhok decided that because it had been his last principal residence and he had established a monastery there, his relics should be installed in a golden stupa and kept in Nepal.

To accommodate this stupa they decided to enlarge and beautify his monastery. Sangyum Kuzhok, therefore, opened the door of great generosity. Under the direction of great mahasiddha Chatral Rinpoche and with the assistance of Ngagchang Khetsun Zangpo, renowned thangka painter Phuntsok Zangpo (His Holiness Dudjom Rinpoche's personal artist), and dharma patron Ang Tamdrin Sharpa, along with many others, a much bigger and more beautiful temple was constructed. At the same time under the close supervision and instruction of Kyabje Chatral Rinpoche, very expert Nepalese craftsmen were called to build a gold-plated copper stupa, six feet tall with many engravings and inset with many precious and semi-precious stones, including *zi*.[242]

After all the preparations and necessary arrangements had been completed, on the full moon day of the twelfth month of the Earth Dragon year, TRE 2115, January 21, 1989, the dharmakaya kudung departed the

Paris airport and arrived the next day, the sixteenth day of the twelfth month, January 22, 1989, at the Kathmandu airport in Nepal. The kudung was received by Kyabje Chatral Rinpoche, Kyabje Dilgo Khyentse Rinpoche, Kyabje Trulshik Rinpoche, and many other great teachers, tulkus, ngagpas, khenpos, monks and nuns, and male and female lay practitioners. Devotees of monasteries of the Nyingma, Kagyu, and Sakya schools had arranged big receptions and parades with musicians, dancers, children in costumes, and people in traditional dress (Sherpa, Bhutanese, Tibetan, and Nepalese) waving colorful banners. In all, tens of thousands of people participated. Filled with great joy and appreciation, they lined both sides of the road from the airport to the monastery, holding white scarves, incense, and flowers, reciting mantras and prayers on their malas. Originally it had been arranged to have the precious kudung carried by elephant, but the box was too large, so the procession proceeded by motor vehicle led by an elephant.

Yellow-robed monks and white-robed ngagpas, blazing with the three-vajra realization[243] combined with devotion and joy, received Kudung Rinpoche and placed it in his monastery, Orgyen Dongak Chökhorling. Everyone made offerings and touched their heads to the body case.

146

> Jigdral, Lake-Born Buddha's regent in these dark times;
> Yeshe Dorje, a light for deluded beings;
> Supreme Lama; once that peaceful sleep befell,
> Everywhere, heart disciples humbly petitioned.

147

> Alas! Peerless Protector,
> Though your form-body is gone,
> Your dharmakaya relics,
> Each begs, should rest in his land.

148

> Letters, each one a longing melody,
> From India, Nepal, Sikkim, Bhutan,
> Flew, as birds, with singular devotion,
> Again, again, coming before Sangyum.

149

> Then, long-life dakini-consort chose
> Hospitable Nepal, from the rest.
> Since that had been the protector's home,
> She decreed his relics should rest there.

150

> Source of merit for gods and men,
> Revered dharmakaya relics:
> For this precious body's resting place,
> A splendid new temple was decreed.

151

> First among the protector's heart disciples,
> Bright shining light of the Dzogchen teachings,
> Great siddha Chatral Sangye Dorje, with
> Yogis and yoginis, prayed and blessed the site.[244]

152

> From within the bright clarity of three vajras,[245]
> Blessing earth, invoking earth's blessings, they broke ground
> There; for visible and invisible beings
> To enjoy, they celebrated ritual feasts.

153

> Afterward, all the world's finest craftsmen
> Seemed to come together as one body,
> All applying their skills with devotion,
> To raise this temple to the three jewels.

154

> Three stories high, supremely beautiful,
> Beautiful with relics of body-speech-mind,
> Beautiful within and without, a delight,
> This temple was built to shape, beautiful.

155

> Then the resplendent dharmakaya relics,
> Surrounded by brocades, silks, spices, and jewels,
> Hundreds of thousands of rich offering clouds,
> Reposed in the sky ship's heavenly expanse.

156

> This great flying iron-winged whale filled space
> With thousands of dragons' roars and fiery whirlwinds.
> An iron bird, this sky mansion, swifter than wind,
> Landed from western skies on eastern earth.

157

> There, fortunate tens of thousands waited,
> Crying with joy and sorrow for the relics,
> With hundred thousand signs of deep devotion,
> They begged to keep the monastery's relics.

*Everyone is amazed by the visions of spheres and other miraculous images seen
in the space near the golden stupa of His Holiness Dudjom Rinpoche.*

Soon after, at the request of Kyabje Dilgo Khyentse, the precious kudung
was taken to Zhechen Monastery. Then the king, ministers, and subjects of
Bhutan requested that the kudung be transported to Paro, Bhutan. On a
plane commissioned by the royal family, the dharmakaya relics were sent on
the eighteenth day of the twelfth month of the Earth Dragon year, TRE
2115, January 24, 1989. King Jigme Senge Wangchuk, all the queens, the
Royal Grandmother, Azhe Phuntsok Chödrön, the Royal Mother, Azhe
Kalzang, many dragshuls,[246] khenpos, tulkus, lamas, ngagchangs,[247]
gomchen,[248] tsünma,[249] lineage holders, practitioners, and so forth totaling
hundreds of thousands of individuals received the kudung with great honor
and respect. Then for a week they made elaborate ganachakra offerings.

On the twenty-fifth day of the twelfth month, February 1, 1989, the
kudung was returned on the royal airplane to Kathmandu where it was

His Holiness Dudjom Rinpoche

His Holiness Dudjom Rinpoche, Jigdral Yeshe Dorje

Her Eminence the Dudjom Sangyum Kuzhok Rigdzin Wangmo

The face of Kudung Rinpoche seen through the glass in the golden stupa

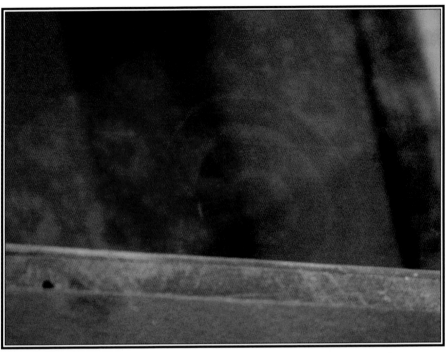

Rainbowlike spheres of light appeared in the center of this monastery window outside the golden stupa of His Holiness Dudjom Rinpoche.

Disciples, including Kyabje Chatral Rinpoche, witness the miraculous visions.

His Holiness Dudjom Rinpoche and Dudjom Sangyum Rigdzin Wangmo

*The great self-born blissfulness is **fearless** of the four demons.*
*One's own **primordial wisdom** of self-awareness, which is without*
*gathering and parting, is the innate nature, the great **vajra** holder*
of the absolute truth, which brings forth the blessings of perceiving
everything as the pure, divine mandala.

Spontaneous poem in His Holiness Dudjom Rinpoche's own blessed handwriting (above),
containing a condensed teaching which expresses the essence of his name

Rainbowlike spheres of light and a vision of Tso Pema
appeared in the center of this monastery window.

again received with great honor at the airport. Then it was taken to the
Orgyen Dongak Chökhorling and installed in the golden stupa. The lord of
the yogis, Kyabje Chatral Rinpoche, and the crown jewel of all the scholars
and siddhas, Kyabje Dilgo Khyentse Rinpoche, together with many great
lamas and tulkus, the two assemblies, and devotees from all over the world,
with devotion and meditation made offering to the golden stupa of
Kudung Rinpoche for forty-nine days. During this time many people perceived beautiful rainbow light and spheres of light outside and inside the
monastery. Within the spheres many saw buddhas and bodhisattvas and
Kyabje's image in various sizes amidst beautiful landscapes of lakes and
mountains. They were seen by both the renowned and unrenowned alike.
Everyone was amazed, and in their hearts the unshakable devotion was
established that brings ultimate benefit.

158

Wonder of wonders, these blessed relics!
Land after land dispatched its envoys,
Each one, for each country's sake, begging
Again, again, that the relics come there.

159

Dilgo Khyentse—Guru Rinpoche's regent—
And Rabjam Tulku[250] made heart decrees that
The relics come to Zhechen Monastery
And confer on all glorious blessings.

160

As samsara and nirvana's sun, the relics,
Moved vibrant rays of compassion and love
Over mind's ocean of the good people of Bhutan,
How could wondrous nirmanakaya play not shine?

161

Bhutan's king, queen, their family, ministers,
Abbots, tulkus, clergy, yogis, yoginis,
Others, all stirred by joy and devotion,
Made ocean clouds of Kuntuzangpo offerings.

162

Lucky men and women, none excluded,
Felt base iron of body, speech, and mind
Turning into gold through the alchemy of blessings,
As the relics returned to Nepal's monastery.

163

    These relics, a wish-fulfilling jewel,
    Crowned the banner of three devotions.
    Each worldly and spiritual wish,
    As it came to mind, was fulfilled.

164

    Living disciples wherever they are,
    All those seeking the path of lasting joy:
    Even though your body has passed away,
    Still you help them. Who but you could do this?

165

    Good, good, these precious dharmakaya relics:
    Each place, each time they came among the faithful,
    Many, many of those still needing help were helped.
    Never, never, was there a protector like you.

166

    Khen Lob Chö, lords of the three buddha families,
    Whose fame reaches beyond samsara and nirvana:
    In the place they first formed their karmic connection,
    A perfect stupa still stands. Seen once, it liberates.

167

    Circled by mountains, majestic garlands,
    Is a nation in step with modern times:
    Nepal, between India and Tibet,
    Is dharma's central land in this dark age.

168

Then, the relics revered by gods and men,
The very same as the dharmakaya,
Emanating thousands of blessings,
Were enthroned in the golden stupa.

169

Protector and regent of Padma Buddha,
Dilgo Khyentse—Terchen Lama—along with
Rich lord of siddhas, Sangye Dorje, and
Many great aryas, all gathered at once.

170

Bhikshus aglow in lustrous red-gold light,
Yogis resplendent in red and white robes,
Two revered assemblies like sun, moon, stars,
With thousands of lights of four visions, shone.

171

From vast depths of oceans of past merit,
Generous patrons, never faint hearted,
Heaped up inexhaustible waves of wealth:
Kuntuzangpo's offering clouds filling space.

172

Vajra meditation, intensely still mountain,
Vajra awareness, vast gleaming tides of mist,
Vajra sounds, tones weaving high and low, along with
Vajra of body-speech-mind, infinite love.

173

Perfectly, on the face of an expansive sky,
Perfectly distinct large and small rainbow circles
Perfectly mirror the peaceful-wrathful three roots.
Perfectly, they bless happy and lucky beings.

174

    Unending vajra chain of profound awareness,
    Self clarity: through secret paths of the six lamps,
    All inherently perfect aspects of clear light
    Are seen, with ease and no meditation, through you.

175

    Guru yab yum, vidyadharas, king and subjects,
    Ocean of heroes, dakinis, dharmapalas,
    In a shimmering rainbow, through compassion and
    Wisdom came happily there. No doubt about that.

This is how his dharmakaya mind entered dharmadhatu, the beneficial activity of his kudung, and its taking residence in the golden stupa for the benefit of future beings; and with this brief account the tenth heap of light-beams is concluded.

His Holiness Dudjom Rinpoche

THE ELEVENTH HEAP OF LIGHTBEAMS:
a brief list of his disciples

Through his kindness, the sunshine of his teaching, many lotus blossoms bloomed in the Buddhist garden—numerous disciples, who had the capability to mature themselves and others, who upheld the general Buddhist teaching, particularly the Nyingma, throughout the world. Students so numerous came that it is difficult to list them all. According to the capability of my knowledge some are listed here, beginning with Dilgo Khyentse Rinpoche Rabsal Dawa and Chatral Rinpoche Sangye Dorje Trogyal Dorje,[251] and Dodrubchen Rinpoche, Palyul Pema Norbu,[252] Trulshik Rinpoche, eleventh Minling Trichen Kunzang Wangdu, and continuing with Minling Chen Gyurme Khyentse Norbu, Minling Chung Gyurme Ngagwang Chökyi Dragpa, Kangyur Rinpoche Longchen Yeshe Dorje, Dungse Thinley Norbu, Dungse Shenphen Dawa, Yogi Trulshik Dorje, Yardrok Taklung Tsetrul, Kathok Zhingchong Tulku, Kathok Önpo Tulku, Dzogchen Tulku, Palyul Chogtrul, Palyul Dzongnang Tulku, Dorje Drag Rigdzin Chenmo, Dorje Drag Chuzang, Zhechen Rabjam Tulku, Serdung Khachöd Tulku, Sera Drubde, Chogtrul Jigme Kunkhyab Dorje, Tulku Jigme Chöying Norbu Döndrub, Khokhyim Tulku, Gyurme Yönten Gyatso, Kathok Bero Tulku, Gönjang Tulku, Tsike Chokling, Namnying Tulku, tenth and eleventh Peling Sungtrul (Pema Ösel Gyurme Dorje and Kunzang Pema Rinchen Namgyal, respectively), Sogtse Tulku, Chungdzong Degyal Tulku, Chungdzong Tulku Lama Tsewang, Sogyal Tulku, Chagdud Tulku, Tarthang Tulku Kunga Deleg, Gyatrul Rinpoche, Powo Bakha Tulku, Gangteng Tulku Kunzang Pema Namgyal, Lachen Tulku, Lachung Tulku Chödor Nyima, Özer Tulku, Taklung Tsetrul Pema Wangyal, Khyentrul Jigme, Chogtrul

Rangdröl, Golok Sertha Tulku, Khordong Tertrul Chime Rigdzin, Tulku Thondup, Ladakh Chöje Tulku, Golok Tulku, Ritrul Rigdzin Chögyal, Dakong Tulku, Tulku Garab, Tulku Jampal, Orgyen Chemchok Düpa Tsal, Kharchen Rinpoche, Ladakh Nono Rinpoche, and so forth are all the tulkus who were his disciples.

Polo Khenchen Dorje Kunga Gyaltsen, Nyoshul Khenchen Jamyang Dorje, Golok Khenchen Thubten Tsondrü, Doshul Khenchen Palden Sherab, Mewa Khenchen Thubten, Khenpo Pema Sherab, Khenpo Tsewang Gyatso, Khenpo Rigdzin Dorje, Riche Daza Khenpo Sönam Tobgyal, Ngari Khen Yeshe Zangpo, Khen Thubten Norbu, Sangyum Kuzhok Tsedzin Khandro Rigdzin Wangmo, Shugseb Jetsün Tulku, Rigdenma Sherab Tseten Yudrön, Semo Dechen, Dodrub Khandro Dechen, Pashö Könchog Chödrön, Kongpo Bhaga Ani, Rahor Khenpo Thubten, Menyag Khenpo Pema Rabgye, Khenpo Thubchö, Golok Khenpo Dazer, and Khenpo Drugchung are great khenpos upholding the kama and terma and nine-yana teaching in the world.

Then Tertön Pegyal Lingpa, Lhodrag Tertön, and Tertön Namkha' Drime were his disciples. Riwoche Ngagchang Lama Tsewang Lhagyal, Rebkong Ngagchang Sherab Dorje, Lobpon Norbu Lama, Rebkong Ngag-chang Dönden, Riwoche Ngagchang Könchog Jungne, Gazha Ngagchang Naro, Ngagchang Kadag, Ngagchang Dawa Chödrag, Ngagchang Orgyen Tendzin, Golok Drubla Yeshe Rabsal, Doshul Ngagchang Lama Dorje Namgyal, Drubtsön Lama Rigzang Dorje, Doshul Gelong Lama Chimed Namgyal, Ngagchang Lama Tharchin, Troga Tulku, Lama Gyurdrag, Ngagchang Khetsun Zangpo, Tulku Dawa, Mön Ngagchang Lama Nagpo Pema Wangchen, Mön Ngagchang Lama Karpo, Mön Ngagchang Nying-khula, Mön Ngagchang Lobpon Pema Longdröl, Mön Shingkhar Lama, Lama Kudre Chödrag Gyaltsen, Mön Gelong Sangye, Mön Gelong Karpo, Mön Gelong Namdröl Zangpo, Lama Kunzang Wangdu, Drejong Chög-yal Palden Döndrub, Gyetön Tsewang Paljor, Mije Tsewang Rigdzin, Kazi Sönam Tobgyal, Shar Khumbu Tengpoche Tulku, De-u Rinpoche, Dza-trul, Dragtrul, Nagtrul, Ja Lama Sönam Chökyi Gyaltsen, Riwoche Lama Rinchen Phuntsok, Lowo Mentang Ngagchang Chimed, Gazha Sinthang Ngagchang Changchub, Parti Lama Kunzang, and Yölmo Lama Dawa were disciples. This is a brief listing of the disciples from the Nyingma School of Tibetan Buddhism.

Then the twelfth Drugchen Pema Wangchen, Khenchen Thrangu Tulku, Dorje Lobpön Tenga Tulku, Nenang Pawo, Palpung Wöngen, Palpung Beru Khyentse, Ladakh Togden, Ladakh Tagna, Drigung Yudra Tulku, Dazang Tulku, Tulku Chökyi Nyima, Je Khenpo Kunleg of Bhutan, and Gomchen Sönam Zangpo are some of the principal disciples from the Kagyu School.

Then Dzongsar Khyentse Thubten Chökyi Gyatso, Chögye Trichen, Trarig Tulku, Dongthog Tulku Tenpai Gyaltsen, Dzongsar Gona Tulku, Sakya Khenchen Sangye Tendzin, and Khenchen Rinchen are the principal disciples from the Sakya School.

Radring Kyabgön and Kundeling Tatsag Jedrung are some of his disciples from the Gelugpa School.

176

> Bringing scripture and realization to new heights,
> Raising the banner of study and meditation,
> Supreme captains, all guides to freedom,
> Lineage masters, the world's safeguard.

177

> On the ground of stainless morality,
> Unwavering mountain of samadhi,
> Unobscured clear eye of wisdom:
> To those who reached this, I bow from the heart.

H.H. Dudjom Rinpoche's students hailed from central and eastern Tibet, Ladakh, Bhutan, Sikkim, Nepal, India, China, Southeast Asia, Europe, and America. Due to the biographer's lack of knowledge and the time to complete the research, this is but a partial list of his students. Those seeking a more exhaustive record must consult other histories and biographies. With this listing, the eleventh heap of lightbeams and this biography are completed.

His Holiness Dudjom Rinpoche

VERSES DEDICATING THE MERIT
OF THIS COMPOSITION

178

By the merit of this composition,
May those lost in deserts of delusion,
Find the sure, secret, vajrayana path,
Wherein the three kayas swiftly appear.

179

In the world, may sickness, famine, war, evil deeds,
All misfortunes of these dark times be pacified.
Through loving acts of compassion and good conduct,
May everyone have the wealth of seven treasures.

180

All Buddha's doctrine, especially the Nyingma,
Soars on the pure banner of study and insight,
Held high by you, Padma's regent and Terchen Lama.
May the whole earth be filled with others just like you.

181

Drunk with ego-clinging's poisoned elixir,
Seeds of peace and joy burned by the three poisons:
Muddled beings cannot tell right from wrong.
May aryas flood them with two benefits.

182

> Great lama, with Buddha's major and minor marks,
> You left long ago for Copper-Glory Mountain.
> More than ten years have passed, one by one, and still
> The glory of your life's story is hidden.

183

> Uniquely, from sacred depths of the dharma conch
> Came ceaseless sounds of liberating dharma,
> Translated into all languages everywhere.
> How sad, now these words are fading from sight, too.

184

> The lama's virtues, seeds sown in the three devotions,
> Warmed by faith, watered by wisdom and joyful effort:
> Wish-fulfilling vajra wisdom, unmarred by false claims,
> Now radiates two benefits through this unique tree.[253]

185

> Vajra master, through your kind acceptance of me,
> Vajra skills, through powers and words, were bestowed, yet
> Vajra of my three doors remaining unrealized,
> Vajra brethren, I, less in worth, more in shame, wrote this.

186

> Lord Lama, kind and gracious, you
> Spoke in nectar to me. But since
> My view of your vast, three secret virtues is small,
> This life story, for now, can be no more than this.

187

    A poor man, seeking to impress,
    Shows all his wealth, yet fails to please.
    Likewise, my biography of the lord lama
    Will hardly make any vajra brethren happy.

188

    Of Terchen Arya's virtues of love and kindness,
    Whoever writes with devotion the best he can
    For the sake of the two merits should not be blamed,
    Thus Buddha said. And so I wrote this for those like me.

189

    Although vast as sky are your three secrets,[254]
    Too small the aperture of my child's mind,
    Flawed my speech. Now, three roots, dharmapalas,
    Devout brothers and sisters, please forgive me!

190

    Of the outer, inner, and secret Terchen Lama,
    May a more clear, correct, and complete biography
    Be written by living heirs and dharma sons.
    I pray with folded hands for this to happen.

191

    May I, from now until enlightenment,
    Lord Lama, through your kind acceptance, do
    My utmost to please your body, speech, and mind, thus
    Fulfilling the aims of boundless teachings and beings.

192

Lord Lama, truly buddha, along with
Loving parents, kind teachers, and others,
All are mostly gone from sight and hearing.
Let pure detachment rise in my mind-stream.

193

Like bubbles, eighteen precious endowments;
Like goods for sale at market, all hoarded wealth;
Like a dream, the gathering of dear friends;
Like a whirlwind, mind never seen nor touched.

194

All the past a thing of memory.
All the present a flash of lightning.
All the future a scarecrow in dreams.
Always unsteady, samsara's deserts.

195

Constant inconstancy is the way of the world.
Again, again, though the lama's words were heard,
Hard, hard-headed hearers remained stone deaf.
Many, many good chances are almost all gone.

196

Through faith, joy, renunciation, and wisdom,
Pure study and practice of the precious teachings,
As well as holding, safeguarding, perfecting them,
May the whole rest of my life be meaningful.

197

Buddhahood—two benefits for self and others—
Comes about in only one way, without error:
Precious bodhichitta, the wish-fulfilling jewel,
May it always keep increasing, never decrease.

198

Like a sweet garland of pure golden mountains,
Root lineage lamas and all the buddhas:
Through constant and undoubting faith and
Strong devotion, may all blessings come.

199

Drawn by emotions, carelessly soiling
The white garments of samaya and vows,
May I cleanse them with trekchö and four powers
And have the strength fittingly to restore them.

200

Either from three samadhis or by meditation,
Within the emptiness form body of pure light,
Purifying habits of mind with four fixed nails.
May I transform all dharmas into three vajra states.

201

Within body's field, mandala of five chakras,[255]
As clear light moves in the right, left, and middle channels,
Clarity and wisdom, white and red streams reverse flow;[256]
May the four joys of empty bliss ripen and bloom.[257]

202

> Completely beyond categories of thought,
> Pure from the beginning, wisdom's deep bright peace:
> Within vast dharmakaya, free from yay and nay,
> May I perfect the no-focus completion stage.

203

> Pure from the beginning, wisdom's great peace,
> Unborn, unceasing true nature, unblocked,
> Rigpa's emptiness reaching past three times to the fourth:[258]
> Dharmakaya lama beyond thought, may I realize you.

204

> Innate energy, rigpa's unceasing vajra chain,
> Innate nature, clear light wisdom's body,
> Innate sounds, self-arising, pervasive:
> Innate sambhogakaya lama, may I realize you.

205

> From the impartial display of great compassion
> Arise ceaseless sparks of wisdom and kind loving,
> Two streams of benefits for beings, as needed,
> Nirmanakaya lama, may I realize you.

206[259]

> Through all lifetimes, may the feet of pure lineage lamas
> Never stop adorning my crown chakra of great bliss;
> Through strong faith, may my mind and the lama's become one,
> And fulfill all good wishes for heaps of the two aims.

207

> May the strong sun of the stainless Nyingma teachings,
> As long as ego-grasping stands against vast space,
> Emit bright rays of study and meditation,
> Filling three realms with lotus fields of benefits.[260]

208

> Through streams of love and compassion filling heart vases,
> May Buddhist teachings and practice spread everywhere.
> All lineage lamas who bring the two benefits,
> May their lotus feet be firm, their heart-wishes come true.

209

> May I, those close to me, and all mother-beings
> Be well, never sick, vigorous, never infirm,
> Enjoy life without death, wealth and fame without loss.
> May all good wishes always be richly fulfilled.

210

> May good fortune flow from the four-kaya buddhas.
> May good fortune flow from dharma, virtuous from first to last.
> May good fortune flow from sangha glorified by three trainings.
> May good fortune flow from the three jewels in three times.

211

> Ocean of three lineages, three roots, vidyadharas,
> Through your compassion, grant blessings and attainments.
> May beings pervasive as sky reach the rainbow body,
> All of them gaining buddhahood in one lifetime.

Padma Samye Ling in the summer of 2007

COLOPHON

Through the following circumstances and conditions, the man who had the fortune to be one of Kyabje's lesser disciples hailed from Dotöd Doshul Palrong, the region in eastern Tibet dominated by the holy Dokham Mount Tsaritra, which, among the twenty-one sacred glacier mountains of Tibet, Zhingchong Zegyal Mayo Gapa adopted as his domain. The naga protector Genyen Dorje Wangdrag Tsal, also known as Lugyal Dachong, enjoyed the smoothly flowing river known as Palchu. On the banks of that river, my father, Pang Gyalchog, the hidden yogi, who later received the full vinaya ordination and the name Pema Tsultrim, was born into the Pang clan, in which many scholars and siddhas of the old and new schools of Tibetan Buddhism had taken birth. My mother, Pema Lhadze, was born in the Mayang clan, renowned for its honesty, kindness, and gentility; for producing courageous warriors and eloquent public speakers; a family respected in all the villages of the eight and a half valleys of Doshul. These two kind parents provided me with the eighteen endowments and made sure I entered the gate of dharma.

I, the monk Tsewang Dongyal of the Ma-Pang clan, content with his life and health, completed this in the Buddhist Era 2546, the Guru Rinpoche Era 2542, the Tibetan Royal Era 2129 (Water Horse year, seventh month, early morning of the day when Guru Padmasambhava transformed into Khyeuchung Khading Tsal), Western Year 2002, August 17, at the naturally sacred location with its many forested mountains and flowering meadows, with various-sized birds singing beautiful songs, with various-sized animals moving about leisurely; at this land of excellent earth, excellent water, excellent wind, excellent vistas; at this place of many excellent dharma friends

The author with his brother, Khenchen Palden Sherab Rinpoche (right), and their father, Lama Chimed Namgyal (center), at Padma Samye Ling in 1999

who study, contemplate, meditate, and engage in other dharma activities as well, where support for such activities is always available, where not a single excellent hermitage quality ever praised by the gracious teacher Buddha and Guru Rinpoche and other great masters is missing; where above the beautiful meadows is the glorious Samye of America, Padma Samye Ling, Inconceivable Lotus Land, Glorious Copper-Color Mountain. Its second floor is the sambhogakaya temple of the sambhogakaya buddha, Thousand-Armed, Thousand-Eyed Avalokiteshvara, ever vigilant on behalf of all sentient beings. Here also is great mother Prajnaparamita and glorious Vajrasattva; protector and buddha of long-life Amitayus; Yamantaka, king of the wrathful deities; gracious Tara; and all the buddhas of the three roots represented as statues of various sizes. There are thangkas of great master Shantarakshita, Guru Padmasambhava, Dharma King Trisong Deutsen, the eight Medicine Buddhas, Thousand-Armed, Thousand-Eyed White Umbrella, Manjushri, Chenrezig, the sixteen Arhats. The *Kangyur* and *Tangyur*, heaps of the nine-yana teachings gloriously shining all over the world in many languages, now impartially fill this room. In this very place the biography was completed.

May the precious activities of study and recitation increase. May the peace and happiness of beings increase. May the two accumulations increase. May the life and health of myself and others increase. May this become the cause for ever-increasing realization, experience, and goodness of all sentient beings.

SARVA MANGALAM SHUBHAM GEO KUNTU TASHI!

There has never existed an ordinary sentient being who could explain fully the enlightened body, speech, mind, qualities, and activities of a buddha. From the ocean of outer, inner, and secret activities of the Lord Protector, according to my capability I have had the great fortune to explain no more than a dew drop. Without hesitation, in this book I compiled just a fraction of the stories related directly or indirectly to his life that I thought might in some degree benefit future, clear-sighted seekers of historical information regarding events inside and outside Tibet of this present time. Some readers devoted to His Holiness may think that I have added material not directly related to his life. Please, forgive this.

The very devoted and generous American practitioner Orgyen Chötso sponsored the publication of this book in order to commemorate the hundredth anniversary of His Holiness Dudjom Jigdral Yeshe Dorje, Garwang Drodul Lingpa Tsal, opening the major and minor marks of his lotus body on this planet earth. It is published by Pema Samye Chökhorling Nyingma Monastery of Deer Park, Varanasi, where the gracious teacher first kindled the light of the four noble truths and the teachings of nonviolence.

May it bring great benefit and auspicious circumstances to the planet.

*Dharma Protectors Ekajati, Mahakala, Dorje Legpa, Rahula,
Mahadeva Lhachin, Gyalpo Marutse*

Appendix 1: About the Chronology

De Lo ('*das lo*) or calculating time from the mahaparinirvana of the kind and gracious teacher, Lord Buddha

There are many different approaches for establishing the specific date of the parinirvana, and each of them arrives at a different result. Here I follow the chronological system of Sri Lanka, which is very well known today. According to that system Buddha entered parinirvana in 544 BCE on the Western calendar, that is, 2,546 years ago as of this writing in CE 2002.

Trung Lo (*khrung lo*) or calculating time from the birth of Guru Rinpoche

I used the above system for dating the mahaparinirvana as my foundation. In the life stories of Guru Rinpoche—and the many sutras and tantras that make reference to his birth—it is stated that he was born eight or twelve years after the mahaparinirvana in the Monkey year. I accepted the figure of eight years. In addition there is a "full count" (*hril lo*) and a "divided count" (*ched lo*) system for recording months and years. The former tabulates a year comprised of just over twelve full lunations. The latter considers the waxing half of the moon as one month, and the waning half as a second month. Just a little over twelve of these *ched-lo* months is tabulated as one year. Hence, a divided-count year is only half as long as the full-count year. I follow the position that states that the eight-year figure is arrived at using the *ched lo* system. Hence, in the *hril lo* system, the birth of Guru Rinpoche took place in a Monkey year, four years after the mahaparinirvana, that is, 540 BCE.

Gyal Lo (*rgyal lo*) or calculating time from the inception of the monarchy in Tibet, i.e., the Tibetan Royal Era (herein abbreviated as TRE)

Nyatri (*gnya' khri*) Tsenpo was the man who according to legend descended from the sky and was proclaimed Tibet's first king, the progenitor of the Yarlung Dynasty. As with the other two systems, there are many different arguments supporting this or that date for his enthronement. Without further analysis I simply accepted the calculation of the Astrological and Medical College of the Tibetan government-in-exile, which is 127 BCE.

In addition to these systems, which like the Western calendar calculate time based on the number of years elapsed since a particular significant event, there are two systems for determining dates based on a sixty-year cycle count. One of these is called *rabjung* (*rab 'byung*; Skt. prabha), which is derived from the name of the first year of the sexagenary cycle expounded in the Kalachakra Tantra. Because the Kalachakra was introduced into Tibet in 1027 CE, the first rabjung commenced in that year. The second rabjung began sixty years later in 1087 CE, the third in 1147 CE, and so on. We are currently in the seventeenth rabjung, which began in 1987 CE. Drogön Chögyal Phagpa was a renowned master of the Kalachakra and, as the tutor of Kublai Khan, is thought to have introduced the system in Mongolia. This system is also known as *kartsi* (*skar rtsis*), i.e., based on the constellations, or as the "white system" (*dkar rtsis*) of India. The other sixty-year count, very popular in Tibet, is called *jungtsi* (*'byung rtsis*), i.e., based on the elements. Because of its close resemblance to the Chinese system, it is also called the "black system" (*nag rtsis*) of China.[261] The jungtsi system designates each year in the cycle by one of the sixty combinations of the twelve animals with the five elements.

The Tibetan calendar is lunar based and the new year, losar, often falls in the Western month of February. The following list provides the names of the Tibetan months, starting with the first month of the year: (1) *mchu zla ba*; (2) *dbo zla ba*; (3) *nag pa zla ba*; (4) *sa ga zla ba*; (5) *snron zla ba*; (6) *chu stod zla ba*; (7) *gro bzhin zla ba*; (8) *khrums stod zla ba*; (9) *dbyug pa zla ba*; (10) *smin drug zla ba*; (11) *mgo zla ba*; (12) *rgyal zla ba*.

Appendix 2: An Essay on Tibetan Poetry

Prose and Verse in the Biography

Tibetan biographies of saints are written in verse (*tshigs bcad*), prose (*tshigs lhug*), or a combination of verse and prose (*spel ma*). Furthermore, verse can be either adorned (*snyan tshig*) or unadorned (*rang bzhin brjod pa'i rgyan*), that is, with or without rhetorical embellishments like word play, extended metaphors, and patterns of repeated words. There are no end rhymes in Tibetan verse. Khenpo's biography of His Holiness is a combination of verse and prose. All the poetry here is adorned. Saints' biographies are a highly stylized genre, in both form and content. For example, Khenpo's choice of eleven chapters, or *Heaps (tshom bu) of Lightbeams*, as discussed in the Introduction, symbolically represents His Holiness's life as fulfilling the eleven bhumis of the path to enlightenment, but it also makes the book an eleven-heap (*tshom bu*) mandala offering to His Holiness. All saints' lives reenact the outlines of Guru Padmasambhava's life, as told most completely in *The Life and Liberation of Padmasambhava*: a special birth, attended by miraculous signs; prodigious learning and skills at a young age; impressive teaching and other beneficial activities; the garnering of significant students; the display of miraculous abilities; a time of death predicted or chosen by oneself; and finally, a death and mahaparinirvana accompanied by miraculous signs.

In Tibetan texts of mixed prose and verse, the main part of the text may either be verse or prose. Often, in doctrinal and philosophical texts, the author writes both the root verses and a commentary on them, and the main text is considered the verses. In this biography, the prose is the central part of the text, while the poetry is threaded through to achieve other effects, such as embellishment and illustration. Included here are 211 four-line verses, written by Khenpo, each numbered within the text, and six songs written by His Holiness, all in the key sixth chapter, which is devoted to his beneficial activities on behalf of the six realms of beings. Khenpo's first twenty verses comprise the traditional homage that opens every work on the dharma. Groups of verses are included in every chapter, and the biography ends with the dedication verses, comprising the largest group of verses, thirty-four in all (178-211). Verses will be referenced parenthetically by their numbers within the text. Four verses have been included here (84, 91, 93, 127), which were excluded from the original Tibetan version of this biography.

Khenpo's verses are not merely ornamental, and they could stand on their own as an abbreviated biography of His Holiness's life. What function, then, do they serve in the prose text? Including verses is very traditional, but Khenpo's use of the interpolated verses is very modern. This biography, written as third-person narration, memorializes the life of a great contemporary spiritual master who touched the lives of many, but who was also Khenpo's root teacher, to whom Khenpo was personally devoted. Khenpo's verses give a personal voice to his deep love, veneration, and appreciation for His Holiness and His Holiness's teachings. Similarly, Khenpo uses His Holiness's songs as a vehicle to give the reader, who may never have met Dudjom or heard him speak, an immediate experience of the voice of this great master.

ON THE POETIC FORMS: VERSE AND SONG

The four-line stanza (*tshigs bcad rkang bzhi can de yang*) is the classic verse form in Tibetan poetry. While all the lines in a verse contain the same number of syllables, the lines can be as long as twenty-nine syllables, as in Khenpo's praise to the dharmapalas (18), or they can be as short as seven syllables, as in many of Khenpo's happiest and saddest verses, those on His Holiness's youth and the end of his life. The flexibility of the four-line verse makes it a perfect vehicle for poetic virtuosity of the kind Tibetans value, such as: doubling words at the beginning of lines, or at both the beginning and elsewhere (*zung ldan*) (13, 18, 67, 75, 93, 165, 195); or doubling words in each line, but not next to each other (*bar du chod pa'i zung ldan*) (53, 108, 140); or starting and ending a line with the same word (*bar du chod pa'i zung ldan*) (83); or starting a line with the same word that ended the previous line (*rkang pa'i thog mtha' la yod pa'i rjes 'khrid*) (106, 110, 126); or repeating a word or phrase in the same position in every line (7, 11, 73, 117, 172, 173, 185, 193, 195, 204, 210) (*kun tu zung ldan*); or making what we would call an acrostic (9, 74, 146). For example, Khenpo spells out His Holiness's name, Jigdral Yeshe Dorje ("Fearless Wisdom Indestructible"), in a verse (2) praising him as the embodiment of the dharmakaya, sambhogakaya, and nirmanakaya, by starting each of the first three lines with part of his name, and concluding with the epithet "[t]hree lineages' lama":

> Jigdral, unmoving from the dharmakaya,
> Yeshe, compassion beyond all times and directions,
> Dorje, powerful sign pointing to the perfect path:
> Three lineages' lama, at your feet I bow.

These effects are not fully translatable into English, because the parts of the name also always have ordinary meanings within the verse. In the example above, we spelled His Holiness's name out in Tibetan, but in the praise to Yeshe Tsogyal (9), we put her whole name in line 1 and used the ordinary meanings of her name in the other three lines (but not always as the first word). In the Yeshe Tsogyal verse, Khenpo indirectly praises her as the double emanation of Saraswati and Tara. By separating the parts of her name and using them in telling epithets, he is able both to name her and evoke her other aspects. In line 1 of the Tibetan, *yeshe* or "wisdom" alludes to Yeshe Tsogyal herself. In line 2, *mtsho* or "lake" alludes to both Yeshe Tsogyal and to Saraswati, since Saraswati's name in Sanskrit means "[l]ake-born essence (*mtsho byung dpyid*)." In line 3, *gyal* is part of the expression "the buddhas (*gyal kun*)." In line 4, Yeshe Tsogyal is praised by one of Tara's epithets, "swift heroine (*myur ma dpa' mo*)," which emphasizes her identity with Tara, the "great mother" of the buddhas, an identity which is underscored by the crescendo of "m" sounds here, leading to the final *ma* or "mother" toward the end of the last line.

Four-line verses can easily be strung together, as they are here, to sustain a narrative development or to write a doctrinal treatise, as in Shantideva's *A Guide to the Bodhisattva's Way of Life*. Unlike four-line verses, His Holiness's songs (*nyams mgur*) are considered the free-form poetry of a realized being. These songs have a more complex structure and movement than short verses. His Holiness's songs involve subtle shifts of voice, tone, mood, and meaning, and they move seamlessly from the traditional to the personal register. This happens even in a song of only one stanza, as in the case of His Holiness's first song, beginning "In Ogmin, in the midst of Copper-Glory Mountain's palace," where His Holiness's voice becomes increasingly personal, before dissolving into the universal mandala of all buddhas, bodhisattvas, and practitioners. Songs do not have any set number of lines, as in the four-line verses. The lines may also be long or short, but usually the whole song is written in lines of equal length. All His Holiness's songs have lines of equal length, except the last, but they do not all divide into stanzas.

Since Tibetan verse is written straight across the page just like prose, the only way stanzas in a long song can be demarcated is by the use of an opening or concluding refrain or a formulaic structure, repeated in stanza after stanza, as in His Holiness's song beginning "I, a silken lion, do not need a palace," where each of the five stanzas opens similarly. One cannot really speak of stanzas, however, in a song like His Holiness's second song, starting, "Primordially unchanging, innate nature of clear light," because, while the first part seems to divide into stanzas, the stanzaic structure is not maintained throughout.

The development in a song is very different from that in a single verse or a group of short verses. His Holiness has a superlative command of the Tibetan song, which he writes in distinctive and innovative ways. His songs, at their most intriguing, involve a unique kind of counterpointing, as in the song written to commemorate the building of a temple in Kongpo Buchu. This is really three different songs written in very different styles. The first is a traditional invocation of blessings; the second, in a more personal voice, uses His Holiness's favorite images of noble animals like the snow lion, to suggest that, just as the snow lion's turquoise mane "will surely brighten" in the right circumstances, the attainments of practitioners will similarly flourish at the site of the new temple. But the third set of verses changes the tenor of the entire piece from a song about a particular occasion to a timeless teaching on the essence of the spiritual path. Whenever, he says, yogis and vidyadharas come, "anywhere and everywhere . . . the two goods dawn." For the practitioner, fortunate circumstances are not tied to place and time, but only to the connection with the teacher and teachings.

In Tibetan verse, the use of a refrain is not uncommon to link a group of verses all dealing with the same topic, as in the famous cycle of the *Thirty-Seven Bodhisattva Practices* by Acharya Ngulchu Thogme Zangpo, where each verse ends with the refrain "this is the practice of the Victorious Sons." His Holiness's use of refrains, however, is remarkable. In a number of his songs here, he writes deceptively simple stanzas, with refrains and other repeated syntactical structures that culminate in a final stanza which brings the entire prior development to a stunning conclusion, as in the song starting "I, a silken lion." His Holiness wrote this song as he was going into exile from Tibet. In the face of what many could view as the devastating loss of his homeland and a future fraught with uncertainty, His Holiness speaks in a voice of utter simplicity, joy, and confidence about his situation, turning it into a triumph over every conceivable eventuality. First, he speaks as the lion: "I, a silken lion, do not need a palace. / The lion's glacial heights are my palace. / Anywhere I like, I shake my turquoise mane, / Roaming about, enjoying any snowy ravine." Then he assumes the guises of the eagle, tiger, and golden bee, until the final stanza, when he, already famous throughout Tibet, identifies himself with the simple wandering yogi who, because he is homeless, has dominion over the entire universe. "I, the yogi, do not need a family home. / All the yogi's good places are my family home. / Since the two aims are instantly realized, / Anywhere I go I like, heading out at ease."

His Holiness's special techniques of repetition and counterpointing are brought to new heights in the last long song beginning "In the pure land." This is a cycle of long stanzas, all containing the same structure, as well as internal and concluding refrains. Small changes in each stanza add up, in the end, to a complex statement. The meaning emerges here less from the sequence of stanzas than from their essential identity and circularity. Ostensibly, this is a song invoking blessings, but it is also a profound and immediate teaching on the Dzogchen view, as we shall see.

THE ROLE OF KHENPO'S VERSES IN THE BIOGRAPHY

Khenpo's verses are one long homage to His Holiness and to the entire Nyingma tradition His Holiness did so much to preserve—with its siddhas, scholars, tertöns, and lineage masters, starting from its foundations in Buddha Shakyamuni, Khenchen Shantarakshita, Guru Padmasambhava, King Trisong Deutsen. In one remarkable verse (13), Khenpo names more than twenty scholars and siddhas, a feat even in the monosyllabic Tibetan language, because the rules of verse require alternating male and female sounds. Not only do the names have to be listed in correct hierarchical order, but in a poetically pleasing order. Among the first twenty verses containing traditional homages, five are devoted to His Holiness and His Holiness's incarnations (1, 2, 15, 16, 17). Khenpo also singles out for praise other of his teachers (14) and personal protectors (19, 20), and he transposes parts of the Tibetan names of three of them into the three Sanskrit words, *Prajna* (wisdom), *Virya* (joyful effort), and *Shila* (morality) (14), which correspond, respectively, to *Sherab* (Palden *Sherab*), *Tsondrü* (Thubten *Tsondrü*), and *Tsultrim* (Pema *Tsultrim*), which are the names of his elder brother, one of his early teachers, and his father.

In the first three chapters, the verses function to set the factual account of His Holiness's life into the larger context of the Buddhadharma and, more particularly, Tibet's history. The first verse in chapter one (21) alludes to Buddha Shakyamuni as "Ze Tsang's son" and positions Tibet in relation to India. Next, in an evocative group of verses, Khenpo praises the special land of Tibet, where "[w]ild and tame beasts move leisurely" (23) and the people are "mild mannered" (24). While he introduces Buddha by his real father's name, he introduces His Holiness by his own previous incarnations, so that the two lineages, human and spiritual, are juxtaposed. The verses in chapter two rehearse some of Tibet's history, by focusing on its early dharma kings. Here, Khenpo traces the origins of His Holiness's illustrious family to the kings of Tibet and to one of Padmasambhava's heart students (35, 36).

In chapter three, Tibet's land is again praised, but this time from the transforming perspective of its sacred history, which Khenpo describes as indelibly inscribed on the earth itself. Alluding to the Tibetans' origins in the union of a monkey and demoness, emanations respectively of Chenrezig and Tara, he writes: "A wild demoness, sleeping on her back, seems to be / Cradling, in the pistil core of her lotus heart, / Samye, revered in samsara and nirvana" (40). And of Pema Kö, His Holiness's birthplace, he says that it was "the place known as holy land: / Perfect unmade image of [dakini queen] Phagmo's body" (41). In an exquisite group of verses (40 through 49), outdoing those in chapter one, Khenpo describes Tibet's land itself as if it were all dressed up, dancing, singing, and chanting with joy, at His Holiness's impending birth: "Mountain tops, like pillars of the sky, / Wear lovely turbans of pure white snow," and forests are draped in "silken mist" (42), while "all the trees' branches join hands, / Heads swaying with joy in fresh breezes" (43). More amazingly, birds and animals recite the six-syllable mantra and the "calling the lama" prayer, and they pass away "[s]till meditating" (47).

Khenpo's use of nature imagery is very special. By intertwining the natural and human worlds, Khenpo inscribes dharma in the entire universe (*snang srid*). The poetic effect of the whole world's welcoming the birth of the sublime tulku is echoed in chapter four, where His Holiness's lineage holders and former disciples are described in terms of nature imagery. From "necks of living flutes" come "songs praising the two aims" (55). The practitioners are "[r]ooted in courage . . . rich in leaves and stems of realization" (54). Their rejoicing is the rejoicing of the whole animate and inanimate universe: "From the ocean's depths of mind, / Waves of deep joy surge again, again, / While vines of bodies bow low, / As eyes glimpse the supreme tulku's face" (56).

Khenpo recapitulates the joyous nature imagery of his early chapters in the tenth chapter which tells of His Holiness's passing, "[w]hen fields of disciples in all directions / were ripe with nectar of the two benefits" (128). But now the earth, instead of dancing and singing with joy, is struck dumb. Earlier, in chapter seven, Khenpo highlighted the natural attraction to His Holiness of all the wisdom beings. They were drawn to him, just as, upon seeing jewels, "[n]o one needs any urging to gather them up" (*ma bskul*) (99). Now he uses that same construction, "without . . . urging" (*bskul ba med*), to picture His Holiness's death as bringing the whole cosmos to a silent standstill: "All at once, without anyone's urging / The continents and mountains, the whole earth / Seemed, for a moment, in peace, to stand still" (143). The grief of those close to His Holiness is again portrayed as a universal grief, this time, of earth and sky: "In the sky of ordinary mind, / Thick storm clouds of misery gather. / Tears of sadness, strong torrents, / Pour down faces, as earth, drenched" (144). To describe everyone's hoarse weeping (145), Khenpo uses the same word (*'dzer*) that he earlier used to describe the songs of praise crowding in the "necks of living flutes" (55). By writing of joy and sorrow with the same words and motifs, Khenpo highlights the impermanence of ordinary reality. As he says in one verse: "Impossible to tell where joy or sorrow starts. / Impossible to undo the laws of karma" (117).

Perhaps the most important effect of the verses is that they course through the entire biography, infusing the prose with the deep feelings of awe, respect, gratitude, and tender love that all who knew His Holiness felt for him. This is the very modern aspect of Khenpo's biography. Although it is written in the strictest traditional form, it is also an intensely personalized memoir. The prose is an account of the public face of His Holiness's life. The poetry is a stylized and beautiful transformation of what transpired invisibly, within the hearts of those who were close to him.

Some of Khenpo's most poignant verses (60 through 68) are those depicting the relation between the child tulku and his tutors. One of them, Lama Pema, in the presence of the child tulku, was "more a child than the child" (61). Lama Khedrub was a stricter tutor, but even he was reduced to tears when Dudjom recited long mantras he had never actually learned (63):

> Right then and there, right in that place
> The teacher, adept at teaching,
> Lama Khedrub, schooled beyond school,
> Let pour down tears of pouring rain.

In verse 63, as elsewhere (53, 154), Khenpo multiplies the force of his praises by repeating the same word with different meanings in set positions in every line—here, the first and third positions of every line—an effect we can only approximate in the English. Furthermore, verse 63 is written in seven-syllable lines, which makes this repetition an especially prized and difficult rhetorical feat. As in the verses praising Yeshe Tsogyal and Dudjom's incarnation as Khyeuchung Lotsawa (9, 53), one of the repeated words here, *drub* (*grub*), has an ordinary meaning, as well as forming part of Lama Khedrub's name. Unable to duplicate this pun in English, we changed the repeated word to "school." Another example is verse 154, praising the temple built for His Holiness's relics, where the word *mdzes*, "beautiful," is the next to last word of every line, an effect we only partially reproduced by repeating it twice at the start and twice at the end of the four lines. Generally, however, we were able to translate such repetitions in a fixed position in each line, even if we did not retain Khenpo's original positioning.

Unlike Western biographies, Khenpo's does not explicitly describe His Holiness's relationships with others; but his verses masterfully imply many such relations, based often on His Holiness's own accounts. In a set of verses recounting how it was predicted that His Holiness's activities would take place predominantly in the West (65 through 68), Khenpo imagines the way Ling Lama Chöjor Gyatso, His Holiness's chief tutor, might have phrased his request, when he asked this holy child to blow a conch shell to see where the sound would be loudest: "E Ma! Unrivaled tulku, bodhisattva, / With lotus steps, kindly come outdoors, / Take this good, sweet-sounding dharma conch / And blow once in each of the four directions"

(66). And, again, in chapter seven, Khenpo dramatizes His Holiness's decision to dedicate himself to preserving the old termas rather than discovering new ones: "Wisdom dakinis swaying in waves of smiles, / Sweetly uttering melodious words, / With their tender hands your own terma code / Held out, but your heart turned to ancient termas" (104). Writing of His Holiness's last illness, when all who were around him were begging him to remain, he consolidates everyone's grief unbearably: "Everyone, a chorus of distress, / Hands raised to the crown chakra, / Let streams of tears rain down while / Whispering in the Protector's ear" (132). In the letter at the front of this biography, Sangyum Kuzhok speaks of His Holiness simply as "my dear husband." While her grief was surely included in the universal "chorus," all the force of Sangyum Kuzhok's noble, joyous, and courageous love is conveyed in Khenpo's verses on the Sangyum's regal decision-making (147, 148, 149), which guided the building and establishment of His Holiness's stupa in Nepal (150 through 175) immediately following his mahaparinirvana, without any time for personal sorrow.

POETRY AS DHARMA INSTRUCTION:
DEATH AND IMPERMANENCE

The poetry in chapters six and nine is the most sublime in this biography. Six of His Holiness's own songs are collected in chapter six. Khenpo's verses in the ninth chapter recapitulate in poetic form some of His Holiness's informal teachings, delivered as casual comments. These verses, uniting His Holiness's teachings and Khenpo's poetic voice, are a testimonial to their personal relationship as root teacher and student. And that relationship is an emblem of all the Nyingma lineage relationships starting with Guru Padmasambhava and his heart students. The most intensely personal, in this sense, is also the most pervasive and defining relation in the dharma, and in this biography. His Holiness was Padmasambhava's regent, and Khenpo, inept as he claims to be, serves here as the surrogate voice of all of His Holiness's devoted students. Many verses, across the chapters, specifically praise His Holiness as Guru

Rinpoche's regent in these dark times (15, 38, 64, 97, 130, 140, 146, 180).

In His Holiness's first song, he portrays himself as a "miserable little child" whose eyes—fancifully characterized as "eye[s of water]-bubbles" (*chu bur gyi mig*)—are so thickly covered with the veils of ignorance that he has no hope of seeing Guru Padmasambhava and his retinue. This image also pervades Khenpo's verses as his own self-characterization in relation to His Holiness. In chapter one, he confesses his inadequacy to write a proper biography of his master: "Inconceivable deeds of the terchen lama, / Such as they were, how can a child's mind hold them?" (17) In presenting His Holiness's own teachings, Khenpo again resorts to the image of a child (119, 120, 121), but this time it is the child of a barren woman (121), and a dream image (120), which includes: "all meeting and parting: / Samsara's dancers dancing. This play, / Duality's child, take not for truth" (119).

In a different register, Khenpo writes a magisterial verse (126) that embodies His Holiness's teaching on emptiness and true nature:

"From true nature, unmarred by thought or effort, what arises
Arises innately from its origins as emptiness.
Emptiness and what arises are not two, truth is thus,
Thus, creation and completion are one in the lama."

This is a highly virtuosic verse, where the last word of every line is the first word of the following line. Khenpo wrote only three such verses, one (110) that introduces the entire set of verses embodying His Holiness's teachings (111 through 127), and another that compares His Holiness to Guru Padmasambhava (106). Not only does Khenpo's verse flow seamlessly and naturally in the Tibetan, but it also echoes the direct, authoritative, and majestic cadences of the *Heart Sutra*. This enshrining of His Holiness's casual words in an ornate and difficult poetic structure is an act of deepest homage, as Khenpo is showing how much he treasures every word His Holiness uttered.

In chapter ten, devoted mainly to the establishment of His Holiness's stupa, Khenpo writes an eloquent set of verses (138, 139, 140, 141) speaking of the collective pain at His Holiness's passing, once again in terms of the images of child and dream, which evoke the "miserable little child" in His Holiness's first song. These three verses are linked by the expressions of grief, "alas," in the opening words of the first and third verses, and by the special imagery of envelopment. The first verse (138) states His Holiness's loss somewhat objectively as a general condition. With the setting of His Holiness's sun, "[s]unk in dharmakaya sleep," the "dream world" of samsara is "once more enveloped by dark ignorance." The next two verses become increasingly more anguished, as the enormity of this loss is brought home to Khenpo's "small child's mind." In the second verse (139), Khenpo uses a very special word, *bsdus*, drawn from nomadic life, here translated as "folded away." He says: "Beyond eye's reach of duality's child, / For now your body is folded away, / How hard is this for the small child's mind." The word *bsdus* describes what happens when a tent's pegs are removed, and it folds into itself. Khenpo's own modern analogy for this word is "the way an umbrella folds up." The verb *bsdus* is also used to describe how all the grazing animals gather together at dusk. This is the more joyful connotation of the word, and we translate it that way in line 2 of verse 153 as "come together." Khenpo uses this verb yet again in the last line of verse 141, when he says of His Holiness's rainbow body that "once again, dharmakaya space enfolds it." No translation, however, can do justice to the poignance of *bsdus* at its nomadic roots.

In verse 140, Khenpo manipulates the rhetoric of word repetition to convey the unbearable loss of His Holiness. In each of the first three lines of this verse, Khenpo repeats the same word twice in each line, but in variant senses—for example, in line 3, "troubled times, troubled beings." But in the last line, he emphasizes His Holiness's absence by *not* repeating any word, but instead the negation "*mi . . . mi*." The two negative expressions formed with *mi—mi dgongs* and *mi mngon*—are linked syntactically and by assonance, but ironically, they enunciate the breaking of the ordinary connection between His Holiness and us, since we are now out of his mind, and he has gone out of our sight.

The consolation for this unbearable grief is found in His Holiness's splendid and majestic last song in chapter six, which is a supreme example of its genre. Each single stanza is as long as some other songs, and His Holiness sustains his repetition, not only of a concluding refrain, but of internal refrains as well, over seven long stanzas. Outwardly, this song pays homage to the three-kaya buddhas, three roots, and dharmapalas, but every stanza is a Dzogchen teaching that insistently rejects the ordinary understanding of the pure lands and objects of refuge. In all of the stanzas, the first four lines invoke an object of refuge. The second four lines characterize the realization of the figure being invoked and identify that figure with the wisdom awareness suggested by his or her attributes. For example, in the root lama's stanza, the root awareness of the lama is highlighted:

> Instant wisdom, in the fourth time, beyond the three times:
> Is this not your realization, Lord?
> Awareness, the root of all phenomena:
> Is this not the root lama?
> Not for a moment have I been separate,
> Never separate, still I was unaware.
> At the instant of awareness,
> The root lama is gone,
> So-called pure lands vanish—
> Within mind's unborn nature, sha ra ra,
> In the play of awareness and empty bliss, ya la la,
> Whatever arises is the lama's true nature.

The main body of each of the stanzas is structured around sets of refrains that are identical except for one changing line. Instead of "[t]he root lama is gone," as in the example above, the stanza on Amitabha says, "Buddha Amitabha is gone." After the two lines ending in "sha ra ra" and "ya la la," His Holiness always inserts a line which relates some aspect of awareness—as ground/wisdom, arising energy/compassion, or playful display—to the realization being. For example, in the root lama's stanza, he mentions the "lama's true nature."

The final lines of every stanza lead to a conclusion entirely reversing the simple opening invocation. In cautioning each time against holding to the solid existence of pure lands and objects of veneration, His Holiness delivers a profound and moving teaching, which speaks to impermanence in general, but, in the context of this biography, also to the grief at the loss of his own presence. For example, in the root lama's stanza, he writes:

Holding to the pure land is a delusion,
The label "buddha's human form" is a hurdle of attachment.
The lama is not outside, look within.
This finding the Buddha through oneself, a la la!
This being happy, always and ceaselessly, e ma ho!
This again is the sublime lama's kindness;
This again, the profound blessing of pith advice.
Let's sing the noble song of supreme happiness.
Let's step to the dance of ultimate fulfillment.

A commonplace of Dzogchen teachings is that the ultimate view is beyond words and thought. Nevertheless, through his eloquent reversals of expectations in every stanza, His Holiness provides a glimpse of what he himself has actually experienced. Again and again, he cautions that the object of refuge "is not outside, look within." But then, he does not say nor imply that the buddha is "within" us. Instead, he uses the Tibetan particle *las*, which means "from," and the classic example of this use is "milk from (*las*) a cow." Buddha and buddhahood are not found within the nonexistent self, but *from* or *through* the eighteen endowments of a fortunate human birth. By remembering this, one is always in the presence of the beloved root teacher, perhaps never more so than in the instant "the root teacher is gone," and the pure land "vanishes."

Within the arc of the two voices, resonating across the chapters of this book, of Khenpo as the little child and of His Holiness as the realized master, is enclosed the whole meaning of the practice of dharma, the path to enlightenment, and this biography. It is a meaning and a mandala to which every reader is ineluctably called by the warm breath of His Holiness, which gently exudes from his timelessly living words.

FINAL VERSES

The dedication prayers close the biography, and space precludes any lengthy discussion of them. Since these are Khenpo's own prayers, he speaks most directly in his own voice in these verses. Apologizing for the inadequacy of the "too small . . . aperture of [his] child's mind" to let in the "vast . . . sky [of His Holiness's] three secrets" (189), he rests any merits of his biography solely on His Holiness's continuing benefits, for as he says in chapter ten: "Even though your body has passed away, / Still you help [others]. Who but you could do this?" (164) Through His Holiness's blessings, Khenpo characterizes this work as a "unique tree" radiating "the lama's virtues, seeds sown in the three devotions" of any lucky reader (184).

Toy-Fung Tung

The writer wishes to thank Acharya Karma Gongde for help with the terms of Tibetan prosody, as well as the following readers for their perceptive comments: Marie Friquegnon, Arthur Mandelbaum, Richard Steinberg, and Carl Stuendel.

NOTES

1. The dorje, or vajra, is a symbol of indestructibility.

2. The next three verses praise each of these three lineages (see Glossary) in turn.

3. Love, power, and wisdom allude to qualities of the three bodhisattvas, the lords of the three families (*rigs gsum mgon po*): Avalokiteshvara, Vajrapani, and Manjushri.

4. Padma Jung, short for Padma Jungne (Skt. Padmakara), is one of the names of Guru Padmasambhava (the Lotus Born), or Guru Rinpoche (Precious Guru). He is an emanation of Dhyani Buddha Amitabha and Avalokiteshvara, and was born miraculously on a lotus in Dhanakosha Lake (sometimes called Sindhu Lake) in the land of Odiyana, northwest of India, four years after the mahaparinirvana of Buddha Shakyamuni. He is the embodiment of all the buddhas of the three times and ten directions and predicted by Shakyamuni Buddha as the great being who would serve as his regent. He is the buddha who attained the transcendental wisdom rainbow body, an ever-youthful immortal body. In the eighth century Shantarakshita encouraged King Trisong Deutsen to invite him to Tibet in order to subdue the forces that were thwarting the establishment of Buddhadharma there. Out of compassion for future generations, knowing that the oral transmission, *kama* (*bka' ma*), of the Buddha's teachings would either become lost or diluted, he hid innumerable dharma treasures of texts and relics, known as *terma* (*gter ma*), throughout Tibet, Nepal, and Bhutan to be discovered by destined disciples, known as *tertöns* (*gter ston*), in the centuries to come. See *Praise to the Lotus Born* by Khenpo Tsewang Dongyal (Dharma Samudra, 2004).

5. The expression "mind (*blo*), heart (*snying*), and chest (*brang*)" is roughly equivalent to "my entire being." Though currently the word "mind" (*blo*) is used in the expression, in ancient times "lungs" (*glo*) was the word of choice.

4666

6. These are the thirty-two major marks and eighty minor marks of buddhahood.

7. Brahma's voice was renowned as powerful and beautiful.

8. Yeshe Tsogyal is considered an emanation of both Saraswati, the goddess of wisdom, and Tara, the female buddha of compassion. At a very early age she was King Trisong Deutsen's queen. Later the king offered his entire kingdom and all that he held most precious to Guru Rinpoche. Hence she became Padmasambhava's spiritual consort and his chief Tibetan female disciple, receiving all the transmissions he gave in Tibet. She is renowned for her photographic memory and later compiled all his teachings, recording them in the symbolic dakini language and script. In this way she and Guru Padmasambhava hid these teachings throughout Tibet and bordering countries, to be subsequently discovered by great tertöns throughout the ages until the present. After living for more than two hundred years and having attained the transcendental wisdom rainbow body through her practice of Dzogchen meditation, she went to Glorious Copper-Color Mountain, the pure land of Guru Rinpoche, without leaving any physical remains behind.

9. Vimalamitra, known in Tibet as Drimed Shenyen, was one of the greatest Indian Buddhist scholars and siddhas and one of the masters and originators of Dzogchen in Tibet, along with Guru Padmasambhava and Vairochana. He came to Tibet in the eighth century and stayed for about twelve years. He left the country for seven years and then at the royal request of King Mune Tsenpo returned for a brief period. His extant works now number over ninety-three treatises and sadhanas based on the sutras and tantras. Among these is his innermost teaching on Nyingthig (*snying thig*), called *Secret Heart Drop of Vimalamitra*. He taught and translated into Tibetan numerous sutras and tantras. He achieved the transcendental wisdom rainbow body, thereby attaining an ever-youthful immortal body, and is said to be now residing at the Five-Peaked Mountain in China.

10. These are the two schools of mahayana Buddhism: Mind Only (Chittamatra, Yogachara) and Middle Way (Madhyamaka). The Mind-Only School maintains that all phenomenal appearances are reflections of mind and that mind exists as the self-cognizant and basic ground of all consciousness. The Middle Way School maintains that all phenomena are encompassed by the two truths, absolute and relative. All phenomena are considered illusory manifestations of the true nature. Even mind, the ground of consciousness, is devoid of substantial existence. Its

tenets are mainly based on the prajnaparamita sutras. Both schools agree that phenomena obey the laws of interdependent coorigination, of cause and effect.

11. Shiwatso is another name for Shantarakshita and means "Protector of Peace." Shantarakshita, considered to be an emanation of Vajrapani, was the head abbot of Nalanda University. He was a renowned logician and philosopher who composed *Ornament of the Middle Way*—the basis of the Yogachara-Madhyamaka philosophical school, which combines the Mind-Only and Madhyamaka schools. In the eighth century King Trisong Deutsen invited him to Tibet in order to establish Buddhism there. When they met, Shantarakshita took the young king's hand and asked him if he remembered their past-life pledge. Shantarakshita told him how he had stayed in the world nine generations waiting for him to take birth. He was the cofounder of Tibetan Buddhism and ordained the first seven Tibetan monks. He taught both the sutras and tantras to many disciples and trained the first Tibetan translators as well as translating many texts himself. Several of the original twenty-five disciples of Guru Rinpoche were also his students. In Tibet he is well known as Khenchen Bodhisattva.

12. King Trisong Deutsen (742-810), considered to be an emanation of Manjushri, was the second of the three great kings of Tibet. The first was Songtsen Gampo (617-698), and the third was Ralpa Chen (806-841). He invited many Indian scholars and yogic masters to Tibet. The most famous were Shantarakshita, Padmasambhava, and Vimalamitra. He, along with Padmasambhava and Shantarakshita, are the cofounders of Tibetan Buddhism. They built the first famous monastic university in Tibet known as Samye Monastery. The king then provided all the necessities for the translation into Tibetan of all the major teachings of the Buddha, known as the *Kangyur,* and the teachings of other great Buddhist masters, known as the *Tangyur.* As the translations were completed, they were immediately put into practice, and thereby those practitioners including the king himself attained the highest realization with the guidance of the living masters, such as Padmasambhava, Vimalamitra, and Shantarakshita. During his reign, he extended the borders of Tibet far beyond their previous limits, making Tibet one of the most powerful nations in Central Asia. King Trisong became a scholar composing over twenty-one books, which encompassed the subjects of philosophy, logic, as well as poetic praises to the buddhas and bodhisattvas. At the age of fifty-six he resigned as king, transferring his authority to his eldest son, Mune Tsenpo (Tsepo [*btsad po*] is the ancient spelling, but is now written as

Tsenpo [*btsan po*]). His second son was Murub Tsenpo, and the youngest son was Mutig Tsenpo. He also had a daughter named Lhacham Pema Sal. Mutig Tsenpo's son was Gyalse Lhaje who is considered to be the immediate reincarnation of King Trisong Deutsen.

13. Thonmi Sambhota lived in the seventh century and served as a chief minister of Tibet's first dharma patron and champion of indigenous literature, law, and culture, King Songtsen Gampo. Sambhota was a great scholar and created an alphabet for the Tibetan language based on the sequence of sounds used to order the Sanskrit alphabet. He wrote eight treatises on Tibetan grammar. Among these eight, only two have survived: *Thirty Lines Explaining the Vowels and Consonants* and *Gender of Tibetan Syllables and Verb Conjugation*. In addition he was the first translator of Buddhism from Sanskrit into Tibetan, translating over twenty-one sutras and tantras related to Chenrezig, the bodhisattva of compassion.

14. "Vairo" refers to Vairochana, a famous Dzogchen master of the eighth century and the greatest translator-editor in Tibetan history. He was one of the twenty-five disciples of Guru Padmasambhava and a disciple of Vimalamitra. He was one of the first seven devotees to take bhikshu vows from Khenchen Shantarakshita and was also a disciple of his. Vairochana wrote more than eight treatises, including the *Commentary on the Heart Sutra according to Tantra*. His translations of the sutras, tantras, and commentaries on the Buddha's teachings number over eighty-five. He was the royal teacher of King Trisong Deutsen. In addition to his scholarship he was a renowned physician and astrologer.

15. "Ka" is the shortened form of Kawa Paltsek. He was one of the great eighth-century translator-editors and one of the twenty-five disciples of Guru Padmasambhava, as well as a disciple of Shantarakshita and Vimalamitra. Due to the strength of his practice, he became renowned as one who could read the minds of others. The Beijing edition of the *Tangyur* contains ten of his scholarly texts, including the *Seventeenfold Appearance of the Sequence of the View*. His translations of the sutras, tantras, and commentaries number over 148. He was also known for the beauty of his calligraphy, the style of which is still emulated today.

16. "Chok" refers to Chok Ro Lui Gyaltsen. He was one of the great translator-editors of the eighth century and a disciple of Guru Padmasambhava, Shantarakshita, and Vimalamitra. He achieved the highest realization by practicing the teachings of those masters. He was a renowned scholar, writing more than

sixteen treatises including the *Detailed Commentary on the Buddha's Third Turning of the Wheel of Dharma* in twenty thousand stanzas. His translations of the sutras, tantras, and commentaries number over thirty-four very large volumes.

17. Zhang Yeshe De was one of the great translator-editors of the eighth century and one of the twenty-five disciples of Guru Padmasambhava, as well as a disciple of Shantarakshita and Vimalamitra. He was a great scholar, writing several treatises, four of which are still extant including the one thousand stanzas of *Distinctions of the View*. His translations of the sutras, tantras, and commentaries number over 364.

18. So Yeshe Wang Chuk of the So clan was a very important disciple of Nubchen Sangye Yeshe.

19. There are three famous masters who came from the Zur clan: Zurchen Shakya Jungne (the third great native-Tibetan lineage holder of the Nyingma kama teachings), Zurchung Sherab Drak, and Zur Sangdag Dropugpa.

20. There are two famous masters of the Nub clan: Nubchen Sangye Yeshe and Nub Namkhai Nyingpo. Nubchen Sangye Yeshe was one of the twenty-five disciples of Guru Padmasambhava, as well as a disciple of Shantarakshita and Vimalamitra. He was the second great native-Tibetan lineage holder of the Nyingma kama teachings. He is the chief exponent of the Anuyoga tantra in Tibet. He was a renowned ngagpa, achieving the highest realization and abilities. King Langdarma, the ninth-century Tibetan ruler who attempted to completely destroy the dharma, was afraid of Nub's spiritual powers. He was a great scholar, writing about five treatises including *Lamp for the Eye of Meditation*. He translated over twenty-six inner tantras mainly related to Yamantaka, the wrathful form of Manjushri.

21. Nyak Jnana Kumara was one of the twenty-five disciples of Guru Padmasambhava, as well as a disciple of Shantarakshita and Vimalamitra. He was the first great native-Tibetan lineage holder of the Nyingma kama teachings. He was a renowned translator and scholar. Four of his treatises are still extant, and they are mainly related to *Secret Essence Tantra—The Net of Magical Illusions*. His translations of the inner tantras and their commentaries number over forty-four.

22. Rongzompa, or Rongzom Chökyi Zangpo, (1012-1131) was a highly accomplished master whom Atisha recognized as the incarnation of the Indian master

Nagpo Chöpa. He was considered to be the immediate reincarnation of two other Indian masters: Smirti Jnana Kriti and Trala Ringmo. He was a renowned scholar, a master of many languages including that of the animals. He wrote *Starting with Könchog* (*A Commentary on Secret Essence Tantra—The Net of Magical Illusions*) and many other texts on philosophy and the inner tantras. In addition he wrote books on animal husbandry, agriculture, and dairy farming.

23. Longchenpa, or Longchen Rabjampa, (1308-1363) was a Dzogchen master admired by all schools of Tibetan Buddhism for the majestic scope of his Dzogchen and tantric writings, which reconciled and synthesized many prior traditions. He is considered to be an emanation of Vimalamitra. Among his works are: (1) the *Seven Treasures*, comprising the *Dharmadhatu Treasure, Wish-Fulfilling Treasure, Doctrine Treasure, Treasure of the Words and Meaning of Dzogchen, Abiding Nature Treasure, Pith Instruction Treasure, Treasure of the Supreme Yana;* (2) *Trilogy of Relaxation and Ease,* comprising *Relaxing the Mind, Relaxing Meditation, Relaxing as Magical Display;* (3) *Three Liberating Methods,* comprising *Self-Liberating with True Nature, Self-Liberating with True Nature of Mind, Self-Liberating with Equanimity;* and (4) *Three Lights Dispelling Darkness,* comprising *Dispelling the Darkness of the Ten Directions (A Commentary on Secret Essence Tantra—The Net of Magical Illusions), Dispelling the Darkness of Ignorance (A Compendium of Secret Essence Tantra—The Net of Magical Illusions), Dispelling the Darkness of Mind (An Overview of Secret Essence Tantra—The Net of Magical Illusions).* He also wrote a set of pith instructions titled *Four Heart Drop Cycles,* which comprises four texts, plus a summary: *Secret Heart Drop of Vimalamitra, Essential Heart Drop of the Lama, Dakini Heart Drop of Padmasambhava, Essential Heart Drop of the Dakini,* and *Profound Quintessential Heart Drop—The Condensed Meaning of the Vima and Dakini Heart Drops.*

24. Lochen Chöpal Gyatso (1654-1718) is also known as Lochen Dharmashri. He was the incarnation of Yudra Nyingpo, one of the twenty-five disciples of Guru Padmasambhava. He was the younger brother of the great treasure finder Terdak Lingpa and with him revived the kama lineage of the Nyingma School of Buddhism. He was a great scholar, an expert on the Sanskrit language, a writer, astrologer, painter, sculptor of ritual images and objects, a master of dance and mudra, a musician, and designer and fabricator of two- and three-dimensional tantric mandalas. At the age of thirteen he took upasaka vows from his elder brother, Terdak Lingpa. At age fifteen he took sramanera vows and at age twenty

took bhikshu vows, which were both bestowed by the great fifth Dalai Lama who named him Ngagwang Chöpel. He became a great teacher of all forms of Buddhadharma. His collected works are published in eighteen volumes.

25. Mipham Rinpoche (1845-1912) was a renowned Nyingma scholar and teacher of the early twentieth century. Even though he had attained the highest realization, he was a simple and humble wandering, hermitage monk. He is considered to be an emanation of Manjushri and Nubchen Sangye Yeshe. His root teacher was the first Khyentse. In addition he studied with Patrul Rinpoche and many other great masters. His printed works fill thirty-two volumes. He wrote diversely from his own direct knowledge on topics from all ten sciences, and these became the textbooks used in all the Nyingma monastic institutions.

26. Nyang-ral Nyima Özer (1136-1204) was the body incarnation of King Trisong Deutsen. He and Guru Chökyi Wangchuk are known as the kings of all the tertöns. Guru Padmasambhava and Yeshe Tsogyal both appeared to him in their physical forms and directly handed him most of his terma teachings, many of which were written in Tibetan letters, making it unnecessary for him to decode the symbolic dakini language and script in which they are often written. He married Lady Jobum-ma, an emanation of Yeshe Tsogyal, and they gave birth to two sons, who along with their descendants became renowned teachers.

27. Guru Chökyi Wangchuk, also known as Guru Chöwang (1212-1270), was the emanation of the enlightened speech of King Trisong Deutsen. He and Nyang-ral Nyima Özer are known as the kings of all the tertöns. His name was given to him by his father, Pangtön Drubpai Nyingpo, who at the time of his birth was chanting the text *Reciting the Names of Manjushri*, and the verse he was chanting contained the line "one who holds the powerful wealth of dharma (*chos kyi dbang phyug*, i.e., chökyi wangchuk) is the king of dharma (*chos kyi rgyal*)." He was descended from Pang Jetsentrom, a powerful mantra adept who saved the life of King Trisong Deutsen. He studied all forms of the dharma, became a great tertön, and revealed many texts, among them the *Tantra Which Known Alone Liberates All*.

28. Lingpa (*gling pa*) is an epithet frequently appended to the name of a tertön. "Ling" means island, and a tertön is likened to an island refuge in the midst of an ocean of suffering. The five Lingpas are:
(1) Dorje Lingpa (1346-1405), who was the body emanation of the translator Vairochana. He was a great visionary tertön, who at the age of thirteen had seven

visions of Guru Rinpoche, and then found his first treasure trove. In all, he revealed
108 treasures. When he died his body remained intact and occasionally recited the
dedication and aspiration prayers. After three years his body was cremated, and
many images of the buddhas appeared in the bones, as well as many ringsel.

(2) Ratna Lingpa (1403-1478), who was the reincarnation of Langdro Lotsawa
Könchog Jungne, one of the twenty-five heart students of Guru Padmasambhava.
When he was twenty-one, Ratna Lingpa had a vision of Guru Rinpoche, who gave
him his *khajang* and also advice. He extracted his first treasure trove at the age of
thirty from Chungchen Rock. It consisted of a cycle of practices on the three roots.
Because all his circumstances were so favorable without any conflict for his
dharma activities, he revealed twenty-five treasures in a single lifetime, treasures
that he had been assigned to discover in three lifetimes, and therefore he was
known by three names: Zhigpo Lingpa, Drodul Lingpa, and Ratna Lingpa. One of
his very famous discoveries is the *Great Perfection Tantra of the Clear-Sky Sun*.
Ratna Lingpa's many scholarly endeavors included collecting all the tantras of the
ancient school, arranging them as one series called *Hundreds of Thousands of
Nyingma Tantras*, and having new copies prepared.

(3) Pema Lingpa (1450-1521), who was a reincarnation of Princess Lhacham
Pema Sal, the daughter of King Trisong Deutsen, and was the greatest tertön of the
Himalayan kingdom of Bhutan. Through his terma he introduced sacred dance
into Bhutan. Local leaders demanded that he prove himself to be an authentic
tertön by revealing terma from Mebar Lake with a large assembly of local people
assembled to witness. Agitated, the young Pema Lingpa, carrying a large flaming
torch, jumped into the lake, disappearing for a short time, and then resurfaced
with a large vase of treasure and an unextinguished torch. Everyone was amazed
and became devoted to him. In the course of his life he revealed many treasures
such as *Embodiment of Samantabhadra's Enlightened Intention* and the *Lama,
Ocean of Jewels*. His powerful teaching became popular throughout Tibet and all
neighboring countries.

(4) Karma Lingpa (fourteenth century), who was born in Dakpo in southern Tibet
and was an incarnation of the famous eighth-century translator Chok Ro Lui
Gyaltsen, the disciple of Guru Padmasambhava and Master Shantarakshita. At the
age of fifteen he revealed the profound teachings of the *Peaceful and Wrathful
Deities*, which included the *Tibetan Book of the Dead (Liberation upon Hearing)*.
His teaching became popular throughout Tibet but in particular for the Nyingma
and Kagyu schools.

(5) Sangye Lingpa (1340-1396), one of the greatest of all tertöns, who was empowered by Guru Padmasambhava directly. He was the incarnation of Prince Murub Tsenpo, who was King Trisong Deutsen's son and Guru Rinpoche's disciple. From the great cavern of Puri, he extracted the texts and esoteric instructions of *Embodiment of the Total Realization of the Lama* and *Cycle of Teachings of the Great Compassionate One,* which are unique among all the earth treasures of Tibet. He found eighteen great treasure troves between his twenty-fifth and thirty-second years. Subsequently he revealed many dharma and dharma object treasures.

29. Thang Tong Gyalpo (1385-1510) was a renowned emanation of Chenrezig and his wrathful form, Hayagriva, and also of Guru Rinpoche via a womb birth. He was a great tertön and teacher. He was also a civil engineer, building 118 ferry boats and constructing fifty-eight iron bridges spanning large rivers throughout Tibet. He had a technique for preventing the iron from rusting, and many of those bridges are still extant. He is known also as the inventor of a popular operatic theater that compassionately introduced fishermen, hunters, and beggars to the dharma and to right, alternative livelihoods.

30. Jatsön Nyingpo (1585-1656) was the reincarnation of Nyangben Tingdzin Zangpo. The latter was a disciple of Guru Padmasambhava, Vimalamitra, and Shantarakshita, and he attained the transcendental wisdom rainbow body. Nyangben Tingdzin Zangpo also served as the prime minister of King Mutig Tsenpo, thus becoming the first Tibetan Buddhist monk to assume a political position. Jatsön Nyingpo was a great tertön and fully ordained monk, perfectly maintaining both his vinaya vows and tantric samaya. He remained in retreat for seventeen years and during that time secretly revealed the practice of *The Gathering of All Dzogchen Objects of Refuge.* Later he revealed treasures in many other areas with large audiences present. On one occasion an army was pursuing him to deter him from revealing treasure. He galloped his horse straight across the mirrorlike face of a very steep rocky mountain. While doing so, he revealed the treasure, to the consternation and wonderment of his pursuers who thereafter became devotees. His teachings became very popular in both the Nyingma and Kagyu schools.

31. Orgyen Terdak Lingpa, also known as Minling Terchen Gyurme Dorje (1646-1714), was the speech incarnation of the translator Vairochana. He discovered many terma and compiled many kama and terma teachings to make them easy for

practitioners to follow. In 1676 he built Mindröling Monastery in central Tibet, which became one of the most important Nyingma centers for both study and practice. He and the fifth Dalai Lama became teacher and disciple to each other. He and his brother, Lochen Dharmashri, are two of the teachers who are renowned for reviving the Nyingma lineage of both kama and terma.

32. Orgyen Tsasum Lingpa Chökyi Gyatso (1697-c. 1741) was born in eastern Tibet, near the holy mountain Jowo Zegyal, and was an incarnation of Nubchen Sangye Yeshe. He was an important tertön and renowned as a crazy wisdom (*brtul zhugs spyod pa*) yogi. To escape the mundane administrative duties of the monastery, he feigned madness and ran naked into the forest. At that same time, around the age of seventeen, he revealed the khajang for the terma he would discover. Shortly thereafter he began to reveal these treasure teachings and ritual objects in both eastern and central Tibet.

33. Jigme Lingpa (1730-1798) is an emanation of Vimalamitra and Prince Lhaje (King Trisong Deutsen's grandson). He was born in central Tibet. He is one the greatest visionary tertöns, as well as a poet, siddha, and scholar. All his knowledge was gained through Dzogchen meditative realization rather than through study. He therefore exemplifies the teachings that assert that once inner wisdom is discovered, all wisdom is spontaneously revealed.

34. Patrul Rinpoche (1808-1887) was one of the great Nyingma masters, well known as a scholar, poet, and teacher. His powerful teachings were very direct and able to uproot and eliminate the errors of practitioners. He wandered from village to village, gathering the population and practicing Chenrezig and Amitabha with them. He promoted peace, love, and harmony among everyone and encouraged them to refrain from the slaughter and hunting of animals. Though he was the teacher of so many great disciples, he remained a humble and simple wandering, hermitage monk. All the offerings he received, he gave to the poor and asked in return that they carve the sacred teachings of the Buddha onto stones (which are known as mani stones), so that benefit to beings and to the teachings was the result. This heap of mani stones became one of the largest in all of Tibet.

35. This is the first Khyentse, Jamyang Khyentse Wangpo, Terchen Pema Ösel Dongak Lingpa (1820-1892), an emanation of King Trisong Deutsen and Vimalamitra and a great tertön and scholar. He was the cofounder of the Rimed ecumenical movement and was therefore the great teacher of all the Buddhist

schools of Tibet. Because of his tremendous realization he was able to recover many lineages that had over time been lost, and is therefore the father of the nine-teenth-century Tibetan Renaissance, the lord of the seven entrusted transmissions.

36. This is the first Kongtrul, Jamgön Kongtrul, Pema Garwang Lodrö Thaye, Yönten Gyatso (1813-1899), who was the great reincarnation of the translator Vairochana and the cofounder of the Rimed movement. He was a great tertön, scholar, physician, alchemist, poet, and siddha. At the encouragement and support of Jamyang Khyentse Wangpo, he brought forth the great gift of *Five Treasuries*: (1) *Treasury of Precious Treasures*; (2) *Treasury of Vast Speech*; (3) *Treasury of All-Encompassing Knowledge*; (4) *Treasury of Pith Instructions*; (5) *Treasury of Kagyu Mantras*.

37. Terchen Chogyur Lingpa, or Terchen Chogyur Dechen Zhigpo Lingpa, (1829-1870) was an incarnation of Prince Murub Tsenpo. He made a great effort to receive the entire kama teaching on the maha, anu, and ati tantras and revealed many great termas directly related to these teachings, such as the *Three Dzogchen Classes*. In addition he revealed many treasures on the three roots, such as the *Heart Practice of the Lamas*, and many precious artifacts. He and Jamgön Kongtrul and Jamyang Khyentse Wangpo were all mutual teachers to and disciples of each other.

38. Dudjom Lingpa.

39. This verse praises teachers personally close to Khenpo by playing on the iden-tity between parts of their Tibetan names and the Sanskrit equivalents, which also designate three of the six paramitas:
• Khenchen Palden Sherab, Khenpo's elder brother, whose name *Sherab* means "discriminating wisdom," which in Sanskrit is *Prajna*
• Khenchen Thubten Tsondrü, under whom Khenpo studied, whose name *Tsondrü* means "joyful effort," which in Sanskrit is *Virya*
• Khenpo's father, the hidden wisdom yogi Doshul Gelong Lama Chimed Namgyal, whose ordination name was Pema Tsultrim; *Tsultrim* means "morality," which in Sanskrit is *Shila*.

40. This is an allusion to the notion of "crossing the ocean of samsara" whereby the root lama is envisioned as a ship's captain.

41. Guru Padmasambhava.

42. Verses 15 through 17 pay homage to the root guru, the subject of this biogra-

phy, His Holiness Dudjom Rinpoche, Jigdral Yeshe Dorje. He was also known by the name Dudjom Drodul Lingpa.

43. This connotes vastness, but the ocean is also the fabled source of the wish-fulfilling gem. The terchen lama's terma discoveries are here indirectly likened to that gem.

44. When Khenpo first began to compose this biography, he made a pledge to bring the project to completion. That inspired determination is expressed in this verse.

45. The ten discordant spheres (*zhing bcu*, the abbreviated form of *bsgral ba'i zhing bcu*) are ten forms of atrocity. Beings indulging in such activities inhabit every region of the universe. If permitted to continue unchecked, they cause great harm to themselves and others. Only compassionate practitioners of the greatest realization can liberate such beings.

46. Guru Padmasambhava.

47. This verse praises particularly the dharmapala Jowo Zegyal, also known as Mayo Gapa, who inhabits one of the twenty-one sacred glacier mountains of Tibet, near Khenpo's birthplace in Kham.

48. Throughout the text, reference is made to the one thousand buddhas of the Fortunate Aeon. The Fortunate Aeon is this aeon in which we are currently living. The historical Buddha, Shakyamuni, is the fourth buddha of this Fortunate Aeon; Maitreya will be the fifth. In addition to the one thousand, all of whom are emanations of Avalokiteshvara, are two who will support the others throughout the entire aeon. They are Manjushri and Vajrapani.

49. Nalada was the ancient name found in the vinaya for the village in the area of Magadha (the modern state of Bihar) in northern India.

50. Tathul (Skt. Ashvajit) was one of the first five disciples of the Buddha.

51. The "eye of dharma" is the "eye of wisdom" which sees the true nature as it is.

52. Nagarjuna (50 BCE-550 CE) was the great founder of the Madhyamaka School, and *Root Verses of the Wisdom of the Middle Way* is his most famous work. He discovered the *Prajnaparamita Sutra in One Hundred Thousand Verses*. Among the eight vidyadharas he is the lord of lotus speech.

53. Vajra dohas are songs or verses of realization regarding the nature of the mind and phenomena, uttered spontaneously without preconception, and are usually associated with the mahasiddhas such as Saraha.

54. For that reason, Tibetan religious paintings (*thang ka*) representing Guru Rinpoche with his twenty-five disciples show Khyeuchung Lotsawa with a bird on his finger.

55. The miracle (*cho 'phrul*) month is a moniker for the first month of the Tibetan calendar. During this month (lunation), Buddha performed a miracle on each of the fifteen days of the waxing moon.

56. For an explanation of rabjung (*rab byung*) see Appendix 1.

57. Dorje Drolö is a wrathful form of Padmasambhava, one of the "eight manifestations," usually depicted riding on a pregnant tigress. Guru Rinpoche manifested this form when subduing negative forces and when hiding innumerable spiritual treasures throughout the Himalayan region.

58. Black Tröma is the female, wrathful buddha whose primary function is to subdue ego-clinging.

59. Ze Tsang (Skt. Shudodanputra) was Buddha Shakyamuni's father.

60. The twelve deeds of the Buddha, which exemplify the path to enlightenment, are: (1) descent from Tushita Heaven; (2) entering Queen Mayadevi's womb; (3) taking birth; (4) becoming expert in all fields of knowledge, including the martial arts, gymnastics, and the outer and inner sciences; (5) marrying Princess Yasodhara and ruling the kingdom; (6) renouncing the kingdom; (7) performing ascetic practices; (8) walking to the bodhi tree with the intention to attain enlightenment; (9) conquering all of Mara's obstacles by unshakable loving-kindness; (10) attaining complete enlightenment; (11) turning the wheel of dharma; and (12) entering mahaparinirvana.

61. This is a reference to Dudjom Rinpoche's many previous incarnations, some of which are praised in the next six verses.

62. Buddha Shakyamuni himself praised Shariputra as having the most supreme wisdom achievements among all his arhat disciples. Khenpo, therefore, praised Shariputra as second only to Lord Buddha in wisdom.

63. Kathok Gyalse Sönam Deutsen is the son of Terchen Longsal Nyingpo and the immediate reincarnation of Rigdzin Dudul Dorje. He and his father were renowned Nyingmapa masters. Both played a critical role in restrengthening the Kathok lineage and monastery (located in Derge and one of the oldest monasteries in eastern Tibet). Vidyadhara Dudul Dorje left his home in Derge as a young man and traveled extensively, discovering terma wherever he went. Finally he settled in Puwo. Later, the king of Derge asked him to return, which he did, but later he returned to Puwo, recommending that Terchen Longsal Nyingpo take his place.

64. Kunzang Tendzin was the son of Kathok Gyalse Sönam Deutsen. After his birth it was Drung Namkha Gyatso, a principal disciple of Terchen Longsal Nyingpo, who kept an eye on him, ever vigilant for his well-being and development. As a young man he traveled to Khawa Karpo (southeastern Tibet) and remained there performing many beneficial activities for the dharma. Later he traveled southward and opened the door to the secret land of Pema Kö.

65. The Tibetan name Dorje is a compound of two words: *rdo* which means "stone" and *rje* which means "lord." The lord of stones is the diamond.

66. Fire puja (*sbyin sreg*; Skt. yajña or homa).

67. Drigum's queen (some say daughter) later conceived a child with the mountain deity Yar Lha Shampo and gave miraculous birth to a son named Rulekye. When Rulekye was grown, he killed Minister Longam. He recovered the king's body, built a tomb for him at Darthang in Chingyul, and then brought Prince Jatri back from Puwo, enthroning him as the ninth Tibetan emperor, Pude Gung rgyal. Rulekye introduced the mining of metals to Tibet, the system of plowing with two oxen, an irrigation system, bridge building, and making glue from leather and charcoal from wood. Because of his many accomplishments he was the first to be given the title of Dzanglön (*mdzangs blon*), which means "loyal and intelligent." He is renowned as one of Tibet's greatest ministers.

68. Taksham Nuden Dorje, or Rigdzin Samten Lingpa, (1655-?) was born in the Pashö area of eastern Tibet. He was a renowned emanation of Atsar Sale, a disciple of Guru Padmasambhava, and companion of Yeshe Tsogyal. At the age of three he attained the great realization of wisdom born in the heart (*rang byung gi ye shes*), trekchö realization, and for long periods he would remain in the meditation posture gazing at the sky. At the age of eleven through the blessings of the wisdom dakinis everything became luminously clear for him, and he no longer saw a dis-

tinction between day and night. He sang songs and began to dance. Villagers called him "warrior dancer." At age seventeen on his way to a hermitage he saw Guru Rinpoche in the form of a ngagpa with his hair piled atop his head in the shape of a cone. From him he received predictions and instructions regarding his future activities. At the age of eighteen he revealed the *Heart Drop of Vajrasattva and Wrathful Kilaya* from the cave of Vairochana (*bee ro'i sgrub phug*). At age twenty he took full ordination as a monk. He revealed over seventeen treasures from different locations in eastern Tibet. One of the most famous is *Embodiment of the Realization of the Yidams*, a cycle of teachings on Hayagriva and Vajravarahi contained in nine volumes. His lineage continues to this day.

69. The "red-faced Tibetans" (*gdong dmar bod*) is an expression for the Tibetan people generally, which is here translated as "Tibet's red-faced race."

70. Nyatri (*gnya' khri*) Tsenpo was the man who according to Tibetan history descended from the sky and was proclaimed Tibet's first king, the progenitor of the Yarlung Dynasty. He is not to be confused with his later descendant Nyatri (*nya khri*), King Drigum Tsenpo's son.

71. King Drigum Tsenpo, a descendant of Nyatri (*gnya' khri*) Tsenpo, was the eighth king of the Yarlung Dynasty.

72. Langdro Lotsawa Könchog Jungne Lotsawa was one of the twenty-five heart disciples of Guru Padmasambhava.

73. Dudjom Rinpoche.

74. Jnana (*ye shes*) means "primordial wisdom" or as stated elsewhere in the text, simply, "wisdom."

75. Mön is the ancient name for Bhutan and Pema Kö.

76. See Appendix 1: About the Chronology.

77. When His Holiness was conceived, his previous incarnation, Dudjom Lingpa, was still living. A great master can reincarnate before actually dying. A single realized consciousness can emanate in many forms and places. This is the display of primordial wisdom (*rig pa'i rol rtsal ma 'gags pa*) which, according to the great master Jamgön Kongtrul, transcends the regimented systems of ordinary beings. He used as an example the single sun that is reflected upon one hundred thousand lakes. An additional example was offered by the future buddha Maitreya, who in

the Sublime Tantra said, "As the water bowls of the disciples are ready, images of buddhas instantly appear." There are no restrictions to the realized mind. Such a mind is completely beyond karma and unlimited in capacity.

78. Nyima means "sun."

79. Orgyen Dorje Chang is the name of Vajradhara, the dharmakaya buddha, and is here used as another name for Guru Padmasambhava.

80. King Trisong Deutsen.

81. Karchen Za, which means "the lady from the Karchen clan," is another name for Yeshe Tsogyal.

82. The topography of the land of Tibet is said to resemble a reclining wild demoness.

83. Phagmo (*phag mo*) is Vajra Varahi, the consort of Hayagriva. The topography of Pema Kö is said to resemble the outline of Phagmo's body.

84. Gandharvas are the members of the celestial orchestra.

85. The "six syllables" are the heart mantra of Chenrezig, and they have been painted and carved all over the landscape of Tibet by devoted practitioners: *Om Mani Padme Hung.* Reciting them invokes compassion for the six realms of sentient beings.

86. What is here referred to as "calling the lama" is listed in the Glossary as *calling the lama from afar.*

87. Only realized dharma practitioners at the time of their death and the period following are able to maintain their meditation and meditation posture. In addition other signs may appear, such as flowers, rainbows, and sweet scents.

88. Guru Rinpoche.

89. The sun's chariot-wheel was turning through the twelve months of the Wood Dragon year and had reached its full intensity in the sixth month, the summer season resonant with thunder storms. The tenth day of the sixth month, the monkey month, is the day on which Padmasambhava's birth is commemorated. In that year it happened to fall on a Sunday. On that day just as the sun was rising, His Holiness was born.

90. Khyeuchung Lotsawa.

91. The purest gold is said to come from the river that runs through Dzambu's kingdom. Dzambu is the lord of wealth.

92. This is a shortened expression for Guru Padmasambhava and his consort Yeshe Tsogyal.

93. Oftentimes in Tibetan dharma texts the Sanskrit and Tibetan mantras are given only in an abbreviated form, e.g., only *argyam*, the first word of the mantra that accompanies the filling of the offering bowls, is printed.

94. This verse is a whimsical rendition of the outings of Dudjom Rinpoche and his tutor, Lama Pema, who is here styled a firm tree atop which the child Dudjom sat, as teacher and student took walks in the countryside. Lama Pema is also the subject of the following verse. Here, the scenery is described in philosophical vocabulary, as being the visible manifestation of relative truth or as the result of the twelve links of interdependent coorigination. The world of ordinary causation, or samsara, is ordered by the twelve interdependent links of coorigination, starting with ignorance and ending in death.

95. In the distant future Dudjom Rinpoche will reincarnate as Möpa Thaye, the last buddha of the one thousand buddhas of this Fortunate Aeon. Of the thousand, Buddha Shakyamuni was fourth.

96. What are here referred to as "three vehicles of true speech" are listed in the Glossary as *three vehicles*.

97. What are here referred to as the "four attractions" are listed in the Glossary as *four attractive behaviors*.

98. The four classes of gods and men referred to here are lay and ordained practitioners, both human and divine. Only by poetic license are gods included here. The teachings indicate that gods can only take upasaka vows.

99. Empowerments, transmissions, and pith instructions here translate the Tibetan terms *dbang, lung,* and *khrid*. Elsewhere in Heap Four these same English terms will translate the terms *smin, grol,* and *rgyab brten*, which together are a metonymic abbreviation for the ripening (*smin*) empowerments, the liberating (*grol*) instructions, and supporting (*rgyab brten*) instruction, i.e., instruction on tormas, the shrine, etc.

100. Longsal Nyingpo (1625-1692), an emanation of one of Guru Padmasambhava's twenty-five disciples, Langdro Lotsawa Könchog Jungne, was born in
Derge in eastern Tibet. Around the age of twenty-eight, he received indications,
which he ignored, that he was to reveal terma. Soon after, he met Rigdzin Dudul
Dorje, who encouraged him to reveal his allotted treasures. At age thirty-two, a
yogi, brown in color and wearing bone ornaments, gave him the necessary
khajang. Longsal Nyingpo knew this yogi to be Guru Padmasambhava. He then
proceeded to reveal terma along with ritual objects and ringsel from various locations in eastern Tibet. He restored Kathok, the oldest monastery in eastern Tibet.
His teachings continue in an unbroken stream.

101. Ngari Pandita Pema Wangyal (1487-1542/1543) was born in the Lowo
Mentang region of western Tibet. (This region is now part of Nepal and known as
Mustang.) He was renowned as the heart emanation of King Trisong Deutsen. His
father was Jamyang Rinchen Gyaltsen, and from him he received many teachings.
His education and development continued with masters from all the schools of
Tibetan Buddhism living in the region. As a result, he was known as a pandita, or
great scholar. At the age of twenty-five he took full ordination and from then on
was known for his strict observance of the vinaya rules. He followed the twelve
ascetic practices. In his late thirties he and his younger brother Rigdzin Legden Je
moved to central Tibet. At Samye Monastery he recalled many incidents from his
lifetime as King Trisong Deutsen. He revealed many termas including
Condensation of the Entire Vidyadhara Cycle, which he extracted from the statue of
Buddha Vairochana at Samye. He continued to transmit the teachings to many disciples. Among his most famous works is his composition *Definitive Distinctions
among the Three Vows*.

102. Khorde rushen (*'khor 'das ru shan*) is the Dzogchen technique that investigates
dualistic thinking and that results in the decisive identification of the borderline—
if such exists—between samsara and nirvana. Where is the borderline? Is it outside,
or inside, or is it in between? The practitioner must decide.

103. *Treasury of Precious Treasures* is a collection of the major termas of each major
tertön of the Nyingma School. This collection was arranged by Jamgön Kongtrul
Yönten Gyatso and published in sixty volumes.

104. Lord Khyentse here means the first Khyentse, Pema Ösel Dongak Lingpa.
For further details see the Glossary listing *seven entrusted transmissions of*

Jamyang Khyentse Wangpo.

105. The *Four Medical Tantras* are: (1) *Root Tantra*; (2) *Exegetical Tantra*; (3) *Tantra of Pith Instructions*; and (4) *Subsequent Tantra*. The authorship of these is usually attributed to Gyuthog Yönten Gönpo, who served as the personal physician of King Trisong Deutsen and who is regarded as an emanation of the Medicine Buddha. Another tradition claims that the Medicine Buddha revealed them at an earlier date to an Indian master and that later they were committed to writing. Then at the time of King Trisong Deutsen they were translated from the Sanskrit originals into Tibetan by Vairochana. These four tantras were then concealed as terma that were later revealed by Tertön Drapa Ngönshe in the eleventh century CE. Many great physicians have composed commentaries on these.

106. The two great Jamgöns (*'jam mgon*) are the first Khyentse and the first Kongtrul. The epithet can be understood like this: as these two masters are inseparable from Manjushri (*'jam dpal*), like him they will protect (*mgon*) all beings.

107. Padmasambhava gave this name to Jedrung Thrinle in one of his own termas.

108. *Gradual Path of the Essence of Wisdom* is a record of the oral teachings of Padmasambhava, written by Yeshe Tsogyal.

109. Senge Rabsal is the coming sixth buddha of the one thousand buddhas of this Fortunate Aeon.

110. In this context "semde" is an abbreviation for all three divisions of Atiyoga: mind class or semde (*sems sde*), space class or longde (*klong sde*), and pith instruction class or men-ngagde (*man ngag sde*). For further discussion of the maha, anu, and ati divisions of tantra, see Dudjom's own *Rejuvenating Medicine of the Heart* in Heap Six.

111. Vajrakilaya is the wrathful form of Vajrasattva, a sambhogakaya buddha who embodies the enlightened activity of all the buddhas. Vajrakilaya is one of the eight herukas of the Nyingma tantras.

112. Nanam Dorje Dudjom was one of Guru Rinpoche's twenty-five main disciples.

113. *Supra tishta ye soha*, "May this realization remain firmly with you!"

114. *Heart Practice That Dispels All Obstacles*: a cycle of teachings revealed by Chogyur Lingpa together with Jamyang Khyentse Wangpo.

115. Dorje Thogme (1746-1796/1797), an emanation of Yudra Nyingpo (one of the twenty-five disciples of Guru Padmasambhava), was born in the Kongpo area of southern Tibet. When he was young, he had visions of Guru Padmasambhava and Yeshe Tsogyal. Under their guidance he began revealing terma. In his twenties, he discovered his khajang at Dongchu Monastery, and elsewhere in the Puwo area he revealed *Nets of Light Long-Life Practice*. Publicly, he revealed many other terma teachings. His consort, Khandro Da Öd Wangmo, maintained these teachings, and through her the lineage was transmitted. She reached the highest realization of Dzogchen.

116. Garwang Sangye Dorje is also known as Phulung Tulku Sangye. His kudung is in third camp at Orissa. After the 1959 Chinese invasion and occupation of Tibet, the Indian government made tracts of land available for Tibetan refugees. These tracts were located in several Indian states. Each tract was large enough to be divided into smaller areas called camps, or settlements, where they were allowed to maintain their spiritual and cultural heritage.

117. Chakrasamvara, Hevajra, and Guhyasamaja are yidam deities of the unsurpassed tantra section of secret mantra belonging to the new translation (*gsar ma*) tradition of Tibetan vajrayana. The first two in particular are associated with the sarma tradition.

118. Jigme Trogyal Dorje (1913-) is more commonly known as Chatral Rinpoche, or in full, Chatral Rinpoche Sangye Dorje Trogyal Dorje. In this text he is also referred to as Chatral Sangye Dorje and Sangye Dorje Tsal. There are several instances in which the honorific Kyabje is added to his name.

119. Dechen Dewe Dorje, also known as Sera Khandro, (1899-1952) was a renowned wisdom dakini. Though born in central Tibet, it was predicted she would make a connection with Dudjom Lingpa. As a young adult, she made the journey to eastern Tibet and established a relationship with his son, Tulku Drimed.

120. In the West Orgyen Tsewang Palbar is commonly known as Tulku Urgyen (1920-1996).

121. The five categories (*rim lnga*): tummo, phowa, bardo, illusory body, and clear light.

122. *Mirror of Poetry* is a text, written in verse, on poetic composition by the famous Indian poet Dandi.

123. The "practice lineages" are commonly used to refer to the Nyingma and Kagyu schools, but in this case it refers specifically to the Kagyu School.

124. Lhatsun Namkha Jigme (1597-16 . . . ?) was the emanation of the great Dzogchen masters Vimalamitra and Longchenpa. The *Heart Practice of the Vidyadhara* and the *Vajra Heart Hymns of the Clouds* have been very popular teachings of the Nyingma School until the present day. At the age of fifty in 1646, complying with the direct requests of Rigdzin Jatsön Nyingpo and Dudul Dorje, he traveled to Sikkim and opened the secret valley Beyul Drejong.

125. *Chart of Nerves and Muscles* is a medical text that includes such topics as pulse diagnosis, body structures, diseases, and treatments.

126. Marpa Lotsawa (1012-1097), known as the "father" of the Marpa Kagyupa school, was the student of Naropa and the teacher of Milarepa.

127. Milarepa (1040-1123), a disciple of Marpa, was one of Tibet's most famous yogis.

128. Gampopa (1079-1153) is equally well known as Dagpo Lhaje, the physician from the Dagpo region of Tibet. He is one of Milarepa's most famous students. Prior to meeting the great yogi, he had been a practitioner of the Kadampa School. Gampopa combined the teachings of these two schools into one. Except for the Shangpa Kagyu, all the different Kagyu schools originated with or were transmitted by his disciples.

129. Five Teachings of Maitreya: (1) *Ornament of Vivid Realization*; (2) *Ornament of the Mahayana Sutras*; (3) *Discriminating between the Middle Way and the Extremes*; (4) *Discerning Phenomena and Their Nature*; and (5) *Sublime Tantra*.

130. Mudra has many different meanings in the tantras; "hand gestures with ritual objects" is one.

131. Lineage blessings, empowerments, and pith instructions (*byin rlabs dbang khrid*).

132. What is here referred to as "tenfold mastery" is listed in the Glossary as *ten qualifications*.

133. The three cities of our vajra body are: (1) five aggregates and five elements (*phung khams gshegs pa gshegs ma*), which are the city of the five male and five

female buddhas; (2) the five sense organs and their objects (*dbang yul sems dpa'
sems ma*), which are the city of the five male and five female bodhisattvas; (3)
the four limbs (*yan lag khro bo khro mo*), which are the city of the wrathful male
and female deities.

134. Garab Dorje was the first historical teacher of Dzogchen.

135. The three immovables are: (1) body (*lus mi 'gul*); (2) channels (*rtsa mi
'gul*); and (3) eyes (*mig mi 'gul*).

136. The three basic practices of the vinaya, or zhi sum (*gzhi gsum*), are: (1)
purification (*gso sbyong gi gzhi*); (2) summer retreat (*dbyar gnas kyi gzhi*), the
last day of which includes the participants taking turns teaching late into the
night or even all through the night (*mtshan thog thag*); (3) coming out of the
retreat (*dgag dbye'i gzhi*), which includes a few days of sightseeing, picnicking,
and partying (*ljongs rgyu*).

137. "Mantra recitation" here renders the Tibetan term nyendrub (*bsnyen sgrub*).

138. The "six strengths" (*gshog drug*) allude to the flying skills of the eagle and
are here a metaphor for the strength of keeping samayas.

139. Taktsang, Tiger's Nest Cave, is an important location near the current town of
Padro (Paro) in Bhutan where Guru Rinpoche transformed into Dorje Drolö.

140. Tashi Gang is an important town in Bhutan.

141. The three places (*gnas gsum*) are: (1) celestial earth (*sa spyod*); (2) celestial
sky (*mkha' spyod*); (3) celestial pure land (*zhing spyod*).

142. Bumthang Valley, located in Bhutan, is one of the holiest pilgrimage destinations in the world. In the valley is a famous body imprint of
Padmasambhava, the Tarpa Ling Monastery established by Longchenpa, and
many other significant sites.

143. Zangdok Palri Monastery, Glorious Copper-Color Mountain Monastery, is
named after Guru Rinpoche's pure land. Both are also known by the name Ogmin
Palri. Kongpo Buchu is one of the acupuncture points according to Tibetan geo-
mancy and the astrological earth chart. In the seventh century King Songtsen
Gampo built temples on this point, as well as many others, to restore and rebalance
the earth energy. Subsequently, Guru Rinpoche and a number of other great

masters and tertöns restored these temples. For the same reason, His Holiness came to settle in this location and proceeded to established five dharma centers all situated very close to one other. The principal temple was known as Dechen Teng. In addition there were Sangchen Ösel Namdröling; Lama Ling, which served mainly ngagpa retreatants and lay practitioners; Rigdzin Gatsal Ling, which was named after his wife, Sangyum Kuzhok, and served as the residence and personal retreat center for His Holiness and the Sangyum. And on a small hill nearby named Jewel Mountain (*nor bu ri*), he built Zangdok Palri Monastery.

144. What is translated as the "three and six flight skills" (*gshog drug rtsol gsum*) is a formulaic expression for the eagle's strength and skill in flight.

145. What are here referred to as "two goods" are listed in the Glossary as *two benefits*.

146. A "dudul stupa" is a specific type of stupa that brings about the pacification and subjugation of negative forces.

147. Khyentse Chökyi Lodrö (c. 1893-1959), the second Khyentse, is the reincarnation of Jamyang Khyentse Wangpo.

148. The eagle's flight skills are being praised with the formulaic expression, "six strengths" (*gshog drug*).

149. "White-robed ngagpas" is an epithet for the lay mantra practitioner, just as "golden-robed monks and nuns" is one for the ordained. It does not mean that they were always attired in that fashion, and at the time in question, they were not.

150. The threefold division of the Nyingma inner tantras is maha, anu, and ati; but His Holiness indicates them with the metonymic abbreviation Do, Gyü, Sem. Do and Gyü refer to the principal texts associated with the anu and maha division, while sem, as has previously been explained, refers not just to the semde texts of Atiyoga, but to the longde and men-ngagde as well.

151. *The Sutra Which Gathers All Intentions* (*mdo dgongs pa 'dus pa*; also, *dgongs pa 'dus pa'i mdo*) is the general condensation of the other Anuyoga tantras often given as six in number. They are: (1) *Expressing the Qualities of Kuntuzangpo within Oneself Tantra*; (2) *King of Empowerments Tantra*; (3) *Supreme Samadhi Tantra*; (4) *Seven Applications of Time Tantra*; (5) *Meaningfulness of Effort Tantra*; and (6) *Display of Samaya Tantra*.

152. The Mahayoga tantras are collectively known as the *Eighteen Mahayoga Tantras*. They are: (1) *Awakened Union Body Tantra*; (2) *Secret Moon Sphere Speech Tantra*; (3) *Assembly of Secrets Mind Tantra* (Skt. *Guhyasamaja*); (4) *Glorious First and Foremost Qualities Tantra*; (5) *Garland of Actions Activity Tantra* (these are the five fundamental root tantras); (6) *Heruka Enjoyment Tantra*; (7) *Glorious Hayagriva Enjoyment Tantra*; (8) *Compassion Enjoyment Tantra*; (9) *Ambrosia Enjoyment Tantra*; (10) *Source of the Twelve Kilayas Tantra* (these are the five branch tantras related to practice); (11) *Pile of Mountains Tantra*; (12) *Splendid Lightning Tantra*; (13) *Array of Samayas Tantra*; (14) *One-Pointed Samadhi Tantra*; (15) *Ultimate Gift of the Elephant Tantra* (these are the five branch tantras related to conduct); (16) *Vairochana's Net of Magical Illusions Tantra* (this is the branch tantra which explains mandalas); (17) *Skillful Lotus Garland Lasso Tantra* (this is the branch tantra which explains the techniques of accomplishment); and (18) *Glorious Secret Essence Tantra—Vajrasattva's Net of Magical Illusions* (Skt. *Guyhagarbha Mayajala*; this is the condensed root text of the other seventeen Mahayoga tantras, making eighteen all together).

153. *Ka gong phur sum* (*bka' dgongs phur gsum*) is another abbreviation. *Ka* is short for *bka' brgyad*, the many cycles of terma related to the eight herukas. *Gong*, which is short for *bla ma dgongs 'dus,* usually refers to a terma of Sangye Lingpa. In this context, however, *gong* signifies all the terma cycles focusing on the primordial nature discovered through practice on the guru. *Phur* is short for *rdo rje phur pa*, or Vajrakilaya, one of the principal yidams of the Nyingmapa. Vajrakilaya practice quickly overcomes all obstacles to enlightenment. *Sum*, the last term in the phrase *ka gong phur sum*, means *three*.

154. The term "major" indicates that the treasures revealed by a particular tertön include teachings from all three categories of both *ka gong phur sum* and *la dzog thug sum* (*bla rdzogs thugs gsum*; an abbreviation for lama, Dzogchen, and Avalokiteshvara). Likewise the adjective "lesser" is applied to a treasure revealer whose terma did not include representative teachings from each of these categories.

155. *Vajrasattva's Net of Magical Illusions* is a shortened name for the root text of the *Eighteen Mahayoga Tantras*, i.e., *Glorious Secret Essence Tantra—Vajrasattva's Net of Magical Illusions*. It should be mentioned again that the title *Secret Essence Tantra—The Net of Magical Illusions* (*Guhyagarbha Mayajala*) can refer to the root tantra in particular or serve as an abbreviation pointing to this entire cycle of

Mahayoga tantras. Furthermore the *Net of Magical Illusions* (*Mayajala*) portion of the title lends its name to another grouping of supplementary tantras related to this cycle called *Eight Divisions of Mayajala*. This grouping includes: (1) *Root Tantra of the Secret Essence* (i.e., *Vajrasattva's Net of Magical Illusions*); (2) *Expressing the Direct Display of the Divine Lady of Magical Illusions*; (3) *Eight Magical Illusions Showing the Mandalas*; (4) *Forty Magical Illusions Showing Activity*; (5) *Supreme Magical Illusions Showing Power*; (6) *Eighty Magical Illusions Showing Perfected Qualities*; (7) *Great Net of Magical Illusions Showing Pervasion in All Sutras*; (8) *Branch Magical Illusions Showing Samaya Mainly*.

156. *Condensed Sutra Mandala of the Great Assembly* is an extraction from *The Sutra Which Gathers All Intentions*.

157. The mind class of Atiyoga includes eighteen tantras, which are: (1) *Cuckoo's Awareness*; (2) *Great Power Shaking It Up*; (3) *Gliding Garuda*; (4) *Gold Nugget from Molten Ore*; (5) *Never-Flagging Victory Banner* (these five are the mother semde tantras translated earlier by Vairochana); (6) *Victory Arising as a Summit*; (7) *Sky King*; (8) *Display of Bliss*; (9) *Strap of General Accomplishment*; (10) *Essence of Bodhichitta*; (11) *Bliss Pervaded*; (12) *Wheel of Life Force*; (13) *Six Spheres*; (14) *Perfection of Ordinary Conduct*; (15) *Wish-Fulfilling Jewel*; (16) *Condensed Awareness*; (17) *Holy Powerful Might*; (18) *Accomplishing the Purpose of Meditation* (these thirteen are the son semde tantras translated later by Vimalamitra, Nyak Jnana Kumara, and Yudra Nyingpo).

158. The space class of Atiyoga comprises the following four tantras: (1) *Black Space Tantra Expressing the Negation of Causes*; (2) *Striped Space Tantra Expressing Variations*; (3) *White Space Tantra Expressing Mind*; (4) *Pervasive Space Tantra Expressing the Conclusion of Cause and Effect*.

159. The *Seventeen Tantras* refer to the tantras of the esoteric instruction class (*man ngag sde*) of Atiyoga. They are: (1) *Natural Arising of Awareness*; (2) *Mirror of the Heart of Vajrasattva*; (3) *Lion's Perfect Expressive Power*; (4) *Absence of Syllables*; (5) *Beauteous Good Auspices*; (6) *Penetration of Sound*; (7) *Mirror of the Heart of Samantabhadra*; (8) *Blazing Lamp*; (9) *Array of Fine Gemstones*; (10) *Coalescence of Sun and Moon*; (11) *Pearl Necklace*; (12) *Natural Liberation of Awareness*; (13) *Sixfold Expanse*; (14) *Naturally Born Perfection*; (15) *Black Wrathful Goddess*; (16) *Blazing Relics of Buddha-Body*; (17) *Mound of Gemstones*.

160. Dor-Min is an abbreviation for the two monasteries Dorje Drag and

Mindröling; Ka-Pal, for Kathok and Palyul; and Zhe-Dzog, for Zhechen and Dzogchen.

161. Khenpos Chen and Chung refer to Minling Chen Gyurme Khentyse Norbu and Minling Chung Gyurme Ngagwang Chökyi Dragpa.

162. *Ka gong* is a further abbreviation of the abbreviation *ka gong phur sum* explained above. (See endnote 153.)

163. Khenchen Dorje Chang, an honorific name for any honored personal teacher, refers to Gyurme Phende Özer, who was one of His Holiness's principal teachers.

164. Shakyamuni Buddha.

165. The fourteenth Dalai Lama.

166. Dharamsala in Himachal Pradesh, northern India, is the seat of the Tibetan government-in-exile and since 1961 the home of His Holiness the fourteenth Dalai Lama.

167. Dzongsar Khyentse Thubten Chökyi Gyatso, the third Khyentse, is the reincarnation of Khyentse Chökyi Lodrö. He is the son of Dungse Thinley Norbu Rinpoche and the grandson of H.H. Dudjom Rinpoche.

168. Dungse (*gdung sras*; child of the body) is the honorific title for a genealogical lineage holder. Thinley Norbu Rinpoche and Shenphen Dawa Rinpoche are Kyabje Dudjom's sons.

169. Four renunciations, or four thoughts that turn the mind, are the contemplation of the preciousness of the human body, impermanence, the infallibility of karma, and the unsatisfactoriness of samsara.

170. The outer refers to the structure itself as container, and the inner to the murals, statues, thangkas, etc. as the contained.

171. Royal Queen Grandmother of Bhutan is Azhe Phuntsok Chödrön. She is grandmother to the current king, Jigme Senge Wangchuk, on his father's side.

172. The thirteen great activities of a vajracharya (*rdo rje slob dpon gyi las chen bcu gsum*) are an elaboration on the list of the ten qualifications of a vajra master. See *ten qualifications* in the Glossary.

173. There are four phases of approach and accomplishment (*bsnyen sgrub las*

bzhi): (1) practice (*bsnyen pa*); (2) intensive practice (*nye bar bsnyen pa*); (3) practice in the context of ritual ceremony (*sgrub pa*); (4) nonstop practice in the context of ritual ceremony for extended periods of time (*sgrub pa chen po*). Approach and accomplishment is an abbreviation for the entire series. All four are instrumental to the actualization of the creation and completion stages.

174. "Instruction manuals" translates the Tibetan *chog khrig*.

175. "Pith retreat instructions" translates the Tibetan *khrid yig*.

176. This letter is a slightly modified version of the translation that appeared in *View* magazine, Issue 10 (1998), a publication of Sogyal Rinpoche's Rigpa Organization.

177. Yeshe Nyingpo was always a part of the name for each of the dharma centers that His Holiness established in North America.

178. The causal vehicle includes the shravakayana, pratyekabuddhayana, and the bodhisattvayana, and emphasizes the causes that must be made to attain enlightenment. Tantric practitioners blazing with bodhichitta and a multitude of skillful means act as if the result, supreme enlightenment, were already in the palm of one's hand.

179. Through the effort of a few dedicated scholars, the collection now totals over a hundred volumes.

180. In late 1977 and early 1978 Dudjom Rinpoche would give the last major teachings of his life, which focused on his own treasures and those of his immediate predecessor, Dudjom Lingpa. The author of this biography chose to signal and honor the special significance of this event by using the elevated diction of the five perfections (*nges pa lnga*). The five perfections are given as the perfect time, the perfect place, the perfect teacher, the perfect retinue, and the perfect teachings. They are the categories used to characterize the transmission of the teachings from cosmic levels, through intermediate levels, and down through the levels of the realms of a variety of species including devas, nagas, and humans.

181. Ka Nying Shedrub Ling is Tulku Urgyen's monastery.

182. *Six Categories of Taking Refuge* is the refuge teachings of Vimalamitra.

183. Of the eight grammar texts composed by Thonmi Sambhota, only two are

extant: *Thirty Lines Explaining the Vowels and Consonants* and *Gender of Tibetan Syllables and Verb Conjugation*. The text referred to here contained these two surviving texts.

184. The title of this commentary is *The Scholar's Beautiful Pearl Necklace*.

185. *Purifying the Limbs and Body through Meditation on the Five Dhyani Buddhas* is a complete cycle of esoteric yoga practices linked to the five dhyani buddhas and focusing on the channels, winds, and essential nuclei. These include physical exercises and breathing techniques that involve the large vase (*bum chen*) and small vase (*bum chung*).

186. This empowerment has as its central deity Thousand-Armed Chenrezig (Avalokiteshvara). The one thousand buddhas are enumerated in detail in the *Auspicious Aeon Sutra*.

187. This verse is from the *Mani Kabum* by King Songtsen Gampo. The text was subsequently hidden but later discovered by Atisha.

188. The eighteen endowments (*dal 'byor bco brgyad*) are divided into two categories. The first category is called the Eight Freedoms (*mi khoms pa brgyad*). They are free from the eight circumstances that are impossible to improve upon: (1) hell realm (*dmyal ba*); (2) hungry ghost realm (*yi dvags*); (3) animal realm (*dud 'gro*); (4) long-life god realm (*tshe ring lha*); (5) barbarians (*kla klo*); (6) wrong views (*log lta can*); (7) an aeon in which buddha's teaching is not available (*sangs rgyas kyis stong pa*); and (8) defective organs (*lkug pa*). The second category is called the Ten Luxuries (*'byor ba bcu*) but is further divided into two groups of five. The first group contains the five luxuries related to oneself (*rang 'byor lnga*): (1) born as a human (*mir gyur*); (2) all the organs are fully functioning (*dbang tshang*); (3) born in a land where the teachings are available (*yul dbus skyes*); (4) not engaged in a negative means of livelihood (*las mtha' ma log*) or forced by circumstances outside one's control, such as slavery or a caste system; and (5) devoted to the teachings (*bstan pa dad*). The second group contains the five luxuries related to others (*gzhan 'byor lnga*): (1) a buddha came (*rgyal byon*); (2) a buddha taught (*chos gsung*); (3) as a buddha taught, so those teachings remain (*bstan pa gnas*); (4) a sangha still exists (*der 'jug*); and (5) teachers are available and able to guide you (*bshes zin*).

189. Khenpo hastened to comment that it is never too late to do mental offerings.

190. As mentioned previously the tenth day of the Monkey month, the sixth month of the Tibetan lunar calendar, is traditionally associated with Guru Rinpoche's miraculous birth. What made this date even more auspicious is that it occurred in the year associated with Guru Rinpoche's birth, i.e., the Monkey year.

191. The qualities of the Buddha are traditionally represented by the eight auspicious symbols (*bkra shis rtags brgyad*). These were offered to Buddha Shakyamuni at the time of his birth. They are: (1) the precious umbrella (*rin chen gdugs*), representing respect; (2) the two golden fish (*gser gyi nya*), representing Buddha's eyes or transcendent wisdom; (3) the inexhaustible treasure vase (*gter chen po'i bum pa*), representing the innumerable qualities of Buddha's body; (4) the excellent lotus flower (*pad ma bzang po*), representing the purity of Buddha's mind; (5) the precious white conch with a spiral that turns to the right (*dung dkar g.yas 'khyil*), representing the sound of dharma which can be heard in all directions; (6) the glorious knot (*dpal gyi be'u*), representing the great love of all the buddhas and the never-ending continuity of the teachings; (7) the supreme banner of victory (*mchog gi rgyal mtshan*), representing victory over negativities; and (8) the precious wheel of dharma (*gser gyi 'khor lo*), representing the teachings of the Buddha.

192. The seven royal treasures (*rgyal srid sna bdun*) are: (1) the precious wheel (*'khor lo rin po che*); (2) the wish-fulfilling jewel (*nor bu rin po che*); (3) the queen (*btsun mo rin po che*); (4) the minister (*blon po rin po che*); (5) the elephant (*glang po rin po che*); (6) the horse (*rta mchog rin po che*); and (7) the general (*dmag dpon rin po che*).

193. *Meditation Instructions of the Nine Yanas* is a text extracted from the *Condensed Sutra Mandala of the Great Assembly*. (See Dudjom's *Rejuvenating Medicine of the Heart* included in this biography for mention of the latter title.) It explains the practices of each of the nine yanas from the Anuyoga perspective.

194. Please consult with your teachers and the Dzogchen texts.

195. Losar (*lo sar*) is the Tibetan new year. See Appendix 1.

196. Shedra (*bshad gra*) is the academic department of the monastery in which the five major fields of knowledge (*rig pa'i gnas chen lnga*) and the five minor fields of knowledge (*rig pa'i gnas chung lnga*) are studied. The five major fields of knowledge are: (1) knowledge of language, grammar, poetry, sounds, music (*sgra rig pa*); (2) knowledge of logic (*tshad ma rig pa*); (3) knowledge of sculpting, painting,

smithing, alchemy, carpentry (*bzo rig pa*); (4) art of healing (*gso ba rig pa*); (5) knowledge of mind (*nang don rig pa*), which is the study of Buddha's teachings.

The five minor fields of study are further subdivisions of the five major ones: (1) knowledge of poetry (*snyan ngag*), e.g., the use of a sweet voice or a rough voice to convey the presence of those qualities in some person, place, or thing; (2) knowledge of stylistics (*sdeb sbyor*) calls our attention to the weight of words, their gender, etc.; (3) knowledge of synonyms (*mngon brjod*); (4) knowledge of theater and dance (*zlos gar*); (5) knowledge of astrology and mathematics (*rtsis*).

197. Six distinctive features (*khyad chos che ba drug*) of the Nyingma are: (1) extraordinary patrons; (2) extraordinary teachers; (3) extraordinary translators; (4) extraordinary location for the translation to occur; (5) extraordinary teachings to be translated; (6) extraordinary gifts presented to the teachers and translators. More details can be found in Khenpo Tsewang Dongyal's two-volume set *Six Pillars of the Nyingma School Commemorating the Legacy of the Most Kind Beings.*

198. *gshin rje'i khram mdos.*

199. *chu sbyin stong zlog.*

200. "Supreme nonfocus" translates the Tibetan *dngos gzhi dmigs med dam pa.*

201. Guru Padmasambhava.

202. *The Gathered Essence of the Cycles of Seven Great Tertöns* is another name for *Granting All Wishes, Joyful Feast of Accomplishment, the Practice on the Heart Essence of the Lama.*

203. Me Ön Sum (*mes dbon gsum*) are the three founding fathers: Songtsen Gampo, Trisong Deutsen, and Tri Ralpa Chen.

204. Khen-Lob-Chö is an abbreviation for Khenpo, Lobpön, Chögyal (*mkhan po, slob dpon, chos rgyal*) who are Khenpo Shantarakshita, Lobpön Padmasambhava, and Dharma King Trisong Deutsen.

205. The Six Ornaments and the Two Supreme Ones (*rgyan drug mchog gnyis*) are: Nagarjuna, Aryadeva, Asanga, Dignaga, Vasubandhu, and Dharmakirti and Shakyaprabha and Gunaprabha. (Sometimes Nagarjuna and Asanga are listed as the two supreme ones. In which case, they are also included in the list of six ornaments. The last two names, Shakyaprabha and Gunaprabha, are then deleted.)

206. Kyabje is here drawing our attention to the entire range of dharma, which can be summarized in two aspects: scholarship (*lung gi bstan pa*), exemplified by the Ten Great Pillars, and practice (*rtogs pa'i bstan pa*), exemplified by the Eight Great Chariots.

207. Tibetan tradition divides the lunar month into the waxing period called "white side" (*dkar phyogs*) and the waning period called "red side" (*dmar phyogs*), also known as the side of wisdom. So the letter was composed on the seventeenth day of the lunar month.

208. Shakyamuni Buddha.

209. In Kyabje's own treatises he calculated the birth of Lord Buddha to have taken place in 961 BCE. The author of this biography as Kyabje's secretary had written this portion of the letter for His Holiness and used the dates as given in the Theravadin tradition of Sri Lanka.

210. The honorific title Very Venerable is a translation of ngagyur tenpai drönme (*snga 'gyur bstan pa'i sgron me*). Ngagyur is a synonym for the Nyingma tradition, and tenpai drönme means "lamp" or "holder of the teachings."

211. Outwardly, the five constituents of the physical body (*phung khams*) are the five elements (*khams lnga*) of the universe: (1) earth (*sa*); (2) water (*chu*); (3) fire (*me*); (4) wind (*rlung*); and (5) space (*nam mkha'*). Inwardly, these are the five aggregates (*phung lnga*): (1) form (*gzugs kyi phung po*); (2) feeling (*tshor ba'i phung po*); (3) perception-conception (*'du shes kyi phung po*); (4) activating mental formations (*'du byed kyi phung po*); and (5) consciousness (*rnam shes kyi phung po*). According to the vajrayana, the elements and aggregates (the container and the contained) have always been enlightened, directly corresponding to the five female and the five male buddhas. The five female buddhas are: (1) Buddha-Lochana (*sangs rgyas spyan ma*; earth); (2) Mamaki (*ma ma ki*; water); (3) Pandaravasini (*gos dkar mo*; fire); (4) Samaya Tara (*dam tshig sgrol ma*; wind); (5) Dhatvishvari (*dbyings phyug ma*; space). The five dhyani buddhas are: (1) Vairochana (*rnam par snang mdzad*; form); (2) Ratnasambhava (*rin chen 'byung ldan*; feeling); (3) Amitabha (*snang ba mtha' yas*; perception-conception); (4) Amoghasiddhi (*don yod grub pa*; activating mental formations); (5) Vajrasattva (*rdo rje sems dpa'*; consciousness).

212. The mandala of the universe consists of peaceful and wrathful deities, both

female and male. For further information consult the many translations of the *Tibetan Book of the Dead (Liberation upon Hearing)*.

213. What are here referred to as the "three treasure bowls" are a metaphor for the *three devotions*. The latter expression can be found in the Glossary.

214. To behold Guru Rinpoche and Yeshe Tsogyal directly in pure perception, to receive from them empowerment, instruction regarding one's lifework, and a powerful name sealing that mission is the true significance of enthronement.

215. Guru Padmasambhava and Yeshe Tsogyal.

216. The Tibetan term used here is *jangbu* (*byang bu*). In this instance Kyabje may be referring to actual terma or to the authorization code. See *khajang* in the Glossary.

217. The symbolic dakini languages and scripts used to encode terma are written on paper of various colors, but most often on yellow paper. See also *nine lineages* in the Glossary.

218. Nabza Karmo (*na bza' dkar mo*) is a variant of Gö Karmo (*gos dkar mo*), the female buddha of the fire element. Both names mean "white robed." She is also the goddess of long life.

219. Nyida (*nyi zla*) is a joined sun and moon disc, symbolizing skillful means and wisdom. The sun represents the female aspect and the moon the male aspect.

220. See *terma key* in the Glossary.

221. This is quite usual. It is very rare that a tertön would share the content of his revelation immediately. Without maturing yourself, you can't mature others. It depends on timing and right circumstances. In this case, this was actually specified in the terma.

222. Casket (*sgrom bu*) is the box in which the terma is concealed, but in this case it is mental.

223. This became the ganachakra offering prayer in the *Heart Drop of the Dakini* sadhana.

224. Three great masters: Padmasambhava, Vimalamitra, and Silamanju who at Yangleshö gathered, consolidated, and refined the Vajrakilaya teachings as we know them today.

225. The eight classes of spirits (*sde brgyad*) can be categorized in many ways; this is one list: (1) gods (*lha*); (2) nagas (*klu*); (3) yakshas (*gnod sbyin*); (4) demons (*bdud*); (5) cannibals (*srin po*); (6) red spirits (*btsan*); (7) arrogant spirits (*rgyal po*); and (8) planetary spirits (*gza'*). Among the eight classes, the gyalpo (*rgyal po*) and senmo (*bsen mo*; female side of the gyalpo class of beings) would bring many problems in this current time, mental problems and clinging, both creating obstacles to practice.

226. Gungtang Mountain Pass in Tibet is the site from which Guru Rinpoche left this world of Jambudvipa in 816 CE for the satellite continent of Ngayab in the southwestern direction.

227. Two tertöns are two of his previous incarnations: Dudul Dorje and Dudjom Lingpa.

228. *I-Thi* (*I thi*) means "It is sealed."

229. Sarva Mangalam (Skt.) means "May all be auspicious."

230. These are the two accumulations (*tshogs gnyis*): (1) of merit (*bsod nams*) through good deeds; and (2) of wisdom (*ye shes*) through meditation.

231. "Terma code" is here translating the Tibetan term *khajang* (*kha byang*).

232. Yarje Orgyen Lingpa, the seventh incarnation of Prince Lhaje, was born in 1323, the Water Pig year, in central Tibet into a family of ngagpas. He studied astrology and medicine thoroughly. At age twenty-three he discovered his khajang at the red stupa at Samye Monastery. From the Rahula statue at the Crystal Cave in Yarlung Shedra Mountain he revealed terma from its different parts: head, central face, heart, snake tail, tip of the tail, and hands. One of the most famous of these discoveries (from Rahula's heart) is *The Life and Liberation of Padmasambhava*.

233. The Jokhang is the premier temple of Lhasa, housing the famous statue of Lord Buddha, which was the dowry of Chinese princess Önchang Kongjo, wife of King Songtsen Gampo.

234. Jokhang.

235. Words that had accumulated over time and that were not part of the original terma are here referred to as extraneous.

236. Rigdzin Godem Chen (1337-1408) was born in central Tibet and was the

incarnation of Nanam Dorje Dudjom. At the cave of Zangzang Lhadrak he discovered his principal terma, Gongpa Zangtal. This treasure is central to the tradition known as the Northern Treasure Lineage, the monastic seat of which was
located at Dorje Drag. The terma was also practiced by the fifth Dalai Lama and
is an important teaching among Nyingmapas today. Rigdzin Godem Chen was
one of several vidyadharas who opened the hidden land of Sikkim.

237. Bhutan.

238. Nyang-ral Nyima Özer, Guru Chöwang (Guru Chökyi Wangchuk), Rongzompa, Longchenpa.

239. *Life-long dakini* refers to Kyabje's wife, Sangyum Kuzhok. She represented
the long-life female buddha Gö Karmo.

240. This is to have actualized the fourth of the four visions of togal (*chos nyid
zad sa*), which is to have achieved the dharmakaya.

241. According to the tantras, when a person begins to die, the energy of the
right and left channels begin to merge into the central channel. Externally, the
breath becomes very irregular.

242. Zi (*gzi*) is a unique precious stone found only in Tibet.

243. The realization of vajra body, vajra speech, and vajra mind.

244. These were the ground-breaking ceremonies for the monastery that would
house the stupa containing His Holiness's kudung.

245. These are the three vajra states.

246. Dragshul (*drag shul*) is the Bhutanese name for a minister of state.

247. Ngagchang (*sngags 'chang*) is a synonym for ngagpa.

248. Gomchen (*sgom chen*) literally means "big meditator" and is another
synonym for ngagpa. In Bhutan the term also refers to the laity who support the
monastery.

249. Tsünma (*btsun ma*) is a literary and honorific name for nuns.

250. Rabjam Tulku is Dilgo Khyentse's grandson and the tulku of Zhechen
Monastery.

251. These two great teachers, Dilgo Khyentse Rinpoche and Chatral Rinpoche, also reciprocated the favor by teaching His Holiness.

252. In the West he is known more commonly as Penor Rinpoche.

253. "This unique tree" refers to the present biography of the peerless lama, whose own wisdom shines out from its inner core. Thus, the lama's virtues are styled the seeds of this "tree," nurtured by the devotion, joyful effort, and knowledge of the writer.

254. Here the three secret virtues are referring to Kyabje's vajra body, vajra speech, and vajra mind.

255. This verse describes the completion stage with a focus (*mtshan bcas rdzogs rim*). The five chakras (*rtsa 'khor lo lnga*) are: (1) the great bliss crown chakra (*spyi bo bde chen gyi 'khor lo*); (2) the luxurious enjoyment speech chakra (*mgrin pa long spyod kyi 'khor lo*); (3) the dharma heart chakra (*snying ga chos kyi 'khor lo*); (4) the emanation navel chakra (*lte ba sprul pa'i 'khor lo*); and (5) the bliss-preserving secret chakra (*gsang gnas bde skyong gi 'khor lo*).

256. Here, the meditation of bliss involving tsa-lung tummo practice is meant.

257. The four joys of empty bliss are the four stages of bliss (*dga' bzhi*): (1) bliss (*dga' ba*); (2) supreme bliss (*mchog dga'*); (3) extraordinary bliss (*khyad par gyi dga' ba*); and (4) coemergent bliss (*lhan skyes kyi dga' ba*).

258. The fourth time is the timelessness of primordial nature by which past, present, and future are transcended.

259. This verse is Kyabje's own.

260. An alternate reading of verse 207 is: "May the strong sun of the stainless Nyingma teachings / Never set in the sky of grasping beings, / But keep on shining with study and meditation, / Filling three realms with lotus fields of benefits." Writing verses that can be read in two totally different ways is a prized feat in Tibetan poetry.

261. The Indians were typically seen as wearing white clothing, and the Chinese as wearing black.

GLOSSARY

A

Anuyoga – see *two stages.*

arhat (Skt.; Tib. *dgra bcom pa*) – one who has conquered the inner defilements.

arya (Skt.; Tib. *'phags pa*) – designates one who is "noble" (or "selfless" according to Buddha's usage) and used in Buddhist texts to denote a highly achieved being who has attained the first bhumi, a level of attainment which is truly egoless, or higher.

B

bhikshu/bhikshuni – see *ordination.*

bodhisattva/bodhichitta vow – see *three vows.*

C

calling the lama from afar (*bla ma rgyang 'bod*) – devotional prayers that invoke the enlightened blessings of the lineage into the practitioner's heart. In addition they keep alive the connection to the practice and the lineage. They are a reminder of the nature of outer phenomena and inner mind.

channels, winds, and essential nuclei – see *two stages.*

chuba (*phyu pa*) – the Tibetan national dress for both men and women. It looks something like a kimono but is worn with a belt, which creates a fold in the upper part that is often used as a pocket.

completion stage – see *two stages.*

crazy wisdom – translates both tulzhug chöpa (*brtul zhugs spyod pa*) and heruka chöpa (*he ru ka spyod pa*) and refers to the powerful actions that awaken others from the sleep of duality, dogmatism, and ego-clinging.

creation stage – see *two stages.*

D

dharma (Skt.; Tib. *chos*) – the path to enlightenment as taught by Shakyamuni Buddha.

dharma nectar medicine or dütsi chö men (*bdud rtsi chos sman*) – a ceremonial blessing substance prepared in conjunction with a *drubchen*. These pills are compounded of 1,008 herbs, minerals, and other medicinal substances and with blessing relics from Buddha Shakyamuni, Guru Padmasambhava, and other great masters, past and present.

dharma protector (Skt. dharmapala; Tib. *chos skyong*) – either a wisdom or a worldly deity who serves as a guardian of the Buddhist teachings.

dharmakaya relics – see *kudung*.

drubchen (*sgrub chen*) – great accomplishment ceremonies held for periods of seven or more days and consist in maintaining constant and extensive ritual practice (including ganachakra, lama dancing, mandala creation, fire puja, dharma nectar medicine preparation, etc.) and meditation on a particular deity.

Dzogchen (*rdzogs chen*) or Great Perfection – the ninth and ultimate vehicle of Buddha Shakyamuni. It is called "Great Perfection" because all phenomena are included in this primal perfection. These teachings were transmitted into Tibet via the lineages of three principal teachers: Guru Rinpoche, Vimalamitra, and Vairochana. Dzogchen is customarily divided into three classes: the semde (*sems sde*) or mind class, the longde (*klong sde*) or space class, and the men-ngagde (*man ngag sde*) or pith instruction class. The men-ngagde is divided into two major categories: trekchö (*khregs chod*), which facilitates a profound letting-go that releases the practitioner into the primordial nature; and tögal (*thod rgal*), which might be described as an inner voyage shuttle that opens a pathway to the direct perception of how things are. These two correlate to the primordial purity of all phenomena and the spontaneous presence of the Buddha's qualities in all beings. See also *two stages; four visions; six lamps*.

E

Eight Great Chariots – see *eight practice lineages*.

eight herukas – see *kabgye*.

eight practice lineages (*sgrub brgyud shing rta mched brgyad*) – schools of

Buddhist practice that flourished in Tibet. They are: (1) Nyingma (*rnying ma*); (2) Kadam (*bka' gdams*); (3) Marpa Kagyu (*mar pa bka' brgyud*); (4) Shangpa Kagyu (*shangs pa bka' brgyud*); (5) Sakya (*sa skya*); (6) Jordrug (*sbyor drug*); (7) Dorje Sum gyi Nyendrub (*rdo rje gsum gyi bsnyen sgrub*); and (8) Zhije Chöd (*zhi byed gcod*). These are also known as the Eight Great Chariots.

eight vidyadharas (*rnying ma'i rig 'dzin brgyad*) – (1) Manjushrimitra; (2) Nagarjuna; (3) Humkara; (4) Vimalamitra; (5) Dhanasamskrita; (6) Prabahasti; (7) Rambuguhya; (8) Shantigarbha; and (9) Padmasambhava. Each of these vidyadharas was entrusted with one of the eight heruka practices at Cool Grove Charnel Ground (*dur khrod bsil ba tshal*) by the dakini Lekyi Wangmo. Padmasambhava received all these eight heruka teachings and in addition teachings on the heruka Lama Rigdzin and so is considered the ninth vidyadhara. See also *kabgye*.

ℱ

five impurities (*snyigs ma lnga*) – (1) decrease in lifespan (*tshe snyigs ma*); (2) increase of wrong views (*lta ba snyigs ma*); (3) increase of negative emotions or the five poisons (*nyon mongs snyigs ma*); (4) increase of mental afflictions (*sems can snyigs ma*); and (5) prevalence of bad times (*dus snyigs ma*) including war, famine, and disease.

five visualizations (*mngon byang lnga*) – the five stages of the creation stage visualizations, which are: (1) moon disk (*zla ba*); (2) sun disk (*nyi ma*); (3) seed syllable (*sa bon*); (4) ritual hand objects (*phyag mtshan*); and (5) entire body of the deity (*lha sku*). See also *three samadhis; two stages*.

four actions or *four activities* (*las bzhi*) – (1) pacifying (*zhi ba*); (2) increasing (*rgyas pa*); (3) magnetizing (*dbang*); and (4) subjugating (*drag po*).

four attractive behaviors (*bsdu bzhi*) – regarding the four attractive behaviors, two relate to generosity and two to the teachings: (1) give generously (*sbyin pa*); and (2) use kind words when doing so (*tshig snyan pa*); (3) teach the proper path that you yourself follow (*don mthun pa*); and (4) practice what you teach (*don spyod pa*). These are the qualities in a bodhisattva that will attract sentient beings to the dharma.

four demon evils (*bdud bzhi*) – four obstacles to the spiritual path. They are the demons of: (1) aggregates (*phung po'i bdud*); (2) emotions (*nyon mong po'i bdud*); (3) death (*'chi bdag gi bdud*); and (4) sensual pleasures (*lha'i *bu'i bdud*).

four endings (*mtha' bzhi*) – (1) the end of birth is death (*skyes mtha' 'chi*); (2) the end of joining is separation ('*dus mtha' 'bral*); (3) the end of accumulating is exhaustion (*bsags mtha' 'dzad*); (4) the end of building is collapse (*brtsegs mtha' 'gyel*), or, alternatively, the end of high rank is falling low (*mtho mtha' lhung*).

four everlasting wealths (*chos pa'i gtan nor bzhi*) – (1) devotion to the root teacher (*bla mar mos gus*); (2) love and affection for samaya brothers and sisters (*mched la brtse gdung*); (3) bodhichitta of compassion toward all mother sentient beings ('*gro la byang sems snying rje*); (4) reduction of grasping due to the knowledge that all compounded things are impermanent (*rtag tu mi rtag dran pa dang nges par 'byung ba*).

four fearless states (*mi 'jigs rnam bzhi*) – (1) fearlessly accomplishing knowledge, wisdom, and realization for one's own benefit (*rtogs pa phun tshogs*); (2) fearlessly overcoming all negative obstacles for one's own benefit (*spangs pa phun tshogs*); (3) fearlessly revealing to others the way to attain knowledge, wisdom, and realization, for their benefit (*lam ji bzhin ston pa*); and (4) fearlessly revealing to others the way to overcome all negative obstructions, for their benefit (*bar gcod kyi chos 'di bzhes ston pa*).

four inspirations (*mos pa bzhi*) – supercharging any situation with beneficent power, an accomplished practitioner inspires responses like those found in the following exemplary relationships: (1) respect for an outstanding leader; (2) joy and devotion for the guru; (3) love for a parent; and (4) affection and goodwill for a friend.

four lamps – see *six lamps*.

four nails (*gzer bzhi*) – (1) the nail of the view of the true nature (*lta ba chos nyid gzer*); (2) the nail of the meditation on the deity (*sgom pa lha yi gzer*); (3) the nail of focusing on the emanation and absorption of light ('*phro 'du dmigs pa'i gzer*); and (4) the nail of continuous mantra recitation (*bzlas pa sngags kyi gzer*).

four powers (*stobs bzhi*) – the four vajrayana methods of purification via Vajrasattva: (1) meditation on the deity (*rten gyi stobs*); (2) recognizing one's errors as errors and resolving to refrain from them in the future (*sun 'byin gyi stobs*); (3) applying meditative techniques as antidotes, such as visualizing Vajrasattva and reciting the hundred-syllable mantra (*gnyen po kun tu phyod pa'i stobs*); and (4) restoration to the natural state, pure from the beginning (*sor chud pa'i stobs*).

four visions (*snang ba bzhi*) – terminology from the tögal division of Dzogchen. The four are: (1) directly perceiving the true nature (*chos nyid mngon sum*); (2) expanding the vision (*nyams snang gong 'phel*); (3) reaching the summit of rigpa (*rig pa tshad phebs*); and (4) exhaustion of duality into the true nature (*chos nyid zad sa*). See also *Dzogchen*; *six lamps*.

fourfold retinue – see *two assemblies*.

G

ganachakra (Skt.; Tib. *tshogs*) – a tantric ritual feast offering, consisting of four assemblages: the fortunate gathering of devotees, the luxurious abundance of offerings, the deities who are the joyous recipients, and proceeding from these three, the deep accumulation of merit and wisdom. Among the many practices of skillful means, ganachakra is one of the most powerful.

Glorious Copper-Color Mountain (also Copper-Glory Mountain; Zangdok Palri) – the pure land of Guru Rinpoche.

K

kabgye (*bka' brgyad*) – the eight herukas or principal deities of the Nyingma tantras. They are: (1) Manjushri Yamantaka the Body (*'jam dpal sku*); (2) Hayagriva the Lotus Speech (*padma gsung*); (3) Yangdag the Heart-Mind (*yang dag thugs*); (4) Nectar the Enlightened Qualities (*bdud rtsi yon tan*); (5) Vajrakilaya the Enlightened Activity (*phur ba phrin las*); (6) Mamo Liberating Sorcery (*ma mo rbod gtong*); (7) Malign Mantra (*dmod pa drag sngags*); (8) Mundane Offering and Praise (*'jig rten mchod bstod*). See also *eight vidyadharas*.

kama (*bka' ma*) – the unbroken, transmitted canon of the Buddha's oral teachings and the commentaries on those teachings composed by the great masters. See also *terma*; *Kangyur*; *Tangyur*.

Kangyur (*bka' 'gyur*) – division of Nyingma *kama*; the collection of all the major teachings of the Buddha. See also *Tangyur*.

khajang (*kha byang*) – authorization code that gives the locations of the treasures allotted to the tertön and instructions on how and when to reveal them. A synonymous term is *terma key* (*gter gyi lde'u mig*). The tertön may come across his khajang or terma key unexpectedly, or he may discover it according to detailed instructions. Another related term is *jangbu* (*byang bu*), which can refer either to the authorization code or to the terma itself.

khenpo (*mkhan sprul*) – honorific title which is a contraction of the two titles khenpo (*mkhan po*), or abbot, and tulku (*sprul sku*).

kudung (*sku gdung*) – Tibetan honorific term for mortal remains. In the context of dharma it means the *relics* of a highly realized being. The term *dharmakaya relics* (*chos sku ring bsrel*) is used synonymously.

L

lineage learned by seeing and doing (*mthong ba brgyud pa'i phyag bzhes*) – the learning that comes through observation and participation, e.g., making tormas, playing an instrument, or performing a dance. It isn't something that can be spelled out in writing.

M

Mahayoga – see *two stages*.

mirror divination (*pra*) – certain people have a natural ability to perceive symbolic images in a mirror, especially after a certain ceremony related to divination is performed. For highly qualified individuals, symbols in the form of movie sequences can arise, and even an entire written document can appear.

N

ngagpa (*sngags pa*) – an individual who has received vajrayana empowerments, who practices, and who upholds *samaya*. In popular usage it refers to a lay vajrayana practitioner.

ngöndro (*sngon 'gro*) – preliminary or foundation practice. It includes the general outer practices of the four thoughts that turn the mind, and the special inner practices of the hundred thousand accumulations of refuge— prostrations, bodhichitta, Vajrasattva recitation, mandala offerings, and guru yoga.

nine lineages – see *three lineages*.

nine yanas (*theg pa rim dgu*) – compose the complete Buddhist path, consisting of hinayana, mahayana, and the outer and inner yogas. They are: (1) Shravaka Yana (*nyan thos kyi theg pa*); (2) Pratyekabuddha Yana (*rang sangs rgyas kyi theg pa*); (3) Bodhisattva Yana (*byang chub sems dpa' theg pa*); (4) Kriya Yana (*kri ya'i theg pa*); (5) Upa Yana (*u pa'i theg pa*); (6) Yoga Yana (*yo ga'i theg pa*); (7) Mahayoga Yana (*ma ha yo ga'i theg pa*); (8) Anuyoga Yana (*a nu yo ga'i theg pa*); and (9) Atiyoga Yana (*a ti yo ga'i theg pa*), also known as *Dzogchen* (*rdzogs chen*).

Nyingma (*rnying ma*) – the ancient translation school or early dissemination tradition.

O

ordination (*so sor thar pa'i sdom pa ris brgyad*) – within the Buddhist community there are eight types of ordination established by Lord Buddha in the vinaya. (1 & 2) Bhikshu-Bhikshuni vows (Tib. *dge slong pha ma gnyis*) are the vows of full ordination for both men and women. (3 & 4) Shramanera (Tib. *dge tshul pha ma gnyis*) are the vows that establish male and female applicants as a novice monk and nun, respectively. (5) Shikshamana (Tib. *dge slob ma*) are the rigorous preparatory vows for becoming a fully ordained nun. (6 & 7) Upasaka vows (Tib. *dge bsnyen pha ma gnyis*) are the vows of both male and female lay practitioners. An upasaka is a lay Buddhist practitioner who has vowed to uphold any or all of the five vows: not to kill, steal, lie, engage in sexual misconduct, or consume intoxicants. (8) Upavasa (Tib. *bsnyen gnas*) are vows taken for a limited period of time from the morning of one day until sunrise of the following day, and include fasting and silence. See also *ngagpas*, *three baskets*, and *three vows*.

P

protection cord (*srung mdud*) – strings tied with particular knots, blessed, and then given by the lama as a symbol of blessing and protection.

R

relics – see *kudung*.

rigdzin – see *vidyadhara*.

ringsel (*ring bsrel*) – pea-shaped relics that can shower down from the drifting smoke during the cremation of a highly realized practitioner, or be found in the ashes after cremation, or in the salt used to pack a body. Most often they are white but sometimes emerge in various colors. They have the ability to grow and multiply.

rupakaya – see *three kayas*.

S

sadhana (Skt.; Tib. *sgrub thabs*) – term for both a tantric practice sequence and the text upon which it is based. It usually includes refuge, bodhichitta, visualization and mantra recitation, dissolution, and dedication of merit.

samaya – see *three vows.*

Samye (*bsam yas*) – the first monastic university in Tibet, built in the eighth century by King Trisong Deutsen under the guidance of Guru Padmasambhava and Shantarakshita. Samye has a huge three-story temple at the center and large temples on the four sides, eight smaller temples between, and stupas at the four corners. They are surrounded by a high wall topped by 1,008 small stupas and a vajra railing. Outside this wall there are another three temples, which were sponsored by the three queens of Trisong Deutsen. The temples were used as halls for the performance of vajrayana ceremonies, for teaching, translation, and meditation. They were filled with scriptures and religious objects from Tibet, India, and neighboring countries. One of the temples in particular, the Pehar Kordzö Ling, was filled with original, ancient manuscripts from India.

sarma (*gsar ma*) – the new translation school or later dissemination tradition which includes the Sakya, Kagyu, and Gelug schools.

scholarship and practice (*lung rtogs*) – the entire range of dharma can be summarized in two aspects: scholarship (*lung gi bstan pa*; e.g., *Ten Great Pillars*) and practice (*rtogs pa'i bstan pa*; e.g., *Eight Great Chariots*). Though not exactly the same, these two terms can be compared to another pair: analytic meditation (*dpyad sgom*) and abiding meditation (*'jog sgom*). Verses 95 and 180 give them as study and insight; verse 207, as study and meditation. See also *study and....*

seven entrusted transmissions (*bka' bab bdun ldan*) *of Jamyang Khyentse Wangpo* – (1) Oral tradition (*bka' ma*) (see *kama*), i.e., rare oral teachings from all the schools of Tibetan Buddhism propagated by Lord Khyentse; (2) Earth Treasure (*sa gter*); (3) Rediscovered Treasure (*yang gter*), i.e., previously discovered terma now revealed again; (4) Mind Treasure (*dgongs gter*), i.e., revealed from the mind of Lord Khyentse; (5) Recollection (*rjes dran*), i.e., remembrances from many former lifetimes; (6) Pure Vision (*dag snang*), i.e., teaching received from the three roots in pure visions; and (7) Hearing Lineage (*snyan brgyud*), i.e., received in a dialogue with an enlightened being.

seven treasures of the noble ones (*'phags nor bdun*) – (1) devotion (*dad pa*); (2) morality (*tshul khrims*); (3) generosity (*gtong ba*); (4) good education (*thos pa*); (5) respect for others (*khrel yod*) ; (6) self-respect (*ngo tsha*); and (7) intelligence (*shes rab*).

siddha (Skt.; Tib. *grub thob*) – a highly accomplished practitioner of meditation.

siddhis (Skt.; Tib. *dngos grub*) – the accomplishments resulting from the practice of Buddhadharma. A recurrent system of classification refers to them as the *two siddhis* (*grub gnyis*): (1) supreme accomplishment (*mchog gi dngos grub*) and (2) common or ordinary accomplishments (*thun mong gi dngos grub*).

six bardos (*bar do drug*) or intermediate states – (1) bardo of birth and this life (*skye gnas bar do*); (2) dream bardo (*rmi lam bar do*); (3) contemplation bardo (*bsam gtan bar do*); (4) bardo of the moment of death (*'chi kha bar do*); (5) bardo of intrinsic reality (*chos nyid bar do*); and (6) bardo of rebirth (*srid pa bar do*).

six lamps (*sgron ma drug*) – terminology from the *tögal* teachings of *Dzogchen*. The names of the six lamps are: (1) the lamp of originally pure space (*dbyings rnam dag gi sgron ma*); (2) the lamp of self-born awareness wisdom (*shes rab rang byung gi sgron ma*); (3) the lamp of empty spheres (*thig le stong pa'i sgron ma*); (4) the lamp of the long lasso of the water ball (*rgyang zhags chu'i sgron ma*); (5) the lamp of the locket of the heart (*tsit ta sha'i sgron ma*); (6) the lamp of the white smooth channel (*dkar 'jam rtsa'i sgron ma*). For purposes of practice the first four lamps are emphasized. See also *Dzogchen; four visions.*

six paramitas (*pha rol tu phyin pa drug*) – (1) generosity (*sbyin pa*); (2) morality (*tshul khrims*); (3) patience (*bzod pa*); (4) joyful effort (*brtson 'grus*); (5) concentration (*bsam gtan*); and (6) discriminating wisdom (*shes rab*).

six realms (*'gro ba rigs drug*) – and the six classes of beings which inhabit them are: (1) gods (*lha*); (2) asuras (*lha min*); (3) human beings (*mi*); (4) animals (*dud 'gro*); (5) hungry ghosts (*yi dvags*); and (6) hell denizens (*dmyal ba*).

sramanera – see *ordination.*

study and . . . – the following phrases all include study as the first term: (1) study and contemplation (*thos bsam*); (2) study and practice (*bshad sgrub*); (3) study (teaching ['*chad*] + listening [*nyan*]), meditation (*sgom*), and practice (*sgrub*); (4) study (*thos pa'i shes rab*), contemplation (*bsam pa'i shes rab*), and meditation (*sgom pa'i shes rab*), which together are known as the *three wisdoms* (*shes rab gsum*); (5) study (*klog pa*), meditation (*spong ba*), and dharma activity (*bya ba*), which are called the *three wheels ('khor lo gsum)*. See also *scholarship and practice*.

T

Tangyur (*bstan 'gyur*) – division of the Nyingma *kama*; the collection of teachings of the great Buddhist masters other than the Buddha himself. See also *Kangyur*.

Ten Great Pillars – uphold the academic tradition (*bshad rgyud 'degs pa'i ka chen bcu*) in Tibet. These individuals are Thönmi Sambhota, Vairochana, Kawa Paltsek, Chok Ro Lui Gyaltsen, Zhang Yeshe De, Rinchen Zangpo, Dromtön Gyalwa'i Jungne, Ngok Lotsawa Loden Sherab, Sakya Pandita, and Butön Rinchen Drub.

ten qualifications (*de nyid bcu*) – there are many listings of the outer, inner, and absolute accomplishments of a vajra master (*rdo rje slob dpon*), but for an individual to even qualify for this eminent designation, a deep knowledge, proficiency, and aptitude must be exhibited with regard to the following ten subjects: (1) mandala (*dkyil 'khor*); (2) meditation (*ting 'dzin phyag rgya*); (3) postures (*'dug stangs*); (4) mantra (*sngags*); (5) gestures (*stangs stabs*); (6) recitation and chant (*bzlas brjod*); (7) fire puja (*sbyin sreg*); (8) torma (*gtor ma*); (9) action (*las sbyar*); and (10) dissolution (*slar bsdu*).

terchen (*gter chen*) – *tertön* renowned for the scope of his or her discoveries.

terma (*gter ma*) – dharma treasures of texts and relics hidden throughout Tibet, Nepal, and Bhutan (and even in the mind-streams of disciples) by Padmasambhava and Yeshe Tsogyal in the eighth and ninth centuries. The treasures are subsequently discovered at the appropriate time by destined disciples. The tertöns recover these treasures from the earth (*sa gter*), from the sky (*gnam chos*) as pure visions (*dag snang*), and even from their own mind-streams (*dgongs gter*) where they had been concealed. See *three lineages; seven entrusted transmissions of Jamyang Khyentse Wangpo; kama*.

terma key – see *khajang*.

tersar (*gter gsar*) – new terma, i.e., relatively recent treasure discoveries. Examples include *Minling Tersar* and *Dudjom Tersar*. Ter-nying (*gter rnying*) by contrast are the old terma.

tertön (*gter ston*) – a discoverer or revealer of *terma*.

thigle – see *two stages*.

three aspects of suchness – see *three samadhis.*

three baskets (sde snod gsum) – of Buddhist teachings are: (1) vinaya (ethics and morality); (2) sutra (concentration and mental training); and (3) abhidharma (wisdom; the characteristics and analysis of all phenomena, mental and material).

three blazings ('bar ba gsum) – the manifestations of spiritual attainment: (1) blazing blissful warmth in the body (*lus la bde drod 'bar ba*); (2) blazing power of speech (*ngag la nus pa 'bar ba*); and (3) blazing of the realization in the mind (*sems la rtogs pa 'bar ba*). Another listing of the three is as follows. The body of the accomplished practitioner blazes with comfort (*lus la bde ba 'bar ba*), the mind blazes with joy (*sems la dga' ba 'bar ba*), and realization blazes at all times (*rtag tu rtogs pa 'bar ba*).

three delights (mnyes pa gsum) – the activities that render service to the body, speech, and mind of the teacher and all beings.

three devotions (dad pa gsum) – (1) initial, clear, interested devotion (*dangs ba'i dad pa*); (2) strong aspiration devotion (*'dod pa'i dad pa*); and (3) unshakable devotion (*yid ches pa'i dad pa*).

three dharma kindnesses (bka' drin gsum ldan) – (1) empowerment (*dbang bskur*); (2) thorough explanation of tantra (*rgyud bshad*); and (3) pith instruction (*man ngag gnang ba*). Another classification lists them as: (1) food (*lto*); (2) clothing (*gos*); and (3) guidance (*chos*).

three doors (sgo gsum) – a person's own body, speech, and mind. See also *three vajra states.*

three gatherings ('du ba gsum) – attracted by the blazing spiritual attainments of a practitioner: (1) the daytime gathering of visible beings (*nyin mor mi 'du ba*); (2) the nighttime gathering of invisible beings (*mtshan mor mi ma yin 'du ba*); and (3) the perpetual gathering of abundant wealth (*rtag tu zas nor 'du ba*).

three inquiries – see *three unerring modes of thought.*

three kayas (sku gsum) – the three levels at which a buddha's body manifests: in Tibetan, tulku (*sprul sku*), longku (*longs sku*), and chöku (*chos sku*); in Sanskrit, nirmanakaya, sambhogakaya, and dharmakaya. The zugku (*gzugs sku*; Skt. rupakaya) is the form body of a buddha, which includes both the tulku or emanation body and the longku or body of perfect rapture. The rupakaya is the manifestation of the chöku or formless body of a buddha.

three lineages (brgyud pa gsum) or methods of dharma transmission – (1)

mind-to-mind lineage of the buddhas (*rgyal ba dgongs brgyud*); (2) symbolic lineage of the awareness-holders (*rig 'dzin brda' brgyud*); and (3) oral-aural lineage of individuals (*gang zag snyan brgyud*). A listing of nine methods of transmission includes the first three to which six more are added. These *nine lineages* preserve the Nyingma teachings in general and the terma teachings in particular. The additional six are: (4) the lineage handed over by the dakinis (*mkha' 'gro gtad rgya brgyud pa*); (5) the lineage of authority and prophecy (*bka' bab lung bstan brgyud pa*); (6) the lineage of inspiration and entrustment (*smon lam dbang bskur brgyud pa*); (7) the lineage of yellow-scroll words (*shog ser tshig brgyud pa*); (8) the lineage of karmically connected tertöns (*las 'phro gter brgyud pa*); (9) the lineage of the blessings and samaya substances (*byin rlabs dam rdzas brgyud pa*).

three realms (*khams gsum*) – desire (*'dod khams*), form (*gzugs khams*), and formless (*gzugs med khams*) realms. They are also listed as the naga realm below the earth (*sa 'og klu*), the human realm on the earth (*sa steng mi*), and the god realm above the earth (*sa bla lha*).

three roots (*rtsa gsum*) – lama (*bla ma*; Skt. guru), yidam (*yi dam*; Skt. deva; tutelary deity), and khandro (*mkha' 'gro*; Skt. dakini). They are respectively the roots or source of blessing, accomplishment, and action.

three samadhis (*ting nge 'dzin gsum*) – the three meditations through which the creation stage proceeds: (1) suchness samadhi (*de bzhin nyid kyi ting nge 'dzin*); (2) the display of arising compassionate energy samadhi (*kun tu snang ba'i ting nge 'dzin*); and (3) the seed syllable samadhi (*rgyu yi ting nge 'dzin*), the union of wisdom and compassion that becomes the deity. These three are also known as the *three aspects of suchness* (*de nyid gsum*). See also *five visualizations; two stages.*

three secrets – see *three vajra states.*

three trainings (*lhag pa'i bslab pa gsum*) – (1) morality (*lhag pa'i bslab pa tshul khrims kyi bslab pa*); (2) concentration (*lhag pa'i bslab pa ting nge 'dzin gyi bslab pa*); and (3) wisdom (*lhag pa'i bslab pa shes rab gyi bslab pa*).

three (unerring) modes of thought (*tshad ma gsum*) – central to Buddhist epistemology and logic are: (1) direct perception (*mngon sum tshad ma*); (2) deduction and/or induction (*rjes dpag tshad ma*); and (3) subtle deduction (*yid ches rjes dpag tshad ma*), which is the acceptance on faith of the statements contained in authentic scriptural teachings. The *three inquiries* (*dpyad pa gsum*) are the mental processes of examining, probing, and thoroughly understanding the objects of study. These three inquiries are the same as the three modes of thought except that the three inquiries are construed as methods of private study, while the three modes of thought are polished arguments, based on the three inquiries, which are then used in public debate to establish one's own position or to refute opponents.

three vajra states (*rdo rje gsum*) – the indestructible body, speech, and mind of enlightenment. This expression is almost synonymous with the *three secrets* (*gsang gsum*), which are a buddha's and/or one's own vajra body, speech, and mind. The connotation of three vajra states is more cosmic in scope than the three secrets. See also *three kayas; three doors.*

three vehicles (*theg pa gsum*) – hinayana, mahayana, and vajrayana; also sravakayana (*nyan thos kyi theg pa*), pratyekabuddhayana (*rang sangs rgyas kyi theg pa*), and bodhisattvayana (*byang chub sems dpa'i theg pa*). See *nine yanas.*

three vows (*sdom pa gsum*) – of the vinaya, mahayana, and vajrayana are called the pratimoksha, bodhichitta, and samaya vows. See *ordination* for the pratimoksha vows. The essence of the bodhisattva/bodhichitta vow is the determination to generate, cultivate, and preserve genuine love and compassion for all beings and through the *six paramitas* to lead all beings to complete enlightenment. Samaya (*dam tsig*) is one's own vowed intention to merge with the vajra body, speech, and mind of the Buddha and to preserve that connection with courage, commitment, and joy according to the vajrayana instructions.

three wheels – see *study and....*

three wisdoms – see *study and....*

tögal – see *Dzogchen.*

tormas (*gtor ma*) – ritual objects of many shapes that serve as symbols on many different levels, including the outer cosmic mandala, the inner deity mandala, the deities themselves, all objects of sensual pleasure, as well as the hand objects of the deities. These are often made into cakes ceremoniously offered to deities.

trekchö – see *Dzogchen.*

tsa-lung, tummo, and *trülkhor* – see *two stages.*

twelve ascetic practices (*sbyangs pa'i yon tan bcu gnyis*) – an ordained ascetic is enjoined to (1) beg for food. Once an offering has been received, (2) without delay at a place nearby in a single sitting eat it; and (3) beg no more that day. These three are the disciplines related to food. There are three related to clothing. (4) Always wear the three robes. These robes must be made from (5) coarse material or (6) discarded material. Regarding places to practice, four choices are given: (7) isolated places; (8) under a tree; (9) somewhere exposed; (10) a cemetery. In such locations, remain (11) in meditation posture even during sleep, (12) without making comfortable alterations to the site.

two aims (*don gnyis*) – the bodhisattva's twofold intention to attain enlightenment for the sake of others and self.

two assemblies (*mchod gnas sde gnyis*) – the red-robed, fully ordained monks and nuns, and the white-robed ngagpas, male and female. Also referred to as the *fourfold retinue*.

two benefits (*phan bde gnyis*) of the teachings – temporary (*phan pa*) benefit and ultimate (*bde ba*) benefit. The first is beneficial in this lifetime; the second, of lasting benefit.

two obscurations (*sgrib gnyis*) – the obscuration of afflictive emotions (*nyon sgrib*) and the obscuration of knowledge (*shes sgrib*), which is clinging to subject and object.

two siddhis – see *siddhis*.

two stages (*rim gnyis*) – the kye rim (*bskyed rim*) or creation stage and the dzog rim (*rdzogs rim*) or completion stage of vajrayana meditation.

In the creation stage (related to Mahayoga) everything is seen as the indestructible body, speech, and mind of enlightenment, i.e., the three vajra states. For the followers of Mahayoga, to regard all sights and sounds as the mandala of the peaceful and wrathful deities is relative truth. To remain beyond the three aspects of arising, abiding, and ceasing is ultimate truth. The nonduality of these two truths is the indivisibility of true reality.

The completion stage focuses primarily on the vajra mind. It can be classified into the completion stage with a focus (related to Anuyoga) and the great completion stage without a focus (related to Dzogchen).

The view to be realized according to Anuyoga is that all things are buddhahood from the very beginning. The followers of Anuyoga assert that mind's nature free from conceptual constructs is a limitlessly spacious readiness to respond, its brightness without objectification is primordial wisdom, and their nonduality is great bliss. The path of Anuyoga comprises a common and an extraordinary component. The latter includes the definitive path of skillful means and the liberating path of discriminating awareness. The definitive path of skillful means works with, among other things, the hidden structure of our inherent vajra body. This vajra body is composed of channels (Tib. tsa [*rtsa*]; Skt. nadi), winds (Tib. lung [*rlung*]; Skt. prana), and essential nuclei (Tib. thigle [*thig le*]; Skt. bindu). The practices of tsa-lung (*rtsa rlung*), tummo (*gtum mo*), and trülkhor (*khrul 'khor*) are deeply connected with these structures.

The view of Dzogchen trekchö is the realization of your own primordially pure self-cognizing, uncompounded awareness, abiding beyond representational thought processes, a self-originated big bang (*thig le*), the immense expanse of original freedom. See also *nine yanas*; *three samadhis*; *Dzogchen*.

twofold purity (*dag pa gnyis ldan*) – (1) absence of temporary obscurations (*glo bur gyi dri ma dag pa*); and (2) primordial nature (*ngo bo ye nas dag pa*).

U

upasaka – see *ordination*.

V

vidyadhara (Skt; Tib. *rig 'dzin*) – awareness-holder; those who hold to rigpa; an accomplished practitioner of vajrayana. See also *eight vidyadharas*.

W

white scarf (*dar dkar*) – also mouth scarf (*kha dar*), symbolizing the power of speech, hence leadership, hence prosperity; also neck scarf (*mgul dar*); also *kha btags* (Lhasa colloquial).

Index of Text Titles

The following is a list of titles of texts and teachings mentioned in this namthar. They are alphabetized by the English translation of the title for quick reference and, because many of these titles have been translated in a myriad of ways, we have included the Wylie transliteration of the Tibetan title for accurate identification of the text.

Index of Personal and Place Names

The following is an index of personal names, honorific titles, and/or place-of-origin designations, followed by the Wylie transliteration. The names are alphabetized by their Westernized pronunciation. Names in bold type indicate individuals referred to in this text by alternative names. These alternative names will be found at the end of this list, beginning on page 339.

Individuals Referred to in the Text by Multiple Names

Chatral Rinpoche:
> Chatral Rinpoche Sangye Dorje Trogyal Dorje (*bya bral rin po che sangs rgyas rdo rje khro rgyal rdo rje*), 231, 284
> Jigme Trogyal Dorje (*'jigs med khro rgyal rdo rje*), 91, 284
> Sangye Dorje Tsal (*sangs rgyas rdo rje rtsal*), 201, 284

Chökyi Wangchuk:
> Guru Chöwang (*gu ru chos dbang*), 101, 271, 298

Dechen Dewe Dorje:
> Sera Khandro (*se ra mkha' 'gro*), 284

Dilgo Khyentse Rinpoche:
> Dilgo Khyentse Rinpoche Rabsal Dawa (*dil mgo mkhyen brtse rin po che rab gsal zla ba*), 230

Dorje Wangdrag Tsal:
> Lugyal Dachong (*klu rgyal zla skyong*), 243

Dudjom Jigdral Yeshe Dorje:
> Dorje Dütsal Drag (*rdo rje 'dus rtsal drag*), 22
> Drodul Lingpa (*'gro 'dul gling pa*), 22
> Dudjom Drodul Lingpa (*bdud 'joms 'gro 'dul gling pa*), 44, 276
> Garwang Drodul Lingpa Tsal (*gar dbang 'gro 'dul gling pa rtsal*), 192
> Gyalse Lodrö Drimed Phende Dawai Özer (*rgyal sras blo gros dri med phan bde zla ba'i 'od zer*), 23
> Gyurme Gelek Chogle Namgyal (*'gyur med dge legs phyogs las rnam rgyal*), 22
> His Holiness, too numerous to mention
> Jigdral Dechen Dorje Dragpo Tsal (*'jigs bral bde chen rdo rje drag po rtsal*), 22
> Jnana (*dzny'a na*), 37, 65, 104
> Kyabje (*skyabs rje*), too numerous to mention
> Terchen Lama (*gter chen bla ma*), 37, 44, 65, 169, 235, 237, 259, 276
> Terchen Lord (*skyab rje gter chen*), 37, 44
> Tsojung Gyepai Langtso Ngönme Dawa Sarpa (*mtsho byung dgyes pa'i lang tsho sngon med zla ba gsar pa*), 22
> Yenpa Lode (*yan pa blo bde*), 22

Gampopa:
> Dagpo Lhaje (*dwags po lha rje*), 285

Garwang Sangye Dorje:
> Phulung Tulku Sangye (*phu lung sprul sku sangs rgyas*), 284

LIST OF PHOTOGRAPHS AND ILLUSTRATIONS

All gonpa wall mural photographs are used with permission. © Padmasambhava Buddhist Center.

COLOR PLATES:

1   H.H. Dudjom Rinpoche, from Ani Lorraine's private collection. Photographer unknown.

2   H.H. Dudjom Rinpoche at the Brooklyn Botanical Gardens in the spring of 1980, from the author's private collection. Photographer unknown.

3   Dudjom Sangyum Rigdzin Wangmo in Darjeeling, India, from Dudjom Sangyum's private collection, used with her kind permission. Photographer unknown.

4   Photo collage from the author's private collection. Photographers unknown:
Top left: H.H. Dudjom Rinpoche in the 1970s
Bottom left: H.H. Dudjom Rinpoche
Top right: H.H. Dudjom Rinpoche in the early 1970s
Bottom right: H.H. Dudjom Rinpoche

5   Photo collage. Photographers unknown:
Top left: H.H. Dudjom Rinpoche in Santa Monica, California, from Gyatrul Rinpoche's private collection.
Bottom left: H.H. Dudjom Rinpoche in Santa Monica, California, from Khenchen Palden Sherab Rinpoche's private collection.
Top right: H.H. Dudjom Rinpoche, from the author's private collection.
Bottom right: H.H. Dudjom Rinpoche, from the author's private collection.

6   H.H. Dudjom Rinpoche's kudung, from the author's private collection. Photographer unknown.

7   Visions appearing in monastery window in Boudnath, Kathmandu, Nepal, from the author's private collection. Photographer unknown.

Kyabje Chatral Rinpoche with others in Boudnath, Kathmandu, Nepal, from the author's private collection. Photographer unknown.

8   H.H. Dudjom Rinpoche and Dudjom Sangyum Rigdzin Wangmo, from the author's private collection. Photographer unknown.

Padmasambhava Buddhist Center

Venerable Khenchen Palden Sherab Rinpoche and Venerable Khenpo Tsewang Dongyal Rinpoche have established Padmasambhava Buddhist Center to preserve in its entirety the authentic message of Buddha Shakyamuni and Guru Padmasambhava, and in particular to teach the tradition of Nyingmapa and Vajrayana Buddhism. PBC now includes over twenty centers in the U.S.A., Russia, Canada, and Puerto Rico, in addition to monastic institutions in India, Russia, and the U.S.A.

Padmasambhava Buddhist Center is dedicated to world peace and the supreme good fortune and well being of all.

The Samye Translation Group was founded by the Venerable Khenpo Rinpoches to commemorate and preserve the great ancient tradition of translation that was firmly established during the glorious Tibetan Buddhist era of the seventh through tenth centuries. As a reflection of gratitude for the unique activities of these enlightened translators, the Samye Translation Group publishes dharma books that cover all nine yana teachings of the Nyingma School of Tibetan Buddhism, including shedra philosophical books.

For more information about the Venerable Khenpos' activities, the Samye Translation Group, or Padmasambhava Buddhist Center, please contact:

Padma Samye Ling
618 Buddha Highway
Sidney Center, NY 13839
(607) 865-8068

www.padmasambhava.org

Other Publications
by the Venerable Khenpo Rinpoches

Opening to Our Primordial Nature

Tara's Enlightened Activity

The Dark Red Amulet: Oral Instructions on the Practice of Vajrakilaya

Ceaseless Echoes of the Great Silence: A Commentary on the Heart Sutra

Door to Inconceivable Wisdom and Compassion

Echoes of Dream Boy: Exalting the Realization of the Yogis and Yoginis

Heart Essence of Chetsun: Voice of the Lion (restricted)

*Illuminating the Path: Ngondro Instructions According to the Nyingma
    School of Vajrayana Buddhism*

Jubilant Laughter of the Three Roots: Praise to the Inconceivable Lotus Land

Lion's Gaze: A Commentary on the Tsig Sum Nedek

Praise to the Lotus Born: A Verse Garland of Waves of Devotion

Prajnaparamita: The Six Perfections

The Six Sublime Pillars of the Nyingma School, Volume 1 and Volume 2

*The Smile of Sun and Moon: A Commentary on The Praise to the Twenty-
    One Taras*

PSL Shedra Series:
    Opening the Clear Vision of the Vaibhashika and Sautrantika Schools
    Opening the Clear Vision of the Mind Only School
    Opening the Wisdom Door of the Madhyamaka School
    Opening the Wisdom Door of the Rangtong & Shentong Views
    Opening the Wisdom Door of the Outer Tantras

More information about these and other works by the Venerable Khenpo
Rinpoches can be found online at: www.padmasambhava.org/chiso.

LIGHT OF FEARLESS INDESTRUCTIBLE WISDOM